THE LAW ON
THE
MISUSE OF DRUGS

AUSTRALIA AND NEW ZEALAND
The Law Book Company Ltd.
Sydney : Melbourne : Perth

CANADA AND U.S.A.
The Carswell Company Ltd.
Agincourt, Ontario

INDIA
N.M. Tripathi Private Ltd.
Bombay
and
Eastern Law House Private Ltd.
Calcutta and Delhi
M.P.P. House
Bangalore

ISRAEL
Steimatzky's Agency Ltd.
Jerusalem : Tel Aviv : Haifa

MALAYSIA : SINGAPORE : BRUNEI
Malayan Law Journal (Pte.) Ltd.
Singapore and Kuala Lumpur

THE LAW ON

THE

MISUSE OF DRUGS

by

RUDI FORTSON LL.B. (Lond.)

of the Middle Temple
Barrister

LONDON
SWEET & MAXWELL
1988

Published in 1988
by Sweet & Maxwell Ltd.
11, New Fetter Lane, London
Computerset by Promenade Graphics Ltd., Cheltenham
Printed in Great Britain

British Library Cataloguing in Publication Data
Fortson, Rudi
The Law on the misuse of drugs.
1. Great Britain. Drug abuse. Law.
I. Title
344.104'4463

ISBN 0–421–39620–2

PREFACE

In the wake of rapid cultural changes (internationally) in respect of the use and misuse of drugs, the Misuse of Drugs Act 1971 was enacted with a view to controlling the importation, distribution and use of substances and products considered by the government of the day to be capable of having "harmful effects" likely to constitute a "social problem". But the drug problem—far from being nearer to a solution—has considerably increased in complexity and accordingly, a mass of case law and statutory measures have emerged over the last 17 years.

The Courts have striven to give effect to the letter (and to the spirit) of the relevant legislation but the Courts have also endeavoured to balance various competing interests so as to control drug use on the one hand without unnecessarily making criminals out of people on the other. The upshot is that the law governing this field is becoming increasingly complex.

The object of this book is to guide the reader through the legal complexities—*not* by a cold citation of statutory provisions and authorities, but by attempting to analyse various problems and examining how the Legislature and the Courts have approached each problem. Accordingly, even if the reader does not agree with the analysis (which is entirely my responsibility) it is intended and hoped that he or she will acquire a greater understanding of this area of the law and gain food for further thought.

Because the relevant statutes, statutory instruments and their respective Schedules are continually subject to amendment or modification I have seen little value in blandly reproducing them in their original form. Instead the relevant provisions (as amended) are appropriately set out in the text.

The reader should be aware that since going to press there have been significant legislative developments. The Misuse of Drugs Regulations 1985 (S.I. 1985 No. 2066) have been amended by the Misuse of Drugs (Amendment) Regulations 1988 (S.I. 1988 No. 916). Thus, in regulation 6(4), for "Schedule 3" there shall be substituted "Schedule 2 or 3"; regulation 14(7) is amended to include any drugs specified in Schedule 3 contained in or comprising a preparation which (i) is required for use as a buffering agent in chemical analysis, (ii) has present in it both a substance specified in paragraph 1 or 2 of Schedule 3 and a salt of that substance, and (iii) is premixed in a kit. After regulation 18(2)(*a*) sub-paragraph (*aa*) is inserted so as to include any drug specified in Schedule 3 as described in regulation 14(7) above. Finally, "Quinal-barbitone" has been transferred from paragraph 1(b) of Schedule 3 to paragraph 6 of Schedule 2.

On July 29, 1988 the Criminal Justice Act 1988 was passed although many of its provisions have yet to come into force (see s.171(1), (5) & (7) and see S.I. 1988 No. 1408; S.I. 1988 No. 1676). The Powers of the Criminal Courts Act 1973, s.43(1) (forfeiture) is amended and so closes the gap elucidated in *Hinde* (1971) 64 Cr.App.R. 213 C.A.—see s.69(1) and s.171(6). The Misuse of Drugs Act 1971, s.27(1) (forfeiture) applies to "drug trafficking offences" (s.70; 1988 No. 1676). Since July 29, 1988, The Drug Trafficking Offences Act 1986, s.8 is amended although numerous other amendments to that Act have yet to come into force (see s.103 and Sched. 5).

Other significant reforms relate to searches of detained persons (s.147; S.I. 1988 No. 1676); arrests by customs officers (s.151); remands of suspected drug offenders to customs detention (s.152); authorisation of delay in notifying arrest (s.99); the abolition of the power to make a criminal bankruptcy order (s.101); the reviewing of sentencing by the Court of Appeal (s.35); and the making of Confiscation Order for non-drug trafficking offences (Part VI of the Act).

It is often remarked that the publication of a book is a team effort that tests the patience of the team. I have come to learn just how true that statement is and I should therefore like to thank my publishers for their support, advice and assistance. I should also like to thank my wife, Fiona, for her unfailing patience and encouragement; to my parents for their support and the interest which they have taken in all that I do; and last, but not least, to G. Linis Esq. who opened my eyes to the fact that a book of this nature was called for. Needless to say any errors that exist are my responsibility.

Gray's Inn, London   RUDI FORTSON
July, 1988.

CONTENTS

PART I
THE MISUSE, CONTROL AND CLASSIFICATION OF DRUGS

PART II
THE IMPORTATION AND EXPORTATION OF CONTROLLED DRUGS

PART III
POSSESSION SUPPLY AND PRODUCTION OF DRUGS

PART IV
CONSPIRACY AND ATTEMPT TO COMMIT A DRUG OFFENCE

PART V
ENFORCEMENT

PART VI
A PRACTICAL GUIDE TO DRUG MISUSE

PART VII
THE STATUTORY BODIES

TABLE OF CASES

xi

TABLE OF STATUTES

TABLE OF STATUTORY INSTRUMENTS

PART I

THE MISUSE, CONTROL AND CLASSIFICATION OF DRUGS

AN HISTORICAL SKETCH OF DRUG MISUSE

Until the early 1960s Britain did not have a major social narcotics problem. Today it is conservatively estimated that over four million people in Britain regularly abuse drugs—from cannabis, amphetamines and barbiturates, to cocaine and heroin. It is beyond the scope of this book to examine why drug-taking should have such a wide appeal. The reasons are intensely complicated and probably not fully understood but it should always be borne in mind that not all drug abuse is rooted in delinquency; drugs are often unwittingly abused as well. Secondly, the familiar image of the physically sick addict ignores the fact that many drugs produce harmful effects even if they are not proved to be physically dangerous, for example psychological dependence or drug-related crime.

It is therefore with good reason that the Legislature has move away from narrow terms such as "dangerous drugs" and "poisons" and speaks instead of the "misuse" of drugs; hence the Misuse of Drugs Act 1971.

The emergence of a social drug problem

Drug misuse is an ancient problem. It is easy to overlook the fact that probably the oldest drug is alcohol, which has been used and abused on an international scale since time immemorial. In the Far East, and in Africa, opium and cannabis have been taken socially for thousands of years. The South Americans discovered that chewing coca-leaves stimulates the mind while the Greeks and Aztecs used hallucinogenic herbs and plants in some of their religious ceremonies to create mystical effects. The Egyptians, too, compounded many mind altering potions.

With the advent of the Industrial Revolution (1760–1840) the skills of chemistry and pharmacy were combined to form a powerful industry which made available a host of new drugs to meet a host of new demands.

Opium was principally used for the purposes of stupefaction but no restrictions were placed on its distribution and use until the Pharmacy Act 1868 regulated the sale of the drug. Nevertheless, the drug remained readily obtainable for many years thereafter. As early as 1803 morphine (an opiate) was developed and soon became recognised as a most powerful pain reliever, but it is also highly addictive. Its widespread use to treat the wounded, both in war-time and in peace-time, unfortunately resulted in a large number of patients becoming opiate dependent. Moreover, drugs such as opium and morphine found their way into many commercial substances and products which claimed to alleviate all kinds of ailments.

The discovery of morphine led, in turn, to the discovery of another powerful drug—heroin—produced in London in 1874. Foolishly (with the benefit of hindsight), this drug was also used in many commercial preparations. In the nineteenth century it was thought not to be addictive—it is. It follows from the above that many opiate users became unwillingly addicted.

There were of course substances and products which were wilfully (even fashionably) abused by the consumer.

Thus, cocaine, formerly a popular local anaesthetic, appealed to an eccentric, middle-aged circle of the Victorian middle class, as a stimulant. Sir Arthur Conan Doyle mirrored that fact in his portrayal of the fictional character "Sherlock Holmes" as an occasional user of the drug. Interest in cocaine waned until the 1920s when, once again, a relatively well-heeled set in America, and in Europe, abused it.

Again, amphetamine was originally used to treat depression and narcolepsy, but it's ability to stimulate the mind has, for decades, prompted people to abuse it. Thus, Drinamyl attained notoriety in the 1960s when it was widely abused by delinquent teenagers; by students revising for examinations, and by performers in the entertainment industry. Better known as "the Purple Heart" this product accelerated legislation to control amphetamines.

More recently, Ritalins have become popular with heroin addicts, who use the drug to counteract some of the adverse effects experienced with heroin, for example depression.

Other products contained active constituents, (for example morphine or amphetamine) the effects of which were not fully understood until the manifestations of abuse or side effects were realised.

It is sometimes said that major wars have contributed to the current drug problem but this superficial claim overlooks the fact that the majority of those currently abusing drugs have not seen National Service let alone active service. Certainly major wars have significantly contributed to the development of new drugs and probably encouraged a much wider use of many dangerous substances such as morphine and other pain killers. Amphetamines, too, were regularly prescribed to servicemen, to keep them awake and alert during combat (i.e. "wakey, wakey" pills). Their use could not be sustained since they were addictive and capable of producing aggression, confusion and panic.

Significantly, in the West, relatively few drug abusers deliberately self-administered the first dose of a "hard-drug," for example heroin, until the 1960s. By contrast, opium addiction in the Far East, was a major concern of the world over one hundred and fifty years ago.

Unfortunately, Britain played a major role in the highly profitable "opium trade" of the Far East. In 1830 Britain declined to allow China to put a ban on opium, and 1842 saw Britain's victory in the so-called "opium war." The now widespread abuse of opium generated international alarm, with calls for positive action to eradicate the problem. A series of conferences and treaties followed. Britain honoured its commitment by ratifying several treaties. The Pharmacy Act 1868 regulated the use and preparation of opium. Between 1868 and 1925, three further statutes were passed restricting the use of a number of other substances. Significantly, the Dangerous Drugs Act 1920 codified a number of wartime regulations which outlawed the possession of opium and cocaine for personal consumption. Following the Geneva Convention in 1925, and after representations made by the Egyptian Delegation, the use of cannabis came in for strong condemnation. As a result the Dangerous Drugs Act 1925 regulated the possession and use of that substance. There is some evidence that, after 1925, drug abuse in the United Kingdom (as small as it was) was in decline. Of course domestic laws could have little effect on the drug problem overseas. Accordingly, The League of Nations, and later the United Nations, sought to prevent addiction and drug trafficking throughout the world. Their success has been limited and perhaps frustrated by a cumbersome bureaucratic, method of control based on quantifying the amount of world production and consumption of dangerous drugs. "Taking stock" of drug production is largely dependent on relying on member states submitting estimates of their own production of the relevant drug. Inevitably the drug barons, carrying out illicit production and supplies, either furnish no particulars at all or falsify them. Member States whose "balance sheets" reveal a disturbing quantity of "lost drugs" may be asked to explain the loss, but efficiently policing drug production and supply, in this way and in accordance with International Law, is virtually impossible.

For approximately one hundred years between 1860 and 1960, the addict was seen as a person suffering from illness. In one sense such a perception is justified if one looks purely at the effects various drugs may have on both the body and the mind, but drug abuse cannot be regarded as a disease, as it certainly was regarded in 1926, when the Departmental Committee on Morphine and Heroin Addiction (the "Rolleston Committee") published its

Report (H.M.S.O.; 1926). Medical thinking had not significantly changed when the first Report of the Interdepartmental Committee on Drug Addiction was published in 1961. Again, the suggestion was that drug addicts were "sick"; suffering a form of mental illness.

However, in the wake of rapid cultural changes, narcotic abuse became fashionable on an international scale. The Second Report of the I.C.D.A. (H.M.S.O. 1966) shows that the committee revised its thinking and directed its attack against the black market and doctors who over prescribe.

In the treatment of addicts the role of doctors complicates the picture. A doctor might, for example, prescribe the hard drug itself; or prescribe a substitute, e.g. methadone for heroin, or prescribe nothing at all and instead advise therapy. Often doctors prescribe heroin or cocaine privately. The pharmacist, likewise, often charges a fee for encashing the prescription. From the addict's point of view the cost involved is still cheaper than buying on the black market. But, such a doctor was (and is) in danger of becoming an "easy touch," liable to attract many drug users. He would be encouraged to liberally prescribe; perhaps fearing that to turn users away empty handed was forcing them to resort to the black market and probably to commit offences in order to pay the black market prices. The General Medical Council has considered many cases of doctors prescribing in this way. Some doctors were undoubtedly well motivated while a few were unscrupulous and issued private prescriptions like confetti. Although the existence and enforcement of regulations may seriously reduce the range of drugs a doctor may administer, prescribe and supply, nevertheless they also serve to protect him from manipulative addicts.

The doctor was (and still is) liable to be the victim of another manipulation of the system namely, by unwittingly prescribing controlled drugs to a drug user who was already registered with another doctor. The practice of "double-scripting" is rife and not easy to detect. The addict having increased his supply of drugs through the comparatively cheap medium of the private or national health service might then sell his surplus stock on the black market at street level prices. The income would pay his doctors fees; allow him to buy other drugs and to pay the general household bills. It is partly with this practice in mind that the legislature has sought to enact a structured system of licensing, registration, recording and book-keeping in order to monitor the distribution of controlled drugs.

Much controversy has arisen concerning the "drugs problem" and how to deal with it. Views range between demands for stern penal sanctions on the one hand; to calls for no action at all on the other. The former school advocates the need to deter others; the latter advocates that left alone the "practice" will burn itself out. Between 1868 and 1971 Parliament's approach had been piecemeal. The Pharmacy Act 1868 was designed principally to regulate the use of opium. The Drugs (Prevention of Misuse) Act 1964 sought to restrict the use of amphetamines. Those restrictions were extended to the drug L.S.D. by the Dangerous Drugs Act 1965. For over one hundred years attention was focused on those drugs considered to be "dangerous." In truth little was known about the medical and social effects of many popular drugs from asprin and Librium, to cannabis and cocaine. To control the use of some drugs and not others was unpopular in principle because legislation was thereby demonstrated to be arbitrary in its approach. Parliament ultimately endeavoured to search for a method of control that would be open ended in its scope, and reasonably subtle in its administration. The result was the Misuse of Drugs Act 1971.

The Misuse of Drugs Act 1971 ("the M.D.A.") can be summarised as setting up six main objectives. First, to control the use, production and distribution of all drugs recognised as being medically or socially harmful. Second, to create a body (the Advisory Council) that would give to the government of the day, sound professional advice; comprising of experts in the field of science and social-science. Third, to promote a deeper understanding of the problem by undertaking research. Fourth, to enforce the law by criminal sanctions if necessary. Fifth, to facilitate the treatment of drug-dependants and finally to educate the public.

DRUG CONTROL AND DRUG CLASSIFICATION

Which drugs are liable to control?

The Oxford English Dictionary defines a "drug" as being: "An original, simple, medicinal substance organic or inorganic, used by itself, or as an ingredient in medicine . . . a narcotic or opiate. . . ." The word "narcotic," by contrast has a much narrower meaning: "a substance which when swallowed, inhaled or injected into the system induces drowsiness, sleep, stupefaction or insensibility. . . ."

Oddly, the Misuse of Drugs Act 1971, does not define the word "drug" preferring, instead, to merely list those "substances" which are "controlled" in their use. Clearly all medicines are drugs but not all drugs are medicines. Scientists generally assess a drug's level of safety by reference to its *therapeutic index*, being the ratio between the median *effective* dose as against the median *toxic* dose.

For present purposes drugs can be loosely grouped as follows:
  (i) substances either organic or inorganic, which are used in medicines;
 (ii) drugs present in naturally occurring substances, *e.g.* caffeine in tea and coffee, alcohol, nicotine in tobacco, T.H.C. in cannabis;
(iii) narcotics contained in substances not naturally occurring, *e.g.* in solvent glues, nail varnishes, butane fuels[1];
 (iv) substances cultivated, extracted or created principally for narcotic abuse, *e.g.* L.S.D., psilocin (the "magic mushroom").

The Preamble to the M.D.A. reads "An Act to make provision with respect to dangerous or otherwise harmful drugs. . . . ."

Hence certain drugs are "controlled" and listed as Class A, B, or C type drugs depending on the magnitude of danger or harm attached to them; see section 2(1) and Schedule 2 of the M.D.A. While it is not difficult to predict substances which would fall into the dangerous drugs category, being ones dangerous to health, physically or mentally, it is apparent that Parliament had in mind yet another category of drug which it sought to control, namely, those drugs that are described by the M.D.A. as being "otherwise harmful." The problem lies in identifying those drugs which are liable to fall into this latter category. An indication is given in section 1(2) which imposes a duty on the Advisory Council to keep under review drugs "likely to be misused and of which the misuse is . . . capable of having *harmful effects* to constitute a *social problem* . . . " What then is meant by the phrase "a harmful effect" in the context of section 1(2) of the M.D.A.? Also what type of problem is a "social" one?

Harmful Effects
The first point to note is that, unlike the Preamble to the Act, section 1(2) does not distinguish between "dangerous" drugs and those that are "otherwise harmful." Instead the Legislature preferred to rely on the phrase "harmful effects" as being all embracing. Secondly, Parliament clearly intended to include drugs that were not only capable of causing physical or mental "harm" to the user, directly or indirectly but also drugs which are capable of producing harmful *results*, or *consequences*, amounting to a "social problem." Accordingly, in this wider context, the "harm" encompasses sociological "damage," for example delinquency, or the

[1] But see *R.* v. *Southwark Coroner Ex parte Kendall, The Times*, June 8, 1988.

emergence of a social group of users who are in danger of acquiring no more than psychological dependence to a certain drug, for example barbiturates.

Defining what is a social problem

Any *irregular activity* in the pattern of human behaviour in which some action is required to be carried out, by and on behalf of the community, in order to maintain harmonious co-existence, or to maintain the reciprocation of benefits, may be said to give rise to a social problem. Accordingly, drugs that cause an unacceptably high level of addiction and which place significant demands on the resources of the medical profession, and the social sciences, create a social problem. But suppose the taking of a certain drug does no more than mark adolescent rebellion and causes no physical or psychological harm at all. Such behaviour may be delinquent and therefore a "social problem" but it is also likely to be seen as a harmful effect of the drug misuse and therefore, again, the drug is liable to be controlled.

The emphasis therefore being placed on the recognition of any drug-linked social problem (which need not be based on delinquency), it is evident that all drugs are capable of being controlled by the M.D.A. even if they may not produce any physical or psychological harm (medically speaking). The consequential sociological problem is, in itself, one "harmful effect" of the abuse.

Because the classes of controlled drugs are not closed, substances may be added to, or removed from Schedule 2 by an Order in Council; section 2(2). A draft of that order must be laid before Parliament and approved by a resolution of each House; section 2(5). This is designed to give Parliament the opportunity of vetting any proposed changes of the law. It is also the probable reason why any radical alteration to Schedule 2 is unlikely to occur lest it should spark off a politically damaging response.

Practical considerations of drug classification

Flexibility

It is clearly desirable that the classes of controlled drugs should be kept open and that any alterations made to them are based on sound empirical research. Both the Advisory Council and the Secretary of State may initiate their own research to that end but the Secretary of State cannot lay a draft order before Parliament without first consulting the Advisory Council; see section 2(5). Determining just how flexible the law really is can best be measured by noting the rate at which the law changes in response to the prevailing conditions and state of scientific opinion.

Since 1971 no less than eight "Modification Orders" have been approved; the latest being S.I. 1986 No. 2230.[1a] In the majority of cases the changes have not been particularly startling. However, more sweeping changes have taken place in the last two years, including (after much pressure), controlling certain barbiturates and tranquillizers which have been deliberately abused or taken to excess for a considerable number of years. For the moment the trend is to select with one hand, an increasing number of drugs for the purposes of classification, so as to bring them within the scrutiny of the law but, using the other hand, to grant an extension of the general authority to possess, and supply, a limited number of them; as well as making a number of other concessions. Laudable though it is for the law to be flexible, and to be seen to be so, three other factors must be put into the equation. First, the law must strive to be certain. From the moment of manufacture, until the moment of consumption, a drug will change hands countless times. It may be imported or exported. It will be used for different purposes. Different considerations will inevitably apply at different stages. Nevertheless, the manufacturer and every other party in the chain, must make his arrangements in accordance with the law. He can only do so if he knows where he stands. Second, the law does not exist to make criminals out of people unnecessarily. The wider the net of the M.D.A. is cast, the more likely it is that individuals and companies, will fall foul of the law. Third, consideration must also be given to the impact that such a restriction will have on innocent parties, including the drug manufacturers themselves who can suddenly experience much administrative inconvenience; loss of income and possible legal action. He may also be forced to litigate, at much expense, and challenge the classification of his drug as a "controlled" drug.

Classification should not be arbitrary

This is particularly important where drugs are controlled on the basis that their misuse may have harmful effects sufficient to constitute a social problem. Drugs may or may not be fashionable to misuse. Those which are fashionable and meet the criteria, one would expect to see added to the list, and those ceasing to be so, deleted. Furthermore, it was presumably not the intention of the legislature to control drugs that demonstrably appealed only to an eccentric few and was likely to remain so. In those circumstances the abuse is contained and limited to an isolated group and therefore not likely to constitute a social problem. If flexibility is not

---

[1a] See S.I. 1973 No. 771, 1975 No. 421, 1977 No. 1243, 1979 No. 299, 1983 No. 765, 1984 No. 859, 1985 No. 1995.

maintained so that drugs are classified in keeping with current social and scientific opinion, then the Courts are placed at a considerable disadvantage—at least on the question of sentence—believing the drugs in question to be more or less harmful than they really are.

Challenging the classifications

Most people recognise certain drugs by their "brand name" but the government designates controlled drugs by its chemical address, as it must do for clarity. Since drugs are controlled in this way it follows that many different brands can be affected even if it is, in truth, one brand name that seems to be the target of misuse. Furthermore, a drug which produces an effect *similar* to the misused drug, might also find itself being controlled for that reason, even though the comparable substance is differently chemically constituted and has no history of having been misused at all. The drug may also be controlled, not because it is inherently dangerous, but because its harmful effect is said to be rooted in a social problem.

What then can a company do about it? Its only recourse is to attempt to go behind the making of the Order in Council by asserting that the Secretary of State acted *ultra vires* and the designation was made on a misconceived basis. It goes without saying that such a company sets itself a most formidable task.

Exercising control—mapping the M.D.A. 1971

Because the M.D.A. is designed and intended to regulate the flow of drugs and their use, the following structure is enacted:

(i) Certain drugs are specified as being "controlled:" see Schedule 2 of the M.D.A.

(ii) As a *General Rule* it is unlawful to:
  (a) import or export controlled drugs; section 3
  (b) produce or supply controlled drugs; section 4
  (c) possess controlled drugs; section 5
  (d) cultivate the cannabis plant; section 6
  (e) prepare or smoke opium; section 9
  (f) permit premises to be used for the purposes listed above; section 8
  (g) use utensils or allow others to use them in connection with the smoking of opium; section 9
  (h) frequent opium "dens"; section 9

(iii) It is unlawful for a person in the United Kingdom to assist in or induce the commission of a "corresponding offence" abroad; section 20

(iv) Companies may also be guilty of committing offences; section 21

(v) However, the government may create exceptions to the general rule and:
  (a) allow certain controlled drugs to be imported/exported, produced, supplied or possessed, section 7(1)(*a*)
  (b) allow certain persons to use controlled drugs under licence; section 7(1)(*b*) and section 7(2)
  (c) allow practitioners in the medical, veterinary professions to supply drugs; section 7(3)(*a*)
  (d) allow those practitioners to possess certain controlled drugs; section 7(3)(*b*)

But:

(vi) The government may;
  (a) restrict certain controlled drugs to research use only; section 7(4)(*a*)
  (b) require medical practitioners, etc., to hold a licence before supplying or possessing certain controlled drugs; section 7(4)(*b*).

The M.D.A. provides the legal framework. However it is the regulations which seek to administer its objectives. The bulk of the regulations are to be found in the Misuse of Drugs Regulations 1985 (S.I. 1985 No. 2066) ("the M.D.R."). The earlier Misuse of Drugs Regulations 1973 and it's amending instruments are revoked. Other regulations are considered separately in this work.

Many of the regulations and rules are designed to ensure that certain beneficial drugs remain in proper hands by requiring that drugs be kept secure; that documents are kept of drug transactions; that suitable records be maintained and furnished for possible inspection; that drugs are properly packed, labelled and safely transported; and that the issue of prescriptions be carefully regulated.

Controlling the activities of Doctors/Pharmacists, etc.

Again, the M.D.A. seeks to provide a framework regulating the activities of patients, doctors and pharmacists.

Put in simplified terms the basic framework is as follows:
  (i) A doctor may administer specified drugs; M.D. Regs. 7(2)
  (ii) Certain doctors may supply or offer to supply specified drugs to another; M.D. Regs. 8(4) and 9(4)
  (iii) Prescriptions must meet certain conditions M.D. Regs. 15 and 16

(iv) A doctor who attends a person whom he suspects to be addicted to any drug must normally notify the Chief Medical Officer at the Home Office; M.D.A. 1971, s.10(*h*) and S.I. 1973 No. 799, reg. 3(1)

(v) Only a licensed doctor may prescribe cocaine, heroin or dipipanone to addicts; M.D.A. 1971, s.10; S.I. 1973 No. 799 reg. 4(1)(*b*); and M.D. Regs. 5

(vi) An addict lawfully entitled to drugs may administer them to himself and therefore be in possession of them; M.D.A. 1971, s.5(1) and M.D. Regs. 10(2)

(vii) Such an addict must *not* "double-script"; M.D. Regs. 10(2)(*a*)

(viii) Such an addict must not obtain a prescription by providing false particulars; M.D. Regs. 10(2)(*b*)

(ix) Doctors convicted of certain offences may not be permitted to supply controlled drugs; M.D.A. 1971, s.12

(x) Doctors who act in breach of certain regulations may not be allowed to supply certain controlled drugs; M.D.A. 1971, ss.13 and 14. *And*—such doctors may also be committing criminal offences as a result; M.D.A. 1971, s.18.

PART II

THE IMPORTATION AND EXPORTATION OF CONTROLLED DRUGS

THE IMPORTATION AND EXPORTATION OF CONTROLLED DRUGS

Of all narcotics appearing in Britain, the vast majority of them will have been imported—particularly those drugs which naturally subsist in plants and which cannot be successfully grown in this country. All heroin and cocaine must be imported. Cannabis can be "home produced" but only with varying degrees of success. The home grown plant tends to be less "bushy" than it would otherwise be if grown in more temperate regions of the world. Indeed, in such regions, for example Morocco, Nigeria and Jamacia, the plant grows in such natural abundance that its harvesting, processing and exportation is a remarkably inexpensive exercise. However, the British domestic market accounts for only a part of all drug-importations. Britain's geographical position in the world makes it an ideal "staging post" for the onward transmission of narcotics to other countries. This is because many air routes converge in the United Kingdom making it one of the busiest "junctions" in the world. As we shall see, the movement of controlled drugs, entering and leaving the country, is heavily restricted or prohibited. It is therefore hardly surprising to discover that much court time is devoted to the disposal of cases involving the unlawful evasion of the prohibitions and/or the restrictions so imposed.

The burden of "policing" the flow of imports and exports, and prosecuting offenders, falls chiefly on the Commissioners of Customs and Excise whose existence, powers, rights and privileges are embodied in the Customs and Excise Management Act 1979 (the "C.E.M.A.) which describes the duties to be performed by the Commissioners as "assigned matters" see s.1(1). To increase resources, as circumstances demand, Parliament has imposed a duty on all constables, coast-guards, and members of the armed forces, to assist in enforcing the law in respect of these matters; see section 11 of the C.E.M.A.

Every drug seized on the streets (and which must originally have been unlawfully imported) is of interest to customs officers but, in practice, offences committed at this stage will normally be a matter for the police to investigate pursuant to their powers under the M.D.A. The police try to avoid charging individuals with offences under the C.E.M.A. since all proceedings under that Act should be instituted by order of the Commissioners (section 145). Conversely, the Commissioners of Customs and Excise prefer not to charge offenders with offences under the M.D.A. if they can bring a prosecution under the C.E.M.A. As a result, a defendant accused of drug-smuggling, is likely to find that he faces very different charges depending on which law-enforcement-agency is investigating the matter. Clearly, this is not a happy state of affairs. For example, in the case of a smuggler who imports a quantity of heroin which is wholly inconsistent with personal use, then the police (if they are investigating the matter) are likely to charge the accused with the unlawful possession of drugs with intent to supply them contrary to section 5(3) of the M.D.A. or, alternatively (if others are involved), with conspiracy to evade the prohibition on importation imposed by section 3(1) of the M.D.A.[1] However, the Commissioners of Customs and Excise would, by contrast, charge the accused with an "importation/ exportation offence" under the C.E.M.A.—which is eminently more appropriate. It should also be borne in mind that defences available to an accused under one enactment will not always be available to him under another enactment. Thus, section 28 of the M.D.A. will not apply to offences brought under the C.E.M.A.

THE STATUTORY PROHIBITIONS

Section 3 of the MDA 1971 reads:
> "(1) Subject to subsection (2) below—
>> (a) the importation of a controlled drug; and
>> (b) the exportation of a controlled drug,
> are hereby prohibited.
> (2) Subsection (1) above does not apply—
>> (a) to the importation or exportation of a controlled drug which is for the time being excepted from paragraph (a) or, as the case may be, paragraph (b) of subsection (1) above by regulations under section 7 of this Act; or
>> (b) to the importation or exportation of a controlled drug under and in accordance with the terms of a licence issued by the Secretary of State and in compliance with any conditions attached thereto."

It will be seen that section 3(1) of the M.D.A. merely establishes the existence of two separate prohibitions—it does not, by itself, make it an offence to contravene either prohibition. The reason is that many enactments similarly prohibit or restrict the importation, exportation, or carriage coastwise, of many different goods, substances, or even wildlife. Accordingly, for the purposes

---

[1] *Whitehead and Nicholl* [1982] 3 All E.R. 96.

of the C.E.M.A., the Legislature aptly terms all such goods "prohibited or restricted goods" (see section 1(1)) of the C.E.M.A.) and has created a mere handful of offences to punish an unlawful contravention of the relevant prohibition or restriction.

"Prohibited or Restricted Goods" must be carefully distinguished from "Dutiable Goods". Dutiable goods may be lawfully imported but, customs "duty" or "excise" is payable, before the goods may be cleared. The importance of making this distinction will become apparent.

Given that section 3(1) of the M.D.A. only imposes a prohibition on the exportation or importation of controlled drugs, it is necessary to look to the C.E.M.A. to find the offences arising out of a contravention of section 3(1). Broadly speaking, there are three offences. Section 50 punishes improper importations; section 68 punishes unlawful exportations; and section 170 serves as a "mopping-up" provision, punishing ventures designed to evade the prohibitions. Each offence is widely drawn. Each section uses different language which inevitably creates problems of construction. In practice, offences under section 50 or section 68 are rarely charged whereas offences under section 170 are common place.

It follows that offences for the unlawful exportation or importation of controlled drugs arise by a combination of section 3(1) of the M.D.A. and an offence created under the C.E.M.A. As a matter of convenience the offence may be described, or even charged, as an offence under either or both enactments; but the underlying offence undoubtedly exists under the C.E.M.A. Accordingly, no proceedings for an offence arising out of a contravention of section 3(1) of the M.D.A. may be instituted except by order of the Commissioners of Customs and Excise, see: section 145(1) of the C.E.M.A.[2]

Instituting proceedings

In the majority of cases, few problems are likely to be encountered, but the relevant provisions cannot always be applied literally. As a result some difficulties of construction arise.

The basic restriction on the institution of proceedings appears in section 145 of the C.E.M.A. which reads as follows:

"(1) Subject to the following provisions of this section, no proceedings for an offence under the customs and excise Acts or for condemnation under Schedule 3 to this Act shall be instituted except by order of the Commissioners.

(2) Subject to the following provisions of this section, any pro-

[2] *Menocal* [1980] A.C. 598 and *Whitehead and Nicholl* [1982] 3 All E.R. 96.

ceedings under the customs and excise Acts instituted in a
magistrates' court, and any such proceedings instituted in a
court of summary jurisdiction in Northern Ireland, shall be commenced in the name of an officer.

(3) Subsections (1) and (2) above shall not apply to proceedings on indictment in Scotland.

(4) In the case of the death, removal, discharge or absence of
the officer in whose name any proceedings were commenced
under subsection (2) above, those proceedings may be continued by any officer authorised in that behalf by the Commissioners.

(5) Nothing in the foregoing provisions of this section shall
prevent the institution of proceedings for an offence under the
customs and excise Acts by order and in the name of a law officer of the Crown in any case in which he thinks it proper that
proceedings should be so instituted.

(6) Notwithstanding anything in the foregoing provisions of
this section, where any person has been detained for any offence
for which he is liable to be detained under the customs and
excise Acts, any court before which he is brought may proceed
to deal with the case although the proceedings have not been
instituted by order of the Commissioners or have not been commenced in the name of an officer."

There is a peculiar conflict—if it be a conflict—between the
effect of subsection (1) and subsection (6). On the one hand, proceedings can only be instituted by order of the Commissioners
(subsection (1)) but, on the other hand, no such order is required
if the defendant is detained, or arrested, for a customs offence
(subsection (6)). It is difficult to envisage many cases, involving
the prosecution of a customs offence, which would not be satisfied
by section 145(6), even if an order of the Commissioners is not
obtained under subsection (1). One possible explanation for this
curious state of affairs was given by Donaldson L.J. when he said[3]:

" . . . the section is designed only to ensure that proceedings
under [the C.E.M.A.] are not brought without the commissioners being aware of them. The commissioners will
become aware of such proceedings if the proceedings are
brought by their order. They should also become aware of
them if the accused is detained by any offence under the Act."

In *Whitehead and Nicholl*,[4] the appellants had been convicted of
two counts of conspiracy to evade the prohibition imposed by sec-

[3] See *ibid.* at p. 102h.
[4] *Ibid.*

tion 3(1) of the M.D.A. contrary to section 1(1) of the Criminal Law Act 1977. On appeal, it was contended that the proceedings were invalid on the grounds that; (a) section 3(1) merely imposed a prohibition on importation or exportation; (b) the offence of evading section 3(1) existed under the Customs and Excise Act 1952, s.304 (now, section 170 of the C.E.M.A.); (c), an order of the Commissioners was therefore required to institute proceedings under the customs and excise Acts (see: section 145(1), formerly section 281(1) of the 1952 Act); (d), such an order was required for a conspiracy to commit the offence (see: section 4(3) of the Criminal Law Act 1977); and (e), no such consent had in fact been obtained.

The Court of Appeal dismissed the appeals but only after a non-literal application of section 145(6) (formerly section 281(4) of the 1952 Act). The Court held, first, that the offence arose by a combination of section 3(1) of the M.D.A. and, what is now, section 170 of the C.E.M.A.[5] Second, the underlying offence was an offence under the C.E.M.A. requiring an order of the commissioners to institute proceedings. Third, that no such order was required *if* the appellants had been "detained" within the meaning of section 145(6) of the C.E.M.A. Finally, that the appellants had been so detained.

By section 145(6) of the C.E.M.A., an order is not required " . . . where any person has been detained for any offence for which *he is liable* to be detained under the customs and excise Acts." (Note the words in italics). A contravention of section 170 of the C.E.M.A. is one such offence, but in *Whitehead and Nicholl*, neither appellant had been charged with that, or any other substantive offence, under the Act. A conspiracy to evade section 3(1) of the M.D.A. is not, strictly speaking, an offence under the customs and excise Acts and therefore—if section 145(6) is strictly applied—such a conspirator is not a person "liable to be detained" under the customs and excise Acts.

However, the Court of Appeal held that the words in section 281(4) of the 1952 Act—now section 145(6)—should read " . . . where any person has been detained for conspiracy to commit any offence for which *he would be liable* to be detained under the customs and excise Acts."

On this basis, both appellants had been so detained and therefore section 145(6) of the C.E.M.A. should be construed as including cases of conspiracy to commit an offence for which an accused would be liable to be detained/arrested under the C.E.M.A.

[5] *Menocal* [1978] 3 All E.R. 961 and *Williams* [1971] 2 All E.R. 444.

Section 4(3) of the Criminal Law Act 1977 provides, insofar as it is material;

> "Any prohibition by or under any enactment on the institution of proceedings for any offence . . . ˉ shall apply also in relation to proceedings under section 1 above for conspiracy to commit that offence . . . "

Donaldson L.J. said, *obiter*, in *Whitehead and Nicholl* that section 4(3) confers authority on the Commissioners to make an order in relation to a statutory conspiracy to commit an offence under the customs and excise Acts.

Lawful shipments

Section 3(2) and section 7 of the M.D.A. permit the Secretary of State to except any controlled drug from the relevant prohibitions. This he has done by virtue of Regulation 4(1) of the Misuse of Drugs Regulations 1985, which provides that section 3(1) shall not have effect in relation to the drugs specified in Schedules 4 and 5 of the 1985 Regulations. The drugs listed in Schedule 4 will be exempt provided that they are in the form of medicinal products.

Other controlled drugs may only be imported or exported under and in accordance with the terms of a licence issued by the Secretary of State: see section 3(2)(*b*) of the M.D.A.

Defining the moment of importation or exportation

This is dealt with in the C.E.M.A., by section 5, as follows:

"(1) The provisions of this section shall have effect for the purposes of the customs and excise Acts.

(2) Subject to subsections (3) and (6) below, the time of importation of any goods shall be deemed to be—

  (*a*) where the goods are brought by sea, the time when the ship carrying them comes within the limits of a port;

  (*b*) where the goods are brought by air, the time when the aircraft carrying them lands in the United Kingdom or the time when the goods are unloaded in the United Kingdom, whichever is the earlier.

  (*c*) where the goods are brought by land, the time when the goods are brought across the boundary into Northern Ireland.

(3) In the case of goods brought by sea of which entry is not required under section 37 . . . [*particular documentation required on importation*], the time of importation shall be

deemed to be the time when the ship carrying them came within the limits of the port at which the goods are discharged.

(4) Subject to subsections (5) and (7) below, the time of exportation of any goods from the United Kingdom shall be deemed to be—

    (*a*) where the goods are exported by sea or air, the time when the goods are shipped for exportation;

    (*b*) where the goods are exported by land, the time when they are cleared by the proper officer at the last customs and excise station on their way to the boundary.

(5) In the case of goods of a class or description with respect to the exportation of which any prohibition or restriction is for the time being in force under or by virtue of any enactment which are exported by sea or air, the time of exportation shall be deemed to be the time when the exporting ship or aircraft departs from the last port or customs and excise airport at which it is cleared before departing for a destination outside the United Kingdom.

(6) Goods imported by means of a pipe-line shall be treated as imported at the time when they are brought within the limits of a port or brought across the boundary into Northern Ireland.

(7) Goods exported by means of a pipe-line shall be treated as exported at the time when they are charged into that pipe-line for exportation.

(8) A ship shall be deemed to have arrived at or departed from a port at the time when the ship comes within, or, as the case may be, leaves the limits of that port."

A "port" means any port appointed by the Commissioners (under section 19). The Commissioners may also determine the "limits" of the port: see section 1(1). A large number of Statutory Instruments have ensured that the entire coastline has been embraced. It may happen, of course, that controlled drugs (destined for the United Kingdom) are, say, jettisoned at sea beyond the limits of a port and are lost. In these circumstances no offence would be committed contrary to the C.E.M.A. since there has been no importation within the meaning of section 5.

The term "ship" is broadly defined to include any boat or other vessel whatsoever: section 1(1).

It is not entirely clear why Parliament has provided that "prohibited goods" are deemed to be exported at the moment when the exporting ship or aircraft " . . . departs from the last port or customs and excise airport at which it is cleared before departing for a destination outside the United Kingdom . . . " (section 5(5)). If prohibited goods leave the United Kingdom from a place other

than a recognised port or airport then, clearly, section 5(5) can
have no application. In this event there is no reason why section
5(4)(*a*) should not prevail.

Goods sent by post

The provisions of the C.E.M.A. apply to all goods imported or
exported—no matter how they may have been shipped. But,
almost by way of a "belts and braces" provision, section 16 of the
Post Office Act 1953 (as amended by the Post Office Act 1969;
s.87; or article 9 of the Postal Services (Channel Islands Consequential Provisions) Order 1969; and article 11 of the Postal Services (Isle of Man Consequential Provisions) Order 1973), directs
that the C.E.M.A. shall apply:

> " . . . in relation to goods contained in postal packets to
> which this section applies brought into or sent out of the
> United Kingdom by post from or to . . . any place outside the
> British postal area as they apply in relation to goods otherwise
> imported, exported or removed into or out of the United
> Kingdom from or to . . . any such place."

The postal packets, to which section 16 applies, are specified in
the Postal Packets (Customs and Excise) Regulations 1975 (S.I.
No. 1992), namely:

> " . . . all postal packets, other than postcards and telegrams,
> which are posted in the United Kingdom for transmission to
> any place outside it or which are brought by post into the
> United Kingdom" (reg. 4).

Regulation 5 modifies section 5 of the C.E.M.A. by omitting the
proviso to subsection (2) while modifying subsection (3) so that:
" . . . the time of exportation of goods shall be the time when they
are posted (or re-directed) in the United Kingdom for transmission to a place outside it . . . "

The Commissioners of Customs and Excise may require an officer of the Post Office to produce to an officer of Customs and
Excise, postal packets either arriving in, or about to be despatched
from, the United Kingdom for the examination of that packet
(reg. 12). The customs officer may also open any packet for the
purpose of that examination (reg. 12).

Furthermore, the Commissioners of Customs and Excise may,
by reg. 17, require an officer of the Post Office to deliver a postal
packet to a customs officer if the packet contains goods liable to
forfeiture under (*inter alia*) the C.E.M.A. or the Postal Packet
Regulations of 1975.

IMPROPER IMPORTATION—
SECTION 50 C.E.M.A. 1979

Section 50 of the C.E.M.A. defines the offence arising out of an improper importation as follows:

"(1) Subsection (2) applies to goods of the following descriptions, that is to say—
    (a) goods chargeable with a duty which has not been paid; and
    (b) goods the importation, landing or unloading of which is for the time being prohibited or restricted by or under any enactment.

(2) If any person with intent to defraud Her Majesty of any such duty or to evade any such prohibition or restriction as is mentioned in subsection (1) above—
    (a) unships or lands in any port or unloads from any aircraft in the United Kingdom or from any vehicle in Northern Ireland any goods to which this subsection applies, or assists or is otherwise concerned in such unshipping, landing or unloading; or
    (b) removes from their place of importation or from any approved wharf, examination station, transit shed or customs and excise station any goods at which this subsection applies or assists or is otherwise concerned in such removal,
he shall be guilty of an offence under this subsection and may be [arrested].

(3) If any person imports or is concerned in importing any goods contrary to any prohibition or restriction for the time being in force under or by virtue of any enactment with respect to those goods, whether or not the goods are unloaded, and does so with intent to evade the prohibition or restriction, he shall be guilty of an offence under this subsection and may be detained."

The ambit of section 50(1)

Quite clearly the draftsman was careful to distinguish between "dutiable goods" (s.50(1)(a)) and "prohibited and restricted goods" (s.50(1)(b)). At first blush, a problem of construction arises when we examine the wording of section 50(1)(b). If (b) was merely concerned with the unlawful *importation* of prohibited goods, and nothing else, what then does the draftsman gain by adding the words "landing" or "unloading?" Although it may be tempting to argue that Parliament was merely describing or demonstrating an act of importation, this contention is soon defeated once it is remembered that "importation" is sufficiently defined under the Act by reference to the moment when goods are deemed to be imported under section 5. Therefore, goods may be imported (and the prohibitions against importation evaded) before the goods are even unloaded. However, the solution to the problem lies in recognising that each of the three words ("importation," "landing," and "unloading") represents a wholly separate and distinct prohibition, or restriction, which may be expressly imposed by the relevant enactment. Thus, for the purposes of section 3(1)(a) of the M.D.A. the "importation" of controlled drugs is prohibited. Other statutes, for their respective purposes, prohibit or restrict the "landing" or "unloading" of certain goods but do not seek to prohibit their actual importation.

In *Smith (Donald)*[6] cannabis was sent by air from Nairobi to Bermuda via London. The drug was unloaded at London Airport; transferred to another aircraft and flown to Bermuda. *S.* was convicted of fraudulently evading the prohibition against its importation, (contrary to the Customs and Excise Act 1952 s.304), and its subsequent exportation, contrary to section 56(2) of that Act. The appellant argued that reference to "goods unloaded" in section 45 of the 1952 Act (now section 50 of the C.E.M.A.) was excluded from the category of "goods imported" and therefore since S. merely facilitated the unloading of goods he had therefore not imported them.

The Court of Appeal rejected that argument concluding that section 45 of the old Act, was concerned with the "improper importation" of goods, Willis J. said:

> " . . . it is to be observed that ss.44 and 45 are concerned with the improper importation of goods . . . It seems quite clear that the Act contemplates that goods can be imported before they are either landed from a ship or unloaded from an aircraft . . . it would be strange indeed for Parliament to have excluded from the various categories of 'goods imported' a category of 'goods unloaded' without such an intention being precisely indicated. We cannot think . . . that there can be a category of goods which are simply 'unloaded' and not 'imported' when they are taken off an aircraft . . . until reloaded for onward transmission outside the country."

The result is patently right since to treat "imported goods" and "unloaded goods" as being mutually exclusive is to make a non-

---

[6] [1973] Q.B. 924.

sense of the wording of the Act. It should be noted that the appellant was not charged with an offence under what is now section 50, but with the offence of being knowingly concerned in the fraudulent evasion of a prohibition against the importation of a controlled drug (*i.e.* what is now s.170(2)). When Willis J., described section 45 of the 1952 Act as being concerned with the "*improper* importation of goods" he was careful not to say that section 45 was concerned only with the *unlawful* importation of goods. He clearly recognised that goods might be lawfully imported but, illegally unloaded or landed and therefore Willis J. described section 45 in neutral terms as being concerned with the "improper" importation of goods.

Section 50(2) offences

It is clear that subsection (2) creates two sets of offences—one in relation to "dutiable goods" and another in respect of "prohibited or restrictive goods." Therefore, a person arriving in the United Kingdom and knowing that the goods he is carrying, are subject to a prohibition against importation, will commit an offence contrary to section 50(2)(*a*) if he removes them from a ship in a port, or unloads them from any aircraft.

Curiously, whereas section 50(2)(*a*) applies to goods removed from any aircraft in the United Kingdom (whether or not the aircraft has landed at a recognised "Customs and Excise airport") it seems that no offence is committed contrary to section 50(2)(*a*) if goods are unshipped from a vessel outside the limits of "a port" as defined by section 19(1) of the C.E.M.A.

Section 50(3)

"*Concerned*"

The *actus reus* of the offence is very narrow, particularly when it is compared with the much broader offence of "being knowingly concerned in the fraudulent evasion of the prohibition," against importation, contrary to section 170(2). In essence, section 50(3) is concerned solely with the single word "importation"; whereas section 170(2) is concerned with the evasion of a prohibition. Consequently, if the prosecution are to succeed under section 50(3) they must prove that the accused participated in the actual importation—for example by carrying the drug, or that he was at least in such a position as to be able to lend his assistance if required, in the smuggling operation. Therefore unlike section 170(2), the offence is not a continuing one and cannot therefore include persons who, subsequently, handle the drug—albeit that they are aware of its origin—but who were not parties to the original importation.

The Mens Rea

Again, quite unlike section 170(2), the intent required is expressed by section 50(3) to be an intent to "evade *the* prohibition." The use of the words "the prohibition," implies that the accused must know the relevant prohibition which he is evading. If this is so then, an importer of drugs commits no offence, under this subsection, if he genuinely believes that the drugs are not subject to a prohibition. Similarly, if an importer makes a complete mistake as to the nature of the goods imported, believing for example, that he has smuggled weapons (which he knows to be "prohibited goods") whereas he has unwittingly imported heroin, then no offence under section 50(3) has been committed since he does not intend to evade the prohibition imposed by section 3(1) of the M.D.A. However, the point is not free from difficulty since it is widely thought in legal circles that the *mens rea* required for an offence under sections 50, 68 and 170 is identical, namely that the accused need only know that the goods imported were subject to a prohibition or restriction on their importation.[6a] In any event, a mistaken belief that he is importing cannabis whereas he is importing hereon, is no defence since both commodities are subject to the same prohibition.

It is not necessary for the prosecution to prove dishonesty on the part of the importer. By "evade" Parliament meant no more than an intention on the part of the accused to "get around" the prohibition. "Evade," in this context, does not carry the connotation of fraud or dishonesty as it does in income tax law.[7] It follows that it would be no defence for a cannabis smuggler, knowing of the prohibition, to say that he considered that he was doing nothing wrong, believing that the drug cured most ailments.

UNLAWFUL EXPORTATION—SECTION 68

Section 68(2) of the C.E.M.A. provides, that: "Any person knowingly concerned in the exportation . . . or in the attempted exportation . . . of any goods with intent to evade any . . . prohibition or restriction . . . shall be guilty of an offence . . . "

Oddly, the draftsman has adopted a formula of words which is very different to section 50. It is difficult to see why there should

---

[6a] See *Hussain* [1969] 2 Q.B. 567.
[7] *Hurford-Jones* (1977) 65 Cr. App. R. 263.

be a difference. First, the use of the word "knowingly" appears to add nothing to the subsection since the prosecution are required in any event to prove that the accused intended to evade any prohibition or restriction in force with respect to those goods. Secondly, quite unlike section 50, the requirement that the prosecution must prove an intent " . . . to evade any . . . prohibition or restriction . . . " is ambiguous; it may be sufficient for the prosecution merely to prove that the accused knew that the goods he was exporting were subject to some prohibition; albeit, that he was unaware of the precise one. Thus, it would be no defence for an exporter to say that he believed he was exporting guns (knowing them to be subject to a prohibition on exportation) and not heroin. But, if he believed that he was exporting brandy then, there is no intention to evade a prohibition on exportation since brandy does not come within the category of "prohibited goods or restricted goods" (see section 1(1) of the C.E.M.A.) but "dutiable goods." Furthermore, whereas section 50 is principally directed against the persons who are physically involved in the actual importation, for example either by carrying, or unloading the drug or aiding and abetting its commission, section 68, by contrast, is not so restricted and may include persons who organise an exportation venture and who may never see or handle the goods in question.

FRAUDULENT EVASIONS—SECTION 170

Commercially motivated contraband smuggling almost always involves a high degree of planning and a team of participants to secure the distribution of smuggled goods and to prevent their confiscation by law enforcement officers. An evasion of a prohibition or restriction on the importation or exportation of goods is therefore a continuing process and not confined to the moment when the goods actually enter or leave the country. Accordingly, it is not surprising that statutory measures designed to combat smuggling, cast a particularly wide net. The drawback is that these measures lack precision, and create ambiguity and uncertainty—as section 170 demonstrates.

Thus section 170(1) reads as follows:

"Without prejudice to any other provision of the Customs and Excise Acts 1979, if any person—
   (a) knowingly acquires possession of any of the following goods, that is to say—
        (i) goods which have been unlawfully removed from a warehouse or Queen's warehouse;

> (ii) goods which are chargeable with a duty which had not been paid;
> (iii) goods with respect to the importation or exportation of which any prohibition or restriction is for the time being in force under or by virtue of any enactment; or
> (*b*) is in any way knowingly concerned in carrying, removing, depositing, harbouring, keeping or concealing or in any other manner dealing with any such goods,
> and does so with intent to defraud Her Majesty of any duty payable on the goods or to evade any such prohibition or restriction with respect to the goods he shall be guilty of an offence under this section and may be [arrested]."

Note the words "acquires possession" in section 170(1)(*a*), and the activities required to be proved, in section 170(1)(*b*). Note also that the relevant *mens rea*, in cases of drug smuggling, is an intention to " . . . evade any such prohibition or restriction with respect to the goods."

Now compare the above with the wording of subsection (2) set out below:

> "Without prejudice to any other provision of the Customs and Excise Acts 1979, if any person is, in relation to any goods, in any way knowingly concerned in any fraudulent evasion or attempt at evasion—
> (*a*) of any duty chargeable on the goods;
> (*b*) of any prohibition or restriction for the time being in force with respect to the goods under or by virtue of any enactment; or
> (*c*) or any provision of the Customs and Excise Acts 1979 applicable to the goods,
> he shall be guilty of an offence under this section and may be [arrested]."

General statement of the law

Interpreting section 170 has become something of a judicial nightmare—particularly in the last few years—and it would be idle to pretend that considerable difficulties of reconciliation do not continue to exist between the many cases which have wrestled with drug-related importations. Nevertheless it is clear that a set of rules is not only crystalising but it is also displaying signs of durability. Accordingly, before examining the wording of section 170, and the relevant decisions, it may be of assistance to summarise the basic legal position at this stage.

If the charge is brought under section 170(1) then the prosecution must prove, that:

(1) the accused either—
  (a) knowingly acquires possession of goods; or
  (b) is "knowingly concerned" in carrying, removing, depositing, harbouring, keeping or concealing, "or in any other manner" dealing with goods;
(2) the goods in question are subject to a prohibition or restriction on importation in force under or by virtue of any enactment; and
(3) the accused intended to evade a prohibition or restriction imposed with respect to the goods.

If, however, the charge is brought under section 170(2) then the prosecution must prove that:

(1) the goods in question are subject to a prohibition or restriction on importation or exportation under or by virtue of any enactment; and
(2) a *fraudulent evasion* or attempted evasion of a prohibition or restriction has taken place in relation to those goods; and
(3) the accused is *concerned* in that fraudulent evasion or attempted evasion; and
(4) the accused was concerned in that fraudulent evasion (or attempted evasion) "*knowingly.*"

In respect of each subsection the following propositions currently represent the law. Propositions referable to "importations" apply equally to "exportations" thus:
  A. There must be proof (at least for the full offence) that the goods were "imported."[8]
  B. The Prosecution must prove that the accused knew that the goods were, prohibited or restricted from importation.
  C. But, the prosecution do *not* have to prove that the accused knew:

  (i) the precise prohibition involved; or
  (ii) the class of drug actually imported; or
  (iii) the actual drug imported.[9]
  D. It is therefore a defence for the accused to say that he did not know that the goods imported were subject to any prohibition or restriction on importation.

[8] *Watts & Stack* (1980) 70 Cr. App. R. 187.
[9] *Hussain* [1969] 2 Q.B. 567; *Hennessey* (1978) 68 Cr. App. R. 419, C.A.; *Shivpuri* [1986] 2 W.L.R. 988; *Ellis & Street* (1986) *The Times*, August 12.

E. It is a defence for the accused to say that he believed he was importing goods not subject to a prohibition or restriction but that they came within some other category, for example, "dutiable goods," for example brandy.

F. It is a defence for the accused to say that he mistakenly believed he was importing goods subject to a prohibition when, as a matter of law, they would not have been if his belief had been true.[10]

G. An offence may be committed by a person who is involved in the venture before or after the moment of importation of the goods into the country.

H. Acts committed abroad are nevertheless punishable in England if the prohibited goods are consequentially imported into that country.[11]

Distinguishing section 170(1) from section 170(2)

In *Neal and Others*,[12] Griffiths L.J. contrasted the language of subsections (1) and (2) and commented that:

> "The language of [subsection (1)] is so embracing and casts the net so wide that one is left to wonder what purpose is served by subsection (2) . . . We are satisfied that [subsection (2)] was inserted by the draftsman with the intention of casting his net as widely as words enabled him—note his language, 'if any person' and 'in any way'."

Certainly both subsections are very widely drawn and catch individuals who were not parties to the original smuggling operation. So a person who conceals drugs at a safe house, long after the moment of importation, is caught by either subsection providing that he intended to evade a prohibition against the importation of the goods.

However, there is in fact a significant distinction to be made between the scope of subsections (1) and (2). It will be seen that section 170(1)(*a*) makes it plain that an acquisition of possession of the goods is a necessary prerequisite for an offence under section 170(1)(*a*). Similarly, proof of custody or control over prohibited goods is implicitly required in respect of any of the activities referred to in section 170(1)(*b*) of the Act. By contrast subsection (2) imposes no such restrictions.

It may be said that there is another significant difference namely, that subsection (1) expressly requires proof of an inten-

---

[10] *Taffe* [1984] A.C. 539.
[11] *Wall* [1974] 2 All E.R. 245.
[12] (1983) 77 Cr. App. R. 283.

tion to evade the prohibition or restriction, whereas subsection (2) does not. However, such an ingredient is imparted by the word "fraudulent" in subsection (2), that is to say "fraudulent" in this context means dishonest conduct " . . . deliberately intended to evade the prohibition or restriction with respect to, or the duty chargeable on, goods as the case may be . . . ": *per* Lord Lane C.J.[13]

Evading the prohibition or restriction

The popular image of smuggling is a venture involving the surreptitious landing of contraband at an unofficial point of entry into a country. But the "evasion" of "any prohibition or restriction on importation . . . ," as required by subsection (1) or (2), is wider than simply the single word "importation" as Kenneth Jones J. vividly illustrated in *Neal & Others*[14]:

> "A boat arrives in . . . this country . . . and it has on board cannabis resin. One of the sailors . . . actually carries the cannabis resin ashore. He hands it over to another man . . . who loads it into a van. The van is driven off to some place where the drug is . . . stored . . . and . . . at a later stage, it is transported to yet another building and is stored there and it may be . . . that behind all this operation . . . is some organising person. Now you see, of all those men . . . strictly speaking, only the sailor has imported the drug into this country . . . and that is what importation means, but he and each of those other persons . . . have all taken a part . . . in setting at nought the ban which the law imposes on the importation of the drug."

The illustration effectively demonstrates that the evasion of a prohibition is a continuing process—not an isolated act—and accordingly, offences under section 170 are continuing offences. It follows that arguments which attempt to narrowly construe section 170 so as to include only those persons who were parties to the original smuggling operation must be fallacious. The organiser who never makes an appearance at the moment of importation is as guilty as the sailor who brings the goods ashore. Thus, in *Neal*, above Griffiths L.J. said:

> "Subsection (1) clearly includes those who are not a part of the original smuggling team. For example, it includes anyone

[13] *A.-G. Reference (No. 1 of 1981)* [1982] 2 All E.R. 417, at p. 422; *Borro and Abdullah* [1973] Crim. L.R. 513 not followed.
[14] See *supra*, n. 12.

who acquires possession of goods unlawfully removed from a warehouse, or anyone who hides goods on which duty has not been paid, or anyone who carries goods the importation of which is forbidden; and there can be no warrant for reading into the language of the subsection the qualification 'provided they are part of the original smuggling team' . . . ''

As MacKenna J. pointed out in *Ardalan*,[15] section 170(1)(*a*) (formerly section 304(*a*) of the 1952 Act) embraces an accused who "acquires possession" of prohibited goods. Obviously he can only "acquire" goods after (or before) the moment of importation or exportation. Equally, the person who (contrary to section 170(1)(*b*)) carries, or removes or harbours prohibited goods, can only do so prior to, or subsequent to, the moment of importation. In other words, the very language of section 170(1), itself proves that offences under that subsection are continuing. Since subsection (2) merely widens the scope of subsection (1) it follows that offences under subsection (2) must also be continuing. Persons who are therefore not parties to the actual importation may nevertheless join or leave the venture at any time until the goods cease to be prohibited and are therefore criminally liable for their acts under section 170. Thus in *Green*,[16] a crate containing cannabis arrived at Southampton which was placed in a shed. Customs officers removed the cannabis and substituted a quantity of peat. A month after the importation G rented a garage in a false name. The crate was delivered to the garage where it was stored. The Court of Appeal dismissed G.'s appeal against his conviction under what is now section 170(2). The offence was a continuing one and the evasion did not cease when the drugs were seized. Renting the garage, knowing that it was to be used to store cannabis which had been unlawfully imported, completed the offence.

Again, in *Neal* (above), the provision of a barn on a farm in which six hundred weight of cannabis was concealed behind a false wall was sufficient evidence of being concerned in the unlawful importation of drugs even though there was no evidence as to where, or how, the drugs had been imported.

It will be recalled that in *Green* (above) customs officers removed the drug shortly after it was imported and substituted a quantity of peat. Nevertheless, the Court of Appeal held that because the offence was a continuing one, the evasion did not cease when the drugs were seized. Perhaps encouraged by this decision, it has long been the practice of customs officers to substi-

---

[15] (1972) 56 Cr. App. R. 320.
[16] (1976) 62 Cr. App. R. 74.

tute an innocent substance for the smuggled goods before allowing
the goods to be delivered to the consignee. Accordingly, where
any person was "knowingly concerned" in the evasion of the prohibition on importation of a controlled drug (after the goods were
imported and seized) he will still be guilty of an offence contrary to
section 170(2) of the C.E.M.A.

This startling result has recently been confirmed by the Court of
Appeal in *Ciaparra*.[16a]

> In Bolivia, C's sister addressed two packets containing
> cocaine to C. The packets were unsolicited by C. Customs
> officers intercepted the packets and substituted baking
> powder for the cocaine. Each packet consisted of a note (ask-
> ing C for money) wrapped around a postcard to form a con-
> tainer for the drug. C threw away the note, and the postcard,
> but kept the powder which he believed to be cocaine. He was
> convicted of an offence under section 170(2) in respect of one
> packet (which was sent to his place of work) but he was
> acquitted of a similar charge in respect of the other packet
> which had been sent to his home address. C's appeal against
> his conviction was dismissed.

C contended, on appeal, that (a) the packets were unsolicited,
(b) the importation was complete by the time the packages were
intercepted, (c) the drug had been removed before C received the
packages and therefore, (d), C could not be said to be "knowingly
concerned" with the importation of cocaine. The Court of Appeal
rejected C's contention. There was no dispute that the packets
were unsolicited and that the importation was complete by the
time the packages were intercepted. However, section 170(2) did
not exclude those whose only involvement arose after the importation, provided they knowingly participated. The court's attention
was drawn to *D.P.P.* v. *Doot*,[16b] *Neal*,[16c] and *Ardalan*,[16d] but
not—it would seem—to *Green* (above).

The commentary to *Ciappara*, provided by Professor J. C.
Smith Q.C., is thought provoking but—it is submitted—erroneous. Professor Smith remarked:

> "So he is convicted of being knowingly concerned in the
> fraudulent evasion of the prohibition on the importation of
> cocaine, although, in fact, the only substance he even dealt
> with was baking powder! Surely that cannot be right . . .

[16a] [1988] Crim. L.R. 172.
[16b] [1973] A.C. 807.
[16c] (1983) 77 Crim. App. R. 283.
[16d] (1972) 56 Cr. App. R. 320.

> How can a person properly be said to be concerned in evasion of a prohibition on importation when the importation is complete before he even knows anything about it . . . The onus should surely be on the prosecution to show that there are words justifying the remarkable wider meaning given to the section. It is like saying I am knowingly concerned in killing X if, after finding that X has been killed, I help to dispose of the body."

But the definition of "murder", "manslaughter" (or even "killing") is very different to the wording of section 170(2) of the C.E.M.A. A "killing" denotes a very brief moment in time as does the word "importation". However, it is not the fact of importation which is the continuing element of an offence under section 170(2). It is the *evasion* of a prohibition or restriction on importation which continues. Thus, the evasion continues until the goods cease to be prohibited or, possibly, until the goods are re-exported. The fact that they have been seized in the interim is irrelevant.

Applying the same reasoning, acts done before the moment of importation, with the requisite *mens rea*, are punishable under section 170 even if the acts are performed abroad. So where, in *Wall*[17] W travelled to Afganistan with others and handled packages of cannabis which were later shipped to the United Kingdom, it was held that he had been knowingly concerned in the fraudulent evasion.

The appellant contended that if he had done nothing on the day of importation, and if what he did do earlier was not done in England, then he should not have been convicted. This contention implied that the offence is not a continuing one and therefore overlooked the fact that the court was not restricted to focusing its attention on acts done in England when the goods were imported. There was a clear causal link between the defendant's activities abroad and the eventual arrival of the drug into England. If *Wall* had been decided differently the ramifications would have been colossal. Organisers, operating abroad, who shipped vast quantities of drugs to England could therefore never be convicted of an offence under section 170.

The decision in *Wall* is, in fact, supported by a long line of authorities.[18]

In *Smith (Donald)*[19] Willis J. said: "It was quite unnecessary to

---

[17] See *supra*, n. 11.
[18] See *D.P.P.* v. *Doot* [1973] A.C. 807; *Treacy* v. *D.P.P.* [1971] A.C. 537; *Baxter* [1971] 2 All E.R. 359; *Millar* [1970] 1 All E.R. 577.
[19] See *supra*, n. 6.

prove that the applicant did anything to further the transaction in
this country."

It follows that once steps are taken by an individual to bring
about the fraudulent evasion of the prohibition, an act of remorse
(even if coupled with a wish to abandon the enterprise) will not
save that person from a conviction under section 170 if an importation in fact results.

> In *Jakeman* (1983) 76 Cr.App.R. 223, J was recruited to carry
> a case of cannabis from Ghana to Heathrow, via Paris. She
> withdrew from the enterprise in Paris by abandoning the suit-
> case at the airport. Baggage officials found the suitcase and,
> believing it to have been mis-routed, 'rushed' it to London.
>
> Held, her appeal against conviction was dismissed. Her
> initial actions ultimately brought about the importation.

The result may seem harsh but it is consistent with the wording
of section 170(2)—under which Jakeman had been charged. As
Wood J. observed in that case, the correct approach is to analyse
the offence itself. At best her withdrawal from the enterprise was
good mitigation; but it was not a defence. It was ingeniously contended on the appellant's behalf that she should not have been
convicted unless her guilty state of mind subsisted at the time of
importation. Once again, the argument assumed that the offence is
only committed at the moment of importation which, clearly, it is
not. It will be remembered that in *Neal*, the accused prepared a
hiding place in a barn to store cannabis; he was recruited after the
moment of importation and therefore his mind could not possibly
have been a "guilty" one when the drugs were imported into the
United Kingdom from the Lebanon; nevertheless, he was guilty of
an offence under section 170(2).

Wood J., in *Jakeman*, observed that:

> "What matters is the state of mind at the time the relevant
> acts are done, *i.e.* at the time the defendant is concerned in
> *bringing about the importation*. This accords with the general
> principles of common law. To stab a victim in a rage with the
> necessary intent for murder or manslaughter leads to criminal
> responsibility for the resulting death regardless of any repent-
> ance between the act of stabbing and the time of death, which
> may be hours or days later."

Although—on the facts of this particular case—it is correct to
say, as Wood J. effectively did, that the applicant's initial actions
ultimately brought about the importation, this is a feature which
must not be taken too far. Wood J., went on to say that:

> "For guilt to be established the importation must, of course,

result as a consequence, if only in part, of the activity of the accused."

Construed literally those passages may be thought to suggest that in every case the prosecution must establish a chain of causation between the actions of the accused and the ultimate importation of the drug. This would obviously be impossible to prove in the case of a person who (not being a party to the original importation) committed acts in furtherance of the evasion *after* the drugs had been imported; yet such persons are caught by the section. Furthermore, construed literally, the words of Wood J. would mean that any act which breaks the chain of causation would provide a defence. If this is what was intended then it is hard to accept that the result in *Jakeman* would not have been decided differently since the intervention of the baggage officials, who redirected the suitcase from Paris to London, was itself a *novus actus interveniens*.

A person who is not a party to the original smuggling operation will still commit an offence if he acts in joint enterprise with one or more persons to contravene section 170. A classic example of this situation is *Williams*[20]:

> H., an Indian, asked W if he had contacts for selling cannabis as H was returning to India and could send on 'samples.' W gave H a forwarding address, occupied by X. H said he would send a letter to W informing him of an impending delivery at that address. X opened one such letter in error but decided to tell W that no letter had arrived. Customs officers discovered a parcel containing cannabis at that address shortly thereafter. W was convicted of an offence contrary to section 304 of the 1952 Act [now s.170 of the CEMA]. W contended that the offence had not been made out since an agreement to sell cannabis after it had been imported into the United Kingdom was not a sufficiently proximate act to the original importation to be guilty of the offence charged.
> *Held*, the appeal was dismissed. There may well have been a joint enterprise to unlawfully import but, in any event, what W did was sufficiently proximate to make him guilty of the offence.

Of course W was sufficiently proximate to the actual importation to make him guilty of the offence. It was not necessary for W to be present at the moment of importation; or for W to know when the illicit parcel was being posted; or for W to know that the parcel had in fact arrived in the United Kingdom; indeed it is not

[20] [1971] 2 All E.R. 444.

apparent from the report that there was any evidence that W did know that the cannabis had arrived in the United Kingdom. Even so, the interval of time between the defendant agreeing to receive the drugs, and the moment of importation, was not so great as to make him insufficiently proximate to the importation. Like *Jakeman*,[21] W's initial actions brought about the eventual importation of the drug.

It follows from the above that the fact that the drugs were merely in transit to another country will not protect the shipper once the goods are technically imported. Thus, in *Smith*,[21a]

> packets of cannabis were sent by air from Nairobi to Bermuda, via London. S was a party to the shipment and there was evidence that he knew of the likely route. S was convicted, *inter alia*, of being knowingly concerned in the fraudulent evasion of the prohibition on the importation of cannabis. S argued, on appeal, that he did nothing in this country to further the transaction.
>
> *Held*, the appeal would be dismissed. It was unnecessary for the prosecution to prove such an ingredient. The goods were deliberately "introduced" into this country and were therefore "imported."

A similar point was made in *Berner*[22] where B took goods (this time prohibited from *exportation*) out of the United Kingdom with the intention that they be brought back in again. The fact that they were to be brought back did not mean that the exportation ceased to be prohibited.

Exportation—acts done before or after that moment

There is clear authority for the proposition that acts done before the moment of exportation are caught by the section. Thus, where in *Garrett* v. *Arthur Churchill (Glass) Ltd.*,[23] the defendant handed goods over for export knowing that they were prohibited from exportation, he committed an offence contrary to section 170.

There is no reason, in logic, why the principles applicable to importations should not equally apply to exportations.

---

[21] (1983) 76 Cr. App. R. 223.
[21a] See *supra*, n. 6.
[22] (1953) 37 Cr. App. R. 113.
[23] [1970] 1 Q.B. 92.

At what point of time does an offence under section 170 cease?

How far removed does a person have to be, from the original smuggling operation, before he is no longer liable under section 170?

The answer is of some importance for, in theory at least, a person arrested in London in possession of one gram of so-called "Lebanese Gold" (*i.e.* cannabis resin from the Lebanon) may be said to be evading the prohibition on importation of that drug by dealing with it unlawfully. Moreover, consider the case of a person in England, who plants cannabis seeds taken from a cannabis plant imported by another: is that person guilty of an offence under the same section?

In *Ardalan*,[24] A was recruited to collect packages, which contained drugs, long after they had arrived in the United Kingdom, Roskill L.J. observed that[24a]:

> "If once . . . there can be an offence committed at some point of time and at some place after importation . . . it is difficult to see why there should be any limit to that point of time or place provided always, of course, that the goods . . . are the subject of a prohibition . . . and with intent to evade that prohibition."

Logically, there can be no limit either as to time or place, before the offence is committed, providing—and this is the crucial point—that the acts are done with the intention of evading the relevant prohibition. It is when the prosecution cease to be able to prove the requisite *mens rea* that the cut-off point is reached. In *Neal*,[25] Griffiths L.J. expressed the position thus[25a]:

> "If no more can be proved than that a piece of cannabis changed hands in Piccadilly Circus, no doubt it would be foolish of the prosecution to proceed under [s.170 of the Customs and Excise Management Act 1979] for it would be far-fetched to suggest that the real intent of such a transaction is to evade the prohibition on the import of cannabis."

The holder of a small piece of cannabis may know that the drug comes from the Lebanon but his intention is to use it either for his own or for another's benefit. He is unlikely to use the drug in a manner intended to avoid, or to get round, the ban on its importation.

---

[24] (1972) 56 Cr. App. R. 320.
[24a] *Ibid.* at p. 326.
[25] See *supra*, n. 12.
[25a] See *supra*, n. 12 at p. 291.

In *Watts & Stack*,[26] S was arrested upon leaving a public house, and found to be in possession of cocaine, scales, and other drug-paraphernalia. A large sum of money was found at an address which S had earlier visited and where W was arrested. Bridge L.J. (as he then was) said, *obiter*:

> "Merely to establish that there has been a dealing with the prohibited goods, and that by virtue of the presumptions [see now s.154(2)] they are presumed at some time in the infinite past to have been unlawfully imported, would not, in our judgment, ever justify, without anything further, inviting a jury to conclude that the evidence established an intent to evade the prohibition on importation."

Accordingly, Bridge L.J. reached the conclusion that:

> " . . . on a true construction of section 170(1), in order to establish that any particular dealing with goods was done with intent to evade the relevant prohibition on importation, the onus on the Crown to prove that intent must involve *establishing a link or nexus between the actus reus of the offence and some prohibited importation*."

Just as one must be careful not to construe too literally the words of Wood J. in *Jakeman*,[27] when he said that the importation must result " . . . as a consequence, if only in part, of the activity of the accused . . . " so one must be careful not to treat references made by Bridge L.J. to a "link" or "nexus" as establishing hard and fast ingredients of the offence. But, that said, there is a great deal of force in the dictum of Bridge L.J. in *Watts & Stack* which should not be overlooked. *Watts & Stack* was cited in *Neal* but, most unfortunately, the head-note to *Neal* (as it appears in the Criminal Appeal Reports), states that the dictum of Bridge L.J. was "not applied." In fact, this is not so. It is important to emphasise that their Lordships adopted the dictum for the purpose of stressing the importance of the prosecution leading evidence to prove the necessary intent to evade the prohibition. What the Court of Appeal in *Neal* could not accept was that the words of Bridge L.J. had the meaning attached to them by Counsel for the Appellants who argued that a "nexus between the actus reus of the offence and some prohibited importation" meant that offences under section 170 could only be committed by persons involved in the initial smuggling operation. Such a contention was clearly going too far since Bridge L.J. was careful to use the words "link"

---

[26] See *supra*, n. 8.
[27] See *supra*, n. 21.

or "nexus" to indicate a point of involvement beyond the initial smuggling operation but not so far removed as to be unrealistic and incapable of proving intent.

The appellant's argument in *Neal* ignored the fact that Bridge L.J. was merely describing a method of proving *mens rea*. He was not, it is submitted, setting out to redefine the *actus reus* of the offence.

If Bridge L.J. really did intend to express the construction, for which the appellants in *Neal* contended, then such dictum would at least be in conflict with *Ardalan*,[28] But Bridge L.J. was careful to refer to *Ardalan*, and in any event, it was not the belief of their Lordships in *Neal* that Bridge L.J. intended any such conflict.

The decision in *Watts & Stack* is a revealing example of how easy it is to be misled by the sweeping words of section 170 and to ignore the essential ingredient that there must be an intent to evade the prohibition and that there must be proof that the goods were imported. In *Watts & Stack* there was clear evidence that the accused dealt in cocaine but there was no evidence at all to show that they had imported the cocaine into the United Kingdom. The trial judge held that there was an evasion of a prohibition on importation of goods once goods of that description were shown to have been "dealt with" in the United Kingdom from which an intention to evade the prohibition could be inferred. Astonishing, perhaps, is the fact that the trial judge accepted the argument that the growing of cannabis plants in a back garden in England would be an evasion of the prohibition on the importation of cannabis or, that LSD manufactured in the United Kingdom, would similarly be an evasion of the prohibition on importation of LSD. In neither example of course could it be said that a prohibited importation had taken place. The absence of such a fact was fatal to the argument and accordingly, it was not advanced before the Court of Appeal.

The above examples pose very different situations to the facts in say, *Neal*, where there was evidence that goods had been imported and the prohibition evaded—although there was no evidence as to when or how that importation had taken place. The only issue was whether the defendant was a party to the evasion of the prohibition on importation.

Proving the importation

Arising out of the above it follows that in every case of drug-smuggling the prosecution are faced with the obvious practical

---

[28] *Supra*, n. 8 at p. 192.

problem of proving that the drug was in fact imported. This may
not be very easy if there is no evidence as to the place or the time
of importation of the goods. To get round this difficulty the
Crown, in *Watts & Stack*, argued that what is now section 154 of
the Customs and Excise Management Act 1979 (as it now is)
enacts a series of presumptions in favour of the Crown so as to
place the burden of proving that there had been no importation on
the defendant. The Court of Appeal did not find that contention
attractive. Bridge L.J. said:

> "The Court feels grave doubt as to whether the opening
> words of subsection (2) . . . are apt to refer to an issue as to
> whether goods have been imported or not. We think it more
> probable that those words are directed to an issue, which may
> arise in determining at what rate import duty is to be levied,
> as to the country from which the imported goods have origi-
> nated."

Nevertheless the Court decided the appeal on the assumption
that the contention was correct. The point is not straightforward.
Section 154(2), insofar as it is material, provides that:

> "Where in any proceedings relating to customs and excise any
> question arises *as to the place from which any goods have been
> brought* or as to whether or not—
>   (a) any duty has been paid or secured in respect of any
>   goods; or
>   (b) any goods or other things whatsoever are of the des-
>   cription or nature alleged in the information, writ or
>   other process; or
>   (c) any goods have been lawfully imported or lawfully
>   unloaded from any ship or aircraft; or
>   (d) any goods have been lawfully loaded into any ship or
>   aircraft or lawfully exported or were lawfully water-
>   borne; or
>   (e) any goods were lawfully brought to any place for the
>   purpose of being loaded into any ship or aircraft or
>   exported; or
>   (f) any goods are or were subject to any prohibition of or
>   restriction on their importation or exportation
> then, where those proceedings are brought by . . . the Com-
> missioner . . . the burden of proof shall lie upon the other party
> to the proceedings."

It is important to note that questions arising in connection with
" . . . the place from which any goods have been brought . . . "
(see the opening words of section 154(2)) and questions arising as

to any of the matters listed in section 154(2)(*a*) to (*f*), are separate and distinct.

To demonstrate how devastating these presumptions can be, consider *Mizel* v. *Warren*[29] M bought (in England) a second-hand bracelet from C in 1962. The bracelet was made of white gold and platinum. The bracelet was seized by customs in 1970 on the basis that it was of Belgian manufacture and there was no evidence that duty had been paid on it when it had been imported. However, evidence adduced by M, suggested that it would have been of English *or* foreign manufacture. The Crown Court preferred the evidence called by M. However, the prosecution relied on what is now section 154(2)(*b*), and argued that the place of manufacture formed part of the "description," and that the burden therefore fell on M to prove that the bracelet was manufactured in England. The Divisional Court agreed.

The repercussions of the decision in *Mizel* v. *Warren*[30] are enormous. A person approached by a customs officer in connection with a camera in his possession may be faced with the task of proving that the camera was of British manufacture or, if he cannot do so, of proving that the duty was paid in respect of it—a task that is likely to be quite impossible to fulfil. Again, a person found in possession of cannabis may, likewise, be faced with the task of proving that the drug was grown in Britain.

It may be asked why the Court in *Mizel* v. *Warren* was so concerned with "description" and not with the opening words of section 154(2). Lord Widgery C.J. reflected on this aspect when he said:

> "Some time was spent in the Crown Court in considering the opening words of [section 154(2)] dealing with the place from which any goods have been brought; but it is obvious to me . . . that that is not the point with which we are concerned . . . The argument is concerned with their place of manufacture . . . So we are not interested in the place from whence the goods have been brought; we are very much concerned in whether they have been imported in the sense they began life in a foreign country."

There is, of course, force in this line of reasoning on the particular facts of that case. M did not "bring" the bracelet from any "place." In any event, the opening words of section 154(2) apply, for example, to cases where different rates of duty are payable on goods brought into the United Kingdom from countries outside

---

[29] [1973] 2 All E.R. 1149.
[30] *Ibid.*

the EEC, as opposed to payments on the same goods brought in from countries inside the EEC. In such cases it is important to ascertain the place from which the goods were in fact brought. Identifying the exact country of origin was not relevant to the issue to be determined in *Mizel* v. *Warren*. It was not relevant to ascertain the actual place from which the bracelet was brought at all. It was only necessary to ascertain whether the bracelet was of "foreign manufacture" or not; if it was then it must have been imported. The court was therefore concerned with the description of the goods. "Havana cigars" or "Chinese silk" is clearly a description which includes the country of origin. But the fact that goods are said to be "foreign" is also part of the description.

Given the above, suppose D, an American tourist, is arrested in Piccadilly and found to be in possession of LSD. The prosecution allege that the drug was manufactured in the United States of America and imported into this country by D, D is adamant that he bought the LSD in Piccadilly and believed the drug to be of British manufacture. On such facts, the country of origin is likely to be regarded as part of the description of the drugs and accordingly, the burden will be on D to prove that the substance was manufactured in the United Kingdom and therefore could not have been imported by him.

It is important to note that, for the purposes of section 154(2)(*b*), the presumption arises once it is alleged in the information, writ, or other process, that the goods are of a particular description. In *Mizel* v. *Warren* it was alleged that the bracelet was of foreign manufacture. Evidence was called to support the allegation but the evidence does not appear to have been accepted by the court as being convincing. Nevertheless, it was enough to bring the presumption into play in favour of the Commissioner of Customs and Excise.

PROVING MENS REA FOR AN OFFENCE UNDER SECTION 170(2)

In 1969, the Court of Appeal delivered judgment in *Hussain*[31]—a case which has been the subject of much scrutiny both in the Court of Appeal, and in the House of Lords, but it continues to be the leading authority on the *mens rea* required to be proved for an

[31] (1969) 53 Cr. App. R. 448.

offence under section 170 of the C.E.M.A. The facts are as follows:

> A motor vessel arrived at Liverpool from Las Palmas. The vessel was boarded by an officer who entered a cabin occupied by H and two other crew members. The officer removed the bulkhead panel in the cabin and discovered some ten packets of cannabis resin concealed behind it. H told customs officers that the second engineer and a carpenter (who carried a bucket containing the ten packets) came into his cabin and put the packets behind the bulkhead. H was told he would have his throat cut if he said anything about it. The Chairman directed the jury in the following terms:

> " . . . The question is; has it been proved that the defendant was knowingly concerned in that operation? . . . 'Knowingly concerned in that operation' means co-operating with the smugglers . . . and it does not matter if he did not know precisely the nature of the goods the smugglers were dealing with. He would be just as guilty if he had thought they were dealing with brandy, for instance, but what has to be proved is that he was knowingly and . . . consciously and deliberately concerned in co-operating in what he must have known was an operation of smuggling or getting prohibited goods into this country."

> *Held*, *inter alia*, that "knowingly" in section 304 of the 1952 Act, is concerned with knowing that a fraudulent evasion in respect of goods is taking place. It is not necessary that the defendant should know the precise category of goods the importation of which has been prohibited.

In order to be able to follow the history of this case and to be able to understand the complaints that have been levelled against the decision, it is desirable that the reader should note the following features. First, on more than one occasion the Chairman referred to "smugglers" and "smuggling" but on no occasion did he actually define those terms. This may seem a relatively unimportant omission until it is remembered that the C.E.M.A. applies not only to "prohibited goods" but also to other categories of goods—including "dutiable goods." Second, the Chairman said (by way of example) that it did not matter if Hussain thought he was importing brandy. However, brandy is a *dutiable* commodity: it is not prohibited or restricted from importation. Third, although the Chairman directed the jury that it did not matter whether Hussain knew precisely the "nature of the goods" being dealt with, does this mean that an accused need not know the precise prohibition involved? It has to be noted that if Hussain did not know what was actually being imported, then he would not know which prohibition was being contravened.

As to the first point, the Court of Appeal rejected the complaint swiftly. But, the second and third features pose considerable problems.

In *Hussain*[32] the Court of Appeal isolated the three essential elements of the *mens rea*, which the prosecution are required to prove against an accused, namely:

   (a) knowledge that the goods which are being imported are subject to a prohibition; and

   (b) knowledge that he is concerned in an operation designed to evade that prohibition; and

   (c) knowledge that the prohibition is to be evaded fraudulently.

The burden of proving the above rests on the prosecution because nothing in the C.E.M.A., or the M.D.A., suggests that section 170 or section 3(1) of the M.D.A. is subject to section 28 of the M.D.A. Furthermore, none of the statutory presumptions listed in section 154 of the C.E.M.A. shift the evidential burden on the accused to displace a presumption of knowledge of any of the three elements.

Must an accused know the precise prohibition or goods involved

In *Hussain*, the appellant had submitted that the prosecution was required to prove that the accused knew the precise nature of the goods that had actually been imported—in this case, cannabis resin. This was a very bold submission since one might have anticipated the appellant to have conceded that there was a sufficient *mens rea* if the accused knew that goods of a type subject to a particular prohibition (for example controlled drugs) had been imported. It will be necessary to return to this point when we examine *Hussain* in the light of the decision of the House of Lords in *Courtie*.[33] In the event the Court of Appeal rejected the submission advanced on behalf of the appellant. Widgery L.J. said:

> "It seems perfectly clear that the word 'knowingly' in the section in question is concerned with knowing that a fraudulent evasion of a prohibition in respect of goods is taking place. If, therefore, the accused knows that what is on foot is the evasion of a prohibition against importation and he knowingly takes part in that operation, it is sufficient to justify his convic-

---

[32] *Ibid.*
[33] [1984] 2 W.L.R. 330; [1984] 1 All E.R. 740.

tion, even if he does not know precisely what kind of goods are being imported."

Widgery L.J. made it clear that it is essential that the accused should know that the imported goods are subject to a prohibition on importation, but he added that: " . . . it is not necessary he should know the precise category of the goods the importation of which has been prohibited."

Accordingly, by the jury's verdict, Hussain knew that the packages were being smuggled contrary to a prohibition against their importation and that he was a party to that operation. The fact that he did not know precisely what those packages contained was held to be irrelevant.

Hussain has been held to have been correctly decided in a number of subsequent cases and notably, by the House of Lords in *Taffe*[34] and *Shivpuri*.[35] But, if all that has to be proved is that an accused knew that the goods imported were subject to "a prohibition," does that include a belief (mistakenly but genuinely held) that he was importing goods of a different description (for example firearms instead of heroin) but which would, if true, also have been subject to a prohibition against importation? On a strict reading of the judgment in *Hussain*, the answer must be in the affirmative since it was said in terms that it is not necessary for the prosecution to prove that an accused knew the precise "category of goods" prohibited from importation.

In *Hennessey*,[36] an attempt was made to challenge directly the correctness of the decision in *Hussain* and to renew the submission, (rejected in *Hussain*) that the prosecution had to prove that the accused knew what the imported goods actually were. Thus; in *Hennessey*

> stolen cars were adapted so that cannabis could be hidden in them and then used to bring the cannabis over to the United Kingdom from the Continent. H drove one such car to the Continent and returned to Dover some six days later. Customs officers found 28.14 kilograms of cannabis resin in the vehicle. H said that be believed he was importing pornography into the United Kingdom of a type which would have been prohibited from importation.

Lawton L.J., giving judgment for the court, followed *Hussain* " . . . for the best of reasons—it was correctly decided . . . ," and added:

---

[34] [1984] A.C. 539; 2 All E.R. 626; 78 Cr. App. R. 301, C.A.
[35] [1986] 2 W.L.R. 988.
[36] (1978) 68 Cr. App. R. 419.

"In plain English [Hennessey] was smuggling goods. It matters not for the purpose of conviction what the goods were as long as he knew that he was bringing into the United Kingdom goods which he should not have been bringing in."

The decisions of *Hussain* and *Hennessey* produce harsh results and pose special problems, not least on the issue of sentence. For example, many goods and products or animals (whether dead or alive) are prohibited from importation (see; the Endangered Species (Import & Export) Act 1976). Smuggling often attracts a maximum sentence of two years imprisonment, whereas the penalty for smuggling a Class A drug, is life imprisonment. Accordingly, if heroin is imported whereas the accused believed he was importing an article in contravention of the 1976 Act, he nevertheless faces life imprisonment; the accused's mistaken belief affords him no defence. The sentencer is thus confronted with a difficult sentencing problem. On which basis does he sentence the accused? In *Hennessey*, an application for leave to appeal against sentence was put on the basis that he should not have been sentenced as a drug smuggler but as a smuggler of pornography. The Court of Appeal side-stepped that issue claiming that H's story " . . . was not credible anyway . . . " and secondly, that " . . . he was lucky to be sentenced as leniently as he was."

A second, but far more subtle attack, has been made on the correctness of *Hussain* and *Hennessey*, on the grounds that both cases have wrongly attributed the *mens rea* of one prohibition to offences requiring proof of a very different prohibition and required proof of a corresponding *mens rea*; see *Shivpuri*,[37] considered later in this chapter. If the complaint is valid then the prosecution are put in the very difficult position of having to prove that the accused knew that the goods imported were at least subject to a particular prohibition. Many guilty persons, it is said, would slip through the net as a result.

One solution is to impose a presumption of knowledge on the accused and to shift the burden onto him to prove (on a balance of probabilities) that he neither knew, believed, suspected, nor had reason to suspect that the goods he was importing were the goods alleged, for example controlled drugs. In other words one solution is to direct that section 28 of the M.D.A. applies to drug-related importations.

In respect of offences created by sections 4, 5, 6 and 9 of the M.D.A., section 28(3) already applies to those offences. Obviously the reason why there is no corresponding provision for

[37] See *supra*, n. 43.

the purposes of section 3(1) of the M.D.A. is that Parliament considered that such a course was unnecessary: the difficulty lies in
understanding why Parliament took that view. The basic explanation favoured by many lawyers is that Parliament was satisfied that
Hussain already governed the position and therefore statutory
intervention was not required. The problem with that explanation
is that lawyers have not been agreed on the true *ratio* of *Hussain*.
For this reason two opposing arguments are worth mentioning.

The first argument is that Parliament was not fundamentally
concerned with whether or not an importer made a mistake about
the goods actually imported. That is his problem. All that matters
is that he knew that he was smuggling prohibited goods whatever
their description and whatever the prohibition involved. *Hussain*,
it is argued, is authority for that proposition. Since *Hussain*
already governed the position there was no need for Parliament to
take any further action. The fact that an accused faces different
penalties depending on the goods actually imported was not the
legislature's concern but a matter for the sentencing court. Indeed,
under the M.D.A. different penalties apply to Class A, B and C
drugs (see Schedule 4 of the M.D.A., as amended by the Controlled Drugs (Penalties) Act 1985). Nevertheless, section 28
makes it plain that it is no defence for a person to say "but I
thought I was supplying methaqualone (class C) and not hereoin
(Class A)."

The second argument, which advocates that *Hussain* should be
narrowly construed, starts on the basis that Parliament accepted
the principle that persons who believed that they were dealing with
substances, other than controlled drugs, should not be convicted
of a drugs-related offence. Hence section 28: enacted in the light
of *Warner* v. *M.P.C.*[38] This was so whether a person produced,
possessed, supplied, or *imported*, a drug. It was not intended that
a supplier should be more favourably treated than an importer.
Once it was established that an accused knew that he was dealing
with a drug it really did not matter thereafter what he believed that
drug to be. However, there was no need to extend section 28(3) to
importation cases, because the burden of proving knowledge,
(according to *Hussain*), rests entirely on the Crown and that burden never shifts. Parliament's understanding in 1971 (so the argument runs), was that *Hussain* did not establish the sweeping
proposition that an accused need not be proved to have known
that the goods were subject to a prohibition—any prohibition.
That was not made clear until *Hennessey* was decided in 1978. The
judgment in *Hussain* was understood to mean, in 1971, no more

[38] [1969] 2 A.C. 256.

than that it did not matter whether an accused knew exactly what the imported goods were so long as he knew that they were of a type subject to the same prohibition. Thus, for example, an accused's belief that he was importing methaqualone (class C) whereas he was importing heroin (class A) was not fatal to a conviction under section 170(2) since he knew he was importing drugs. If Parliament knew in 1971, what it now knows, then section 28(3) would indeed have been expressed to apply to section 3(1).

It must be stressed that, for the moment at least, the position is that *Hussain* and *Hennessey* represent the law. All that the prosecution need prove is that an accused knew the goods were prohibited from importation. He does not need to know the precise prohibition involved and still less does he need to know the class of drugs actually imported. But, it is a defence for him to say that he mistakenly believed that the goods imported were not subject to any prohibition and, it is also a defence for him to say that he mistakenly believed he was importing goods subject to a prohibition when (as a matter of law) they would not have been; see *Taffe*.[39] However, because the matter is still regarded as being in a state of flux—and it will be surprising if the House of Lords is not required to look at this matter yet again—it is helpful to trace the history of drug importation offences in so far as it is relevant to do so.

An historical perspective of drug importation offences

Section 304(*b*) of the Customs and Excise Act 1952, was the fore-runner to section 170(2) of the C.E.M.A. and read:

> " . . . if any person; . . . is, in relation to any goods, in any way knowingly concerned in any fraudulent evasion or attempt at evasion of any duty chargeable thereon or any such prohibition or restriction as aforesaid or of any provision of this Act applicable to those goods he may be detained and . . . shall be liable to a penalty . . . "

When *Hussain* was decided in 1969, the relevant prohibition on the importation of various drugs was imposed by section 2 of the Dangerous Drugs Act 1965. Under the Customs and Excise Act 1952 the maximum penalty for contravening section 304 was two years imprisonment unless a different penalty was expressly imposed by a different enactment. But the Dangerous Drugs Act 1965 did not in fact provide a different penalty. Two years later, the Dangerous Drugs Act 1967 (section 7) increased the maximum sentence for drug-smuggling to ten years imprisonment. Thus, whether the drug imported was a Class A, B or Class C drug, the

[39] [1984] A.C. 539.

maximum penalty was the same; ten years imprisonment. It was against this background that *Hussain* was decided.

Widgery L.J. said in *Hussain*, that it is essential that an accused should know that the goods which are being imported are subject to a prohibition but: " . . . it is not necessary he should know the precise category of the goods the importation of which has been prohibited."

These are crucial words but there was uncertainty as to whether or not Widgery L.J. was saying that the *mens rea* for one prohibition would support an offence in connection with the importation of goods subject to another prohibition so that the accused only had to know that the goods were "prohibited goods." The fact that Widgery L.J. referred to "goods" and not to "drugs" is one indication that he was saying precisely that. His reference to knowledge of "a" prohibition (rather than "the" prohibition) is another indication. However, he went on to say that an accused must be proved to be engaged in an operation " . . . designed to evade *that* prohibition . . . " which might, on its own, suggest that proof of the specific prohibition was required.

The M.D.A. swept away the Dangerous Drugs Acts of 1965 and 1967, as well as the Drugs (Prevention of Misuse) Act 1964. New offences were created under the M.D.A., the most important of which are subject to the statutory defences created by section 28. Parts of that section are reminiscent of the judgment of Lord Pearce in *Warner*.[40] A smuggler, charged with offences under the M.D.A. (for example possession with intent to supply) has a defence under section 28(3) of the M.D.A. which he does not have if he is charged under section 170 of the C.E.M.A.

The "Courtie" argument

In *Courtie*,[41] the House of Lords held that the Sexual Offences Act 1967 created several different offences, given that proof of different factual ingredients, attracted different penalties. Each offence would require the requisite *mens rea*.

In *Taffe*,[42] a case involving a rather different point, Lord Scarman said,[42a] *obiter*, that:

> "While there can be no doubt that *Hussain* was correctly decided, it may be that *Hennessey* will not have to be reconsidered in the light of the House's decision to-day in the case of

[40] See *supra*, n. 38.
[41] [1984] 2 W.L.R. 330; 1 All E.R. 740.
[42] (1984) 78 Cr.App.R. 301, C.A.
[42a] *Ibid.* at p. 304.

Courtie. For the court in *Hennessey* appears to have paid no regard to the effect of section 26 of the Misuse of Drugs Act 1971 upon section 304 of the Customs and Excise Act 1952 . . . it would seem likely that these two sections (now consolidated into section 170 of the Act of 1979) have substituted several offences . . . for one offence in relation to all prohibited imports which existed before the Misuse of Drugs Act 1971 was enacted. But the point does not arise and I therefore express no concluded opinion as to whether the decision in *Hennessey* can stand with . . . *Courtie.*"

Those observations have resulted in two further cases reaching the appellate courts, namely, the House of Lords in *Shivpuri* and, more recently, the Court of Appeal in *Ellis, Street & Smith.*[43] The background to these two decisions should now be explained.

In 1971, offences contrary to sections 4, 5, 6 and 9 generally attracted identical maximum penalties depending on the Class of drug involved. Thus, Class A and B drugs attracted 14 years imprisonment while a Class C drug attracted 5 years imprisonment (lesser penalties were imposed for offences of simple possession). Offences committed under the Customs and Excise Act 1952 in respect of drug-smuggling attracted like penalties; section 26 of the M.D.A.

Section 26 was repealed with the passing of the Customs and Excise Management Act 1979 but the same penalties were then re-enacted in Schedule 1 of that Act. However, under the Controlled Drugs (Penalties) Act 1985, the maximum penalty for offences involving a Class A drug, was increased to life imprisonment. Accordingly, each Class of controlled drug now attracted a different maximum penalty. Moreover, unlawfully importing or exporting other prohibited goods attracted a maximum of two years imprisonment (unless a different penalty was stipulated by the relevant enactment).

The impact of *Courtie* is now evident. If separate offences are created, because separate penalties arise out of different factual ingredients which are required to be proved by the prosecution, then this means:

    (a) that separate offences exist where goods are subject to *different prohibitions* attracting different penalties; and

    (b) that, in the case of a drug-related importation, three separate offences exist in relation to Class A, B and C drugs because each class attracts a different penalty.

In other words, if different offences are created under section

---

[43] (1987) 84 Cr. App. R. 235.

170 of the C.E.M.A. then, in the case of a drug smuggling, the prosecution are required to prove as part of the *actus reus* that an accused imported or exported the appropriate *Class* of controlled drug. That being so, is it not also incumbent on the prosecution to prove a corresponding *mens rea*? If the answer is "yes" then *Hennessey*, and possibly *Hussain*, were wrongly decided.

In *Shivpuri*, S believed he was importing a suitcase of cannabis whereas he actually imported harmless vegetable matter and was accordingly, charged with attempting to contravene section 170. The House of Lords feared that if the answer to the question posed above, was in the affirmative, then "the task of the prosecution in proving an offence in relation to the importation of prohibited drugs would in many cases be rendered virtually impossible . . . " (*per* Lord Bridge).

Their Lordships in *Shivpuri* recognised the force of the arguments based on *Courtie*. Lord Bridge traced the history of the legislation, with particular reference to section 28, pointing out that Parliament overcame the "almost insurmountable difficulty . . . of proving the appropriate guilty knowledge . . . " for the purposes of offences under the M.D.A. by placing the burden of proving a lack of knowledge on the accused. Lord Bridge asked why section 28 did not apply to section 3(1) of the M.D.A., concluding that *Hussain* made such a provision unnecessary for the following reasons[43a]:

> "Irrespective of the different penalties attached to offences in connection with the importation of different categories of prohibited goods *Hussain* established that the only mens rea necessary for of any such offence was knowledge that the goods were subject to a prohibition on importation."

It is to be noted that Lord Bridge referred to "goods," not "drugs"; and secondly, that he, like Widgery L.J. in *Hussain*, referred to "a" prohibition, not "the" prohibition. Lord Bridge added[43b]:

> "Had [*Hussain*] been decided otherwise . . . it is surely inconceivable that Parliament, in the 1971 Act, would not have made provision . . . such as . . . section 28(3) applicable to drug related offences connected with importation."

However this observation is not, with respect, a complete answer because by section 28(3) of the M.D.A. it is a defence for the accused to prove that he did not believe or suspect or had

---

[43a] [1986] 2 W.L.R. 988 at p. 996.
[43b] *Ibid.* at p. 996.

reason to suspect that the substance was a controlled drug at all. This is very different from the effect of *Hussain* and *Hennessey* which affords a defendant charged with an offence under section 170(2) no such defence—on the contrary.

Lord Bridge considered that the issue resolved itself once the history of the legislation is traced. Of course that is to assume that Parliament had the foresight to anticipate the decision in *Courtie*, which is highly unlikely. Lord Bridge has bravely attempted to rationalise the relevant history and, to the extent that it is capable of rationalisation, the broad construction of the ratio in *Hussain* is to be preferred. But ultimately rationalising the authorities is proved to be somewhat artificial, and perhaps unnecessary, because in the final analysis it is the wording of the relevant enactment that counts. No matter how hard one tries to scrutinise the decisions of the courts, the colossal difficulties of reconciliation remain. For the moment *Hussain* and *Hennessey* remain the law. The optimistic observations made by the learned editors of Archbold suggesting that *Shivpuri* had not closed the doors to the argument that a mistaken belief that the goods were subject to a wholly different prohibition provided a defence, is unfounded. In *Shivpuri* (above) their Lordships did not expressly approve *Hennessey* and this may have generated confusion and the suspicion that the argument was still open that a person who believes he is importing goods subject to one prohibition, when in fact he is importing goods subject to a different prohibition, does not have the requisite *mens rea*. It is submitted that this construction is a misreading of the opinions delivered in *Shivpuri*. Significantly, Lord Scarman who made the now famous remarks in *Taffe* (above) concerning the implications of *Courtie* also heard the appeal in *Shivpuri*, but said no more in *Shivpuri* than that he agreed with the speech of Lord Bridge. It is not apparent why Lord Scarman in *Taffe* readily accepted that *Hussain* was rightly decided but queried the correctness only of *Hennessey*. This fuelled speculation in legal circles that the judgment in *Hussain* was to be narrowly construed—speculation which was not only proved to be unfounded but which might have ended with the decision in *Shivpuri*. However, in *Ellis, Street & Smith*[44] the appellants imported cannabis believing that they were importing pornography. The facts were therefore identical to *Hennessey*. The Court of Appeal was invited to rule that *Hennessey* was wrongly decided and could not stand with subsequent decisions of the House of Lords. The Court of Appeal had no difficulty in holding that the true ratio of *Hussain* is that it matters not what a person

[44] (1987) 84 Cr. App. R. 235.

believes the nature of the prohibition to be. In *Ellis, Street &
Smith*, the appellants contended that in *Hussain* the defendant
simply did not care what the material was, and accordingly, *Hussain* could be distinguished from *Hennessey*. However, by the
jury's verdict, Hussain must have known as a fact that the goods
were prohibited, even if he did not know of their actual description. O'Connor L.J. said: " . . . if a man does not know what prohibited material is being imported but only knows that it is
prohibited, it follows that he cannot know which prohibition is
being broken."

Applying *Hussain* and *Hennessey*

Once it is proved first, that controlled drugs were imported contrary to section 3(1) of the M.D.A.; second, that the prohibition
was evaded fraudulently; third, that the accused knew that the
goods were subject to a prohibition, and finally that the accused
was concerned in that fraudulent evasion, then the offence under
section 170(2) is made out.

However, a person is to be judged "against the facts as he
believed them to be" (*per* Lord Lane C.J. in *Taffe*)[44a]

> In *Taffe*, T drove his car through the green channel of the
> ferry terminal at Sheerness. The vehicle was stopped. Packets
> of cannabis resin were found in a tyre and more packets of
> cannabis were found on T's person. T maintained that he
> thought the packets contained currency. He mistakenly
> believed that currency was prohibited from importation.
>
> Held, if T's story was true he was entitled to be acquitted.
> Had T indeed imported currency then no offence would have
> been committed and T's mistake of law could not convert his
> reprehensible belief into a criminal offence.

The House of Lords in *Taffe* adopted the reasoning of Lord
Lane C.J. which they found compelling—and so it is, Lord Lane
C.J. said[44b]:

> "He is to be judged against the facts that he believed them to
> be. Had this indeed been currency and not cannabis, no
> offence would have been committed. Does it make any difference that the appellant thought wrongly that by clandestinely
> importing currency he was committing an offence? Counsel
> for the Crown strongly submits that it does. He suggests that a
> man in his situation has to be judged according to the total

---

[44a] [1983] 2 All E.R. 626.
[44b] *Ibid.* at p. 628.

mistake that he has made . . . We think that that submission is wrong. It no doubt made his actions morally reprehensible. It did not . . . turn what he . . . believed to be the importation of currency into the commission of a criminal offence."

It may be said that the result in *Taffe* is inconsistent with *Hussain* and *Hennessey* in that T was not judged on the facts as he believed them to be because T believed currency to be prohibited and that if his belief had been true then he would have had no defence. However, two points should be noted. First, that by the jury's verdict in *Hussain*, and by the defendant's admission in *Hennessey*, both defendants knew that the goods actually imported were subject to a prohibition. Secondly, when a person is judged against the facts, as he believes them to be, he is judged "according to law." Thus, in *Hennessey* (above) H believed that he was importing pornography. The law states pornography is prohibited from importation as of course were the drugs actually imported. Hennessey's belief that the goods were prohibited would, if true, have been correct in law. However, in *Taffe*, T made a mistake of law which saved him. His views on the law were totally irrelevant.

It will be recalled that in *Hussain* the Chairman directed the jury that it did not matter if the defendant did not know precisely what the imported goods were; "He would be just as guilty if he thought [the smugglers] were dealing in brandy." This, of course, was a misdirection since brandy is not prohibited from importation. Accordingly, if *Hussain* believed he was importing brandy then he would have had a defence for the reasons given in *Taffe*. However, this was not a misdirection which the court regarded as being fatal to the conviction.

Meaning of the word "Fraudulently"

This does not mean that a deception must be practised on officers of customs and excise in their presence. It simply connotes a deliberate intention to evade the relevant prohibition or restriction; see the *A-G Reference (No. 1 of 1981)*.[45] The decision of *Borro and Abdullah*[46] to the contrary, was decided *ex tempore* and was therefore not followed by the court.

When must the intent be formed?

In *Jakeman*[47] it was held that what matters is the state of the accused's mind at the time the relevant acts were done, for

[45] [1982] 2 All E.R. 417.
[46] [1973] Crim. L.R. 513.
[47] (1983) 76 Cr. App. R. 223.

example at the time when there was an intention to bring about an unlawful importation. Accordingly, where a courier of drugs abandoned her intention to carrying her suitcase of cannabis into the United Kingdom in Paris, she could not escape conviction under section 170 once the cannabis arrived in the United Kingdom albeit in an unexpected way.

PART III

POSSESSION SUPPLY AND PRODUCTION OF DRUGS

POSSESSION OF DRUGS

An introductory note

Any person approaching the concept of possession for the first time could reasonably be forgiven if he expected the legal principles involved to be straightforward—whereas they are anything but. One might expect to find, for example, that the ingredients of possession are encapsulated in a sentence or two—whereas the ingredients differ from one branch of the law to another. As a general rule, a person has in his possession anything which is in his physical custody, or under his control. Although this bald statement represents the law,[1] it is a statement heavily peppered with qualifications and exceptions, notably in the field of Criminal Law, where a strict adherence to the rule would produce intolerably harsh results. Is a person to be held criminally liable when he does not know, for example, of the existence of the article in his custody, or if he makes a mistake as to it's quality? Once such considerations are taken on board, so as to formulate a fair but workable concept of possession, then the simple rule expressed above must be radically redefined. Furthermore, it is not initially obvious from the general rule that possession involves a mental element yet, in law, proof of a mental ingredient of some sort is required although it is not always clear just what the mental ingredient entails. Such lack of clarity obviously generates confusion and uncertainty in the law.

Not surprisingly, the Misuse of Drugs Act 1971 (the "M.D.A.") does not offer a simple definition of possession. Section 37(3) merely provides that: " . . . the things which a person has in his possession shall be taken to include anything subject to his control, which is in the custody of another."

Possession therefore includes constructive possession. A person who puts a suitcase (knowing that it contains cannabis) into the left luggage office at a railway station while retaining the keys, no longer has custody of the case or its contents but he nevertheless falls within section 37(3) since he retains control by holding the keys. But the Act offers little more by way of assistance. It is important to remember that the Act is designed to *regulate the flow and use* of controlled drugs: it is not designed to "outlaw" the majority of them. It follows that the M.D.A. must distinguish between persons who are *lawfully* entitled to possess controlled

---

[1] *D.P.P.* v. *Brooks* [1974] A.C. 862, P.C.

drugs but are merely restricted as to how they may use them, and those persons who are *unlawfully* in possession of them. Only the latter, of course, will be guilty of the offence of unlawful possession.

For ease of understanding, it may be helpful to approach the law of possession, in the following stages. First, to look briefly at the sections of the Act which make possession of controlled drugs not only unlawful but also a criminal offence. Secondly, to examine what may be *lawfully* possessed under the Act; and, finally, to examine cases of *unlawful* possession.

Making possession unlawful

Section 5(1) is expressed as follows: "Subject to any regulations under section 7 of this Act . . . it shall not be lawful for a person to have a controlled drug in his possession."

Although section 5(1) establishes a general rule that all controlled drugs are unlawful to possess, many exceptions are to be found in the Misuse of Drugs Regulations 1985. One must therefore look initially to the drugs listed in Schedule II of the M.D.A. to see if the drug is controlled. If it is, one then turns to the various schedules set out in the Regulations (which irritatingly do not correspond to the schedules in the M.D.A.) to see if the drug in question comes within one of the exceptions.

Note that section 5(1) merely makes the possession of controlled drugs unlawful. The *offence*, of being in unlawful possession, is created by section 5(2) which provides:

> "Subject to section 28 of this Act and to subsection (4) below, it is an offence for a person to have a controlled drug in his possession in contravention of subsection (1) above."

Three ingredients are required to be proved, by the Prosecution, before an offence under section 5(2) is committed:
  (i) the thing must be in the physical custody or control of the accused,
 (ii) the accused must know, or at least could reasonably have known, of the existence of the thing in question,
(iii) the thing must be proved to be a controlled drug within the meaning of the Misuse of Drugs Act 1971.

For reference, both section 28 and section 5(4) provide an accused with a variety of defences in narrowly defined circumstances, being defences which—for the most part—did not previously exist. Both sections are examined in detail elsewhere but, significantly, the statutory defences so created are all concerned with the state of mind of the person said to be (*inter alia*) in unlawful possession of a controlled drug. Thus, by section 28 it is a defence for the accused to prove that he neither believed, suspected, nor had reason to suspect that what he had was a controlled drug, but it is no defence for him to say that he believed he had cocaine whereas the drug turned out to be heroin. Parliament was therefore making it plain that section 5(2) did not create an absolute offence: unlawful possession requires proof of the requisite *mens rea* before an offence is committed under that section.

Although many cases have considered the meaning of possession, it should be borne in mind that some cases appear to be definitive of a proposition of law, whereas they merely demonstrate a general principle that is already well established. Secondly, there have been many changes to the law since a number of cases were decided. Thus, in *Warner* v. *Metropolitan Police Commissioner*[2] the House of Lords considered the meaning of "possession" but that was, of course, prior to the passing of the Misuse of Drugs Act 1971. Not all the opinions expressed in *Warner* have the significance that they had in 1969. It is however necessary to look at these authorities, since they affect the way in which a case of possession is to be approached, and they have a bearing on the terms in which a jury should be directed by the trial judge.

I. LAWFUL POSSESSION

If there were an absolute rule that nobody is entitled to possess any controlled drug, ridiculous results would follow. A police officer seizing a controlled drug from an addict would himself be guilty of unlawful possession. Accordingly, the Secretary of State (*i.e* the Home Secretary) after consultation with the Advisory Council may, by regulations, permit certain persons to possess particular controlled drugs or, he may make it lawful for individuals to do a number of things in relation to controlled drugs, that would otherwise be unlawful for them to do: section 7. To this end, the Secretary of State may also make different provisions in relation to different controlled drugs; he may affect different categories of persons; he may impose conditions on the right to possess particular drugs, or he may grant an authority to possess them contingent upon the happening of certain events.

The relevant provisions are mainly to be found in the Misuse of Drugs Regulations 1985 (S.I. 1985, No. 2066) which came into operation on April 1, 1986. The Misuse of Drugs Regulations 1973 (S.I. 1973 No. 797) are revoked; similarly the following amending

[2] [1969] 2 A.C. 256.

Regulations are also revoked, namely: S.I. 1974 No. 402; 1975 No. 499; 1977 No. 1380; 1979 No. 326; 1983 No. 788 and 1984 No. 1143.

By section 10 of the M.D.A. 1971, the Secretary of State may also make regulations, as appears to him necessary or expedient, for preventing the misuse of controlled drugs. For example, the Secretary of State may require certain drugs to be kept in a locked safe, or room, or in other secure conditions. The relevant regulations, made under section 10, are embodied in the Misuse of Drugs (Safe Custody) Regulations 1973 (S.I. 1973 No. 798) as amended by S.I. 1974 No. 1449; 1975 No. 294; 1984 No. 1146; 1985 No. 2067; and now S.I. 1986 No. 2322.

The Secretary of State is empowered, by virtue of section 10 of the M.D.A. 1971, to regulate (*inter alia*) the issue of prescriptions or the supply of controlled drugs to drug addicts. This he has done by the Misuse of Drugs (Notification and Supply to Addicts) Regulations 1973 (S.I. 1973 No. 799) as amended by S.I. 1983 No. 1909.

It should be noted that, for the purposes of the Misuse of Drugs Regulations 1985 (S.I. 1985 No. 2066), controlled drugs are listed in five schedules. It is these schedules that must be referred to when considering the extent of the exemptions from section 5(1) and other provisions of the M.D.A. Schedules 1 to 4 have been amended by the Misuse of Drugs (Amendment) Regulations 1986 (S.I. 1986 No. 2 330).

The major exemptions under the Misuse of Drugs Regulations 1985 are summarised and set out below.

Persons who may possess ANY controlled drugs

There are two ways in which it is possible for a person to possess any controlled drug—no matter how dangerous it may be. The first protection is afforded by Regulation 6(7), and the second is afforded by way of a Licence issued by the Secretary of State.

Under Regulation 6(7) six classes of persons are immune from prosecution under section 5(1) when acting in the course of their respective duties, namely:

"(*a*) a constable when acting in the course of his duty as such;

(*b*) a person engaged in the business of a carrier when acting in the course of that business;

(*c*) a person engaged in the business of the Post Office when acting in the course of that business;

(*d*) an officer of customs and excise when acting in the course of his duty as such;

(*e*) a person engaged in the work of any laboratory to

which the drug has been sent for forensic examination
when acting in the course of his duty as a person so
engaged;

(*f*) a person engaged in conveying the drug to a person
who may lawfully have that drug in his possession.''

The last category certainly protects those who convey drugs to
one of the remaining five groups stated above but would seem,
equally, to protect the person who, for example, collects controlled drugs from a pharmacist and delivers them to a person
entitled to receive them under a prescription. Where a person
acts outside the scope of his duties he will lose the protection of
Regulation 6(7) and so will be guilty of unlawful possession.
Thus, a forensic laboratory technician would not be acting in the
course of his duties if he took cannabis resin home to show his
family what it looks like. Curiously, a disturbing omission from
Regulation 6(7) is any specific exemption for court staff, including counsel, jurors or members of the judiciary who frequently
handle controlled drugs as court exhibits. Frankly, it is difficult
to know by what authority court staff may lawfully handle such
exhibits by virtue of any other provision of the M.D.A. or the
Regulations.

Licences

Another method of securing protection is afforded by Regulation 5 which enables the Secretary of State to issue a licence authorising any individual to possess any controlled drug. The licensee
must abide by the terms and conditions attached to the licence.
Failure to do so may amount to the commission of a separate
offence (section 18) but such a breach is unlikely to vitiate the
effect of the licence. However, the Secretary of State is empowered to revoke or modify the licence at any time as he thinks
proper.

Licence fees are controlled by the Misuse of Drugs (Licence
Fees) Regulations 1986 (S.I. 1986 No. 416) and the Misuse of
Drugs (Licence Fees) (Amendment) Regulations 1987 (S.I. 1987
No. 298) and the misuse of Drugs (Licence Fees) (Amendment)
Regulations 1988 (S.I. 1988 No. 311).

Persons who may possess Schedule 2 drugs

The following substances and products, their salts and stereoisomeric forms, are included in Schedule 2 of the M.D. Regs.
1985.

1. Namely:
Acetrophine
Alfentanil
Allylprodine
Alphacetylmethadol
Alphameprodine
Alphamethadol
Alphaprodine
Anileridine
Benzethidine
Benzylmorphine (3
  benzylmorphine)
Betacetylmethadol
Betameprodine
Betamethadol
Betaprodine
Bezitramide
(Carfentanil)[3]
Clonitazene
Cocaine
Desomorphine
Dextromoramide
Diamorphine
Diapromide
Diethylthiambutene
Difenoxin
Dihydrocodeinone
  O-carboxymethyloxime
Dihydromorphine
Domenoxdole
Dimepheptanol
Dimethylthiambutene
Dioxaphetyl butyrate
Diphanoxylate
Dipipanone
Drotabanol
Ecgonine, and any derivative of
  acgonine which convertible
  to ecgonine on to cocaine
Ethylmethylthiambutene
Etonitazene

Etorphine
Etoxeridine
Fentanyl
Furethidine
[Glutethimide][4]
Hydrocodone
Hydromorphinol
Hydromorphone
Hydroxypethidine
Isomethadone
Ketobemidone
[Lefetamine][4]
Levomethorphan
Levomoramide
Levophenacymorphan
Levorphanol
(Lofentanil)[3]
Medicinal opium
Metazocine
Methadone
Methadyl acetate
Methyldesorphine
Methyldihydromorphine
  (6-methyldihydromorphine
Metopon
Morpheridine
Morphine
Morphine methobromide,
  morphine N-oxide and other
  pentavalant nitrogen
  morphine derivatives
Myrophine
Nicomorphine
Noracymethadol
Norlevorphanol
Normethadone
Normorphine
Norpipanone
Oxycodone
Oxymorphone
Pethidine

[3] [. . .] Omitted by the Misuse of Drugs (Amendment) Regulations 1986 (S.I. 1986 No. 2330).
[4] (. . .) Inserted by the Misuse of Drugs Amendment Regulations 1986 (S.I. 1986 No. 2330).

Phenadoxone
Phenampromide
Phenazocine
Phencyclidine
Phenomorphan
Phenoperidine
Piminodine
Proheptazine
Proparide
Racemethorphan
Racemoramide
Racemorphan
Sufentanil
Thebacon

Thebaine
Tilidate
Trimeperdine
4-Cyano-2-dimethylamino-4,
    4-diphenylbutane
4-Cyano-1-methyl-4-phenyl-
    piperdine
1-methyl-4-phenylpiperdine-4-
    carboxylic acid
2-methyl-3-morpholino-1
    1-diphenylpropanecarboxylic
    acid
4-phenylpiperdine-4-
    carboxylic acid ethyl ester

2. Any stereoisomeric form of substance specified in paragraph 1 not being dextromethorphan or dextrorphan.

3. Any ester or ether of a substance specified in paragraph 1 or 2, not being a substance specified in paragraph 6.

4. Any salt of a substance specified in any of paragraphs 1 to 3.

5. Any preparation or other product containing a substance or product specified in any of paragraphs 1 to 4, not being a preparation specified in Schedule 5.

6. The following substances and products are also included, namely:

Acetylihydrocodeine
Amphetamine
Codeine
Dextropropoxyphene
Dihydrocodeine
Ethylmorphine (3-ethyl-
    morphine)
(Fenethylline)[5]
(Glutethimide)[5]
(Lefetamine)[5]
Mecloqualone

Methaqalone
Methylamphetamine
Methylphenidate
Nicocodine
Nicodicodine (6-nicotinyl-
    dihydrocodeine)
Norcodeine
Phenmetrazine
Pholcodine
Propiram

7. Any stereoisomeric form of a substance specified in paragraph 6.

8. Any salt of a substance specified in paragraph 6 or 7.

9. Any preparation or other product containing a substance or

[5] *Ibid.*

product specified in any of paragraphs 6 to 8, not being a preparation specified in Schedule 5.

It will be seen that some of the drugs referred to in Schedule 2 of the 1985 Regulations include some of the most dangerous drugs, *e.g.* heroin, cocaine, dipipanone, methadone, medical opium, morphine, DF 118, and methaqualone. However, because such substances are also recognised as making a valuable contribution to medicine when properly and professionally administered, Regulation 10(1)(*a*) provides that the following classes of persons (set out in Regulation 8(2), are entitled to possess Schedule 2 drugs (and to supply them) namely:

"(*a*) a practitioner
(*b*) a pharmacist
(*c*) a person lawfully conducting a retail pharmacy
(*d*) a person in charge or acting person in charge of a hospital or nursing home which is wholly or mainly maintained by a public authority out of public funds or by a charity or by voluntary subscriptions;
(*e*) in the case of such a drug supplied to her by a person responsible for the dispensing and supply of medicines at the hospital or nursing home, the sister or acting sister for the time being in charge of a ward, theatre, or other department in such a hospital or nursing home as aforesaid;
(*f*) a person who is in charge of a laboratory the recognised activities of which consist in, or include, the conduct of scientific education or research and which is attached to a university, university college or such a hospital as aforesaid or to any other institution approved for the purpose . . . by the Secretary of State.
(*g*) a public analyst appointed under section 76 of the Food Act 1984 or section 27 of the Food and Drugs (Scotland) Act 1956.
(*h*) a sampling officer within the meaning of the Food and Drugs (Scotland) Act 1956.
(*i*) a sampling officer within the meaning of schedule 3 to the Medicines Act 1968.
(*j*) a person employed or engaged in connection with a scheme for testing the quality or amount of the drugs, preparations and appliances supplied under the National Health Service Act 1977 or the National Health service (Scotland) Act 1978 and the Regulations made thereunder;

(k) a person authorised by the Pharmaceutical Society of Great Britain for the purposes of section 108 or 109 of the Medicines Act 1968."

A person who is an authorised member of a group may, in accordance with the terms of his group authority have a Schedule 2 drug in his possession: see Reg. 10(3).

Persons who may possess Schedule 3 drugs

The following drugs are included:

"1(a)Benzphetamine	Meprobamate
(Cathine)	Methylphenobarbitone
Chlorphentermine	Methyprylone
Diethypropion	Pentazocine
Ethchlorvynol	Phendimetrazine
Ethinamate	Phentermine
Mazindol	Pipradrol
Mephentermine	

(b) any 5,5 disubstituted barbituric acid.

2. Any stereoisomeric form of a substance specified in paragraph 1 "not being phenylpropanolamine"—(words added by the Misuse of Drugs (Amendment) Regulations 1986)

3. Any salt of a substance specified in paragraph 1 or 2.

4. Any preparation or other product containing a substance specified in any of paragraphs 1 to 3, not being a preparation specified in Schedule 5."

The drugs in Schedule 3 are less dangerous than drugs listed in Schedules 1 and 2. They include the barbiturates, e.g. methylphenobarbitone. The persons entitled to possess (and supply) these drugs include the following persons (see Reg. 10(1)(b) in conjunction with Reg. 9(2)):

"(a) a practitioner
(b) a pharmacist
(c) a person lawfully conducting a retail pharmacy
(d) a person in charge of a laboratory the recognised activities of which consist in, or include, the conduct of scientific education or research;
(e) a public analyst appointed under section 76 of the Food Act 1984 or section 27 of the Food and Drugs (Scotland) Act 1956
(f) a sampling officer within the meaning of the Food and Drugs (Scotland) Act 1956.

(g) a sampling officer within the meaning of schedule 3 to the Medicines Act 1968.

(h) a person employed or engaged in connection with a scheme for testing the quality or amount of the drugs, preparations and appliances supplied under the National Health Service Act 1977 or the National Health Service (Scotland) Act 1978 and the Regulations made thereunder.

(i) a person authorised by the Pharmaceutical Society of Great Britain for the Purposes of section 108 or 109 of the Medicines Act 1968."

By Reg. 10(1)(c), (in conjunction with Reg. 9(3)(b); (c) and 9(6)—as amended by S.I. 1986 No. 2330), the following persons are also included and may therefore possess any Schedule 3 drug, namely:

" . . . a person in charge or acting person in charge of a hospital or nursing home": per Reg. 9(3)(b)—as amended by SI 1986 No. 2330.

" . . . in the case of such a drug supplied to her by a person responsible for the dispensing and supply of medicines at the hospital or nursing home, the sister or acting sister for the time being in charge of a ward, theatre, or other department in such a hospital or nursing home": per Reg. 9(3)(c)—as amended by S.I. 1986 No. 2330.

A person in charge of a laboratory may possess (and to supply or to offer to supply) any drug specified in Schedule 3 which is required for use as a buffering agent in chemical analysis: see Reg. 9(6)—inserted by S.I. 1986 No. 2330.

Persons who may possess drugs under a practitioner's control

A person receiving, say, amphetamine (as a slimming tablet) or other controlled drugs from a doctor, is entitled to possess them and to take them by reason of Regulation 10(2) which provides:

"Notwithstanding the provisions of section 5(1) of the Act a person may have in his possession any drug specified in Schedule 2 or 3 for administration for medical, dental or veterinary purposes in accordance with the directions of a practitioner: . . . "

Note that only Schedule 2 and 3 drugs are referred to. There was no point in the draughtsman including Schedule 5 drugs since *anybody* may possess these (with or without the directions of a practitioner) by virtue of Regulation 4(2)(b) which provides that:

" . . . Section 5(1) of the Act . . . shall not have effect in relation to . . . (b) the drugs specified in Schedule 5".

The same consideration applies to Schedule 4 drugs in medicinal form which are also excluded from section 5(1): see Regulation 4(2)(a).

The reader may be wondering why no drugs, listed under Schedule 1, are included under this heading. The reason is that Parliament has ensured that certain drugs are not supplied to any patient by any doctor, for example cannabis in all forms, coca leaf (but not cocaine), LSD, psilocin (extracted from the magic mushroom), or raw opium.

"Administration", within the meaning of Regulation 10(2), clearly embraces persons who intend to administer drugs to themselves as well as to others, Regulation 7(3) provides that:

> "Any person other than a doctor or dentist may administer to a patient . . . any drug specified in Schedule 2, 3 or 4."

As Regulation 7(3) gives the general right to administer such drugs, in accordance with the directions of a doctor or dentist, it makes obvious sense to give a corresponding right to possess the drug(s) in question—hence Regulation 10(2).

In cases of self-administration, it is equally important that the drug should be used for the purpose for which it was intended and in a manner that will not cause harm to the user. Accordingly, Regulation 10(2) requires that drugs are administered for "medical, dental or veterinary purposes in accordance with the directions of a practitioner".

Thus, an individual originally in lawful possession of barbituates, will lose the protection of Regulation 10(2) if he uses a drug for a non-medicinal purpose (for example to commit suicide) or if he displays *mal fides* by administering the drug in a way which does not accord with the directions of a practitioner.

> In Dunbar[6] D was a registered medical practitioner who had no patients. He obtained heroin and pethidine for "professional purposes" and administered them to himself. D told police that he intended committing suicide, but at his trial stated that he wished to alleviate his depression. The trial judge ruled that D had no defence to a charge of unlawful possession of the drugs, contrary to section 5(1) M.D.A. 1971, on the basis that Reg. 10(2) had not been complied with since D had not acted "with the directions of a practitioner.

During the course of the appeal the Crown argued that a doctor

6 [1982] 1 All E.R. 188.

who has no patients is not acting in his capacity as a doctor. The Court of Appeal did not find that argument attractive and *held* that a doctor who bona fide prescribed a controlled drug to himself was acting in his capacity as a doctor even though he was the person receiving the benefit.

The decision is patently right. The definition of a doctor is not dependent on whether he has patients or not. Moreover, Regulation 10(2) is designed to ensure the prudent use of controlled drugs (for example for medical purposes) in cases where drugs are in the hands of persons who are not medically qualified. A doctor, treating himself, in a bona fide fashion, clearly more than meets the object of this provision. Like anyone else a doctor who administers a drug to himself for a non-medical purpose—for example for an attempt to commit suicide or simply to abuse the drug—cannot avail himself of the protection of Regulation 10 and is accordingly guilty of an offence under section 5(2).

Persons who may possess Schedule 4 drugs

Drugs falling within Schedule 4 include:

"1. Alprazolam
Bromazepam
Camazepam
Chlordiazepoxide
Clobazam
Clonazepam
Clorazapic acid
Clotlazepam
Cloxazolam
Delorazepam
Diazepam
Estazolam
Ethyl loflazepate
(Fencamfamin)[7]
(Fenproporex)[7]
Fludiazepam
Flunitrazepam
Flurazepam
Halazepam
Haloxazolam
Ketazolam
Loprazolam
Lorazepam
Lormetazepam
Medazepam
(Mefenorex)[7]
Nimetazepam
Nitrazepam
Nordazepam
Oxazepam
Pinazepam
Prazepam
(Propylhexadrine)[7]
(Pyrovalenone)[7]
Temazepam
Tetrazepam
Triazolam
(N-Ethylamphetamine)[7]

2. Any stereoisomeric form of a substance specified in paragraph 1.

3. Any salt of a substance specified in paragraph 1 or 2.

[7] (. . .) Added by S.I. 1986 No. 2330.

4. Any preparation or other product containing a substance or product specified in any of paragraphs 1 to 3, not being a preparation specified in Schedule 5."

Any of the persons mentioned in Reg. 9(2) (above), may possess Schedule 4 drugs. Moreover, *any person* may possess a Schedule 4 drug *provided* that the controlled drug so specified is in a "medicinal product": see Reg. 4(2)(*a*).

All persons may possess Schedule 5 drugs

By Regulation 4(2)(*b*), all drugs specified in Schedule 5 of the 1985 Regulations, are exempt from section 5(1) of the M.D.A. Accordingly, any person may possess such drugs.

Schedule 5, in so far as it is material, provides that:

"1–(1) Any preparation of one or more of the substances to which this paragraph applies, not being a preparation designed for administration by injection, when compounded with one or more other active or inert ingredients and containing a total of not more than 100 milligrammes of the substance or substances (calculated as base) per dosage unit or with a total concentration of not more than 2·5 per cent. (calculated as base) in undivided preparations.

(2) The substances to which this paragraph applies are acetylihydrocodeine, codeine, dihydrocodeine, ethylmorphine, nicocodine, nicodicodine (6-nicotinoyldihydrocodeine), norcodeine, pholcodine and their respective salts.

2. Any preparation of cocaine containing not more than 0·1 per cent. of cocaine calculated as cocaine base, being a preparation compounded with one or more other active or inert ingredients in such a way that the cocaine cannot be recovered by readily applicable means or in a yield which would constitute a risk to health.

3. Any preparation of medicinal opium or of morphine containing (in either case) not more than (0·2 per cent. of morphine calculated as anhydrous morphine base, being a preparation compounded with one or more other active or inert ingredients in such a way that the opium or, as the case may be, the morphine, cannot be recovered by readily applicable means or in a yield which would constitute a risk to health: and see *R. v. Hunt* [1986] 3 W.L.R. 1115, HL.

4. Any preparation of dextropropoxyphene, being a preparation designed for oral administration, containing not more than 135 milligrammes of dextropropoxyphene (calculated as base) per dosage unit or with a total concentration of not more than 2·5 per cent. (calculated as base) in undivided preparations.

5. Any preparation of difenoxin containing, per dosage unit, more than 0·5 milligrammes of difenoxin and a quantity of atropine suphate equivalent to at least 5 per cent of the dose of difenoxin.

6. Any preparation of diphenoxylate containing, per dosage unit, not more than 2·5 milligrammes of diphenoxylate calculated as base, and a quantity of atropine sulphate equivalent to at least 1 per cent. of the dose of diphenoxylate.

7. Any preparation of propiram containing, per dosage unit, not more than 100 milligrammes of propiram calculated as base and compounded with at least the same amount (by weight) of methylcellulose.

8. Any powder of ipecacuanha and opium comprising—

10 per cent. opium in powder
10 per cent. ipecacuanha root, in powder, well mixed with 80 per cent. of any other powdered ingredient containing no controlled drug.

9. Any mixture containing one or more of the preparations specified in paragraphs 1 to 8, being a mixture of which none of the other ingredients is a controlled drug."

II. UNLAWFUL POSSESSION

Two special cases of unlawful possession

At this stage it is appropriate to look at two specific cases of unlawful possession.

(1) "Double-Scripting" nullifies lawful possession

The purpose of the Regulations is to ensure that controlled drugs remain in the hands of those persons entitled to possess them and who will deal with them in a way that produces no harmful effects resulting in a social problem. Since Regulation 10(2) gives all individuals the right to administer drugs specified in Schedule 2 and 3 in accordance with the directions of a practitioner, including controlled drugs supplied to them on prescription from a doctor, the object of the regulations would be defeated if users could simply increase their supply by obtaining prescriptions from more than one doctor at a time.[8]

---

[8] Addicts have the greatest incentive to abuse the system in this way for two reasons. The first is to feed an addiction where tolerance to the drug is higher than each doctor perhaps realises, or would allow to continue without treatment. The second reason is to obtain drugs, ostensibly legally, with the intention of selling them on the black market.

Accordingly, Regulation 10(2) shall not have effect in the case of a person to whom the drug has been supplied by or on the prescription of a doctor if:

"(a) that person was then being supplied with any controlled drug by or on the prescription of another doctor and failed to disclose that fact to the first mentioned doctor before the supply by him or on his prescription; . . . "

Thus, if A obtains drugs from Dr 1 and Dr 2, but fails to inform the latter of the prescription received from Dr 1, then A will be guilty of unlawfully possessing the drugs received from Dr 2. However, A will still be in lawful possession of the drugs received from Dr 1.

(2) Persons dishonestly obtaining drugs

Regulation 10(2) shall not have effect in the case of a person to whom the drug has been supplied by or on the prescription of a doctor if:

"(b) that or any other person on his behalf made a declaration or statement which was false in any particular, for the purpose of obtaining the supply or prescription."

A person who falsely represents to a doctor that he is unable to sleep, and needs a strong barbiturate, commits an offence contrary to section 5(1) if he obtains the drug which he then crushes up and injects for "kicks". The phrase "false in any particular" must refer to a material particular, the falsity of which was intended to induce the doctor to supply the controlled drug. Upon a literal construction of Regulation 10(2)(b) the words " . . . for the purpose of obtaining . . . " means that it is the intention of the recipient that is all important. It would not be necessary to show that the doctor was in fact induced to supply the drug by the false particulars.

THE GENERAL PRINCIPLES OF POSSESSION

The mental element of possession

Given that, in general terms, a person has in his possession whatever is in his physical custody or under his control, it may be thought that possession is a purely physical concept involving no mental ingredient at all whereas, in fact, the law separates the physical element of possession (the *corpus*) from the mental element (the *animus possidendi*) *i.e.* the intention to possess. It is therefore implicit, in every case of possession, that a person must at least know of the existence of the thing which he has or controls but it does not necessarily follow that a person must also be aware of the nature and quality of the thing in question before he may be said to be in possession of it. For the purposes of the M.D.A. 1971, it must be stressed that the provisions of that Act make it plain that it is for the accused to discover for himself the nature of the substance which he has. He will not be liable if he neither believed, nor suspected, nor had any reason to suspect that the substance was a controlled drug (section 28(3)(b)(i)). By contrast, a mistake of fact as to the precise controlled drug possessed is no defence (see section 28(3)(a)). To prove the mental element of possession, the prosecution need only lead evidence to establish that the accused knew of the existence of the "thing" which it is said he has or controls. However, since the provisions of the Act are superimposed onto existing case law, it follows that the fine distinctions which remain relevant (and therefore affect the validity of a judge's summing up at trial) require a close examination of the authorities concerned.

In *Warner* v. *Metropolitan Police Commissioner*[9] W handled two boxes which he believed contained scent. In fact one box contained amphetamine sulphate. W was charged with an offence under section 1 of the Drugs (Prevention of Misuse) Act 1964—now repealed—which provided that "(1) . . . it shall not be lawful for a person to have in his possession a substance . . . specified in the Schedule to this Act . . . ." Amphetamine sulphate was included in the schedule. The House of Lords held that the offence was absolute and not requiring proof of *mens rea*. However, the prosecution were required to prove that the accused knew of the existence of the thing alleged, although a mistake as to its quality was generally no defence. Moreover, special considerations apply in connection with "container cases" and it was a defence for the accused to show that he believed the contents to be of a wholly different character.

Lord Reid observed[9a] that:

> "As a legal term 'possession' is ambiguous at least to this extent: there is no clear rule as to the nature of the mental element required. All are agreed that there must be some mental element in possession, but there is no agreement as to what precisely it must be. Indeed the view which prevailed in *R.* v. *Ashwell* (1885), 16 Q.B.D. 190, and was approved in *R.*

---

[9] [1969] 2 A.C. 256.
[9a] *Ibid.* at p. 391.

v. *Hudson* [1943] 1 K.B. 458, went so far that a person who received a sovereign thinking it to be a shilling was held not to possess the sovereign until he discovered the mistake."

The above passage demonstrates the reluctance of the courts to make persons criminally liable for offences of possession without proof of some mental ingredient. As Lord Scarman remarked in *Boyesen*[10]:

"Possession is a deceptively simple concept. It denotes a physical control or custody of a thing plus knowledge that you have it in your custody or control. You may possess a thing without knowing or comprehending its nature; but you do not possess it unless you know you have it."

Lord Scarman, with whom their Lordships in that case concurred, adopted the description of possession given by Lord Wilberforce in *Warner* v. *M.P.C.*[11] (who also heard *Boyesen*) who said[11a]:

"The question to which an answer is required . . . is whether in the circumstances the accused should be held to have possession of the substance rather than control. In order to decide between these two, the jury should, in my opinion, be invited to consider all the circumstances . . . the manner and circumstances in which the substance, or something which it contains it, has been received . . . On such matters as these (not exhaustively stated) they must make the decision whether, in addition to physical control, he has, or ought to have imputed to him the intention to possess, or knowledge that he does possess, what is in fact a prohibited substance. If he has this intention or knowledge, it is not additionally necessary that he should know the nature of the substance."

When Lord Wilberforce in *Warner* referred to " . . . the intention to possess . . . " he was of course referring to the *animus possidendi* of possession. Again, Lord Pearce in *Warner*, observed[11b] that:

"I think that the term 'possession' is satisfied by a knowledge only of the existence of the thing itself and not of its qualities, and that ignorance or mistake as to its qualities is not an excuse."

[10] [1982] 2 All E.R. 161, 163.
[11] See *supra*, n. 9.
[11a] *Ibid.* at p. 310.
[11b] *Ibid.* at p. 305.

Accordingly, in *Warner*, the majority of their Lordships held that once possession is proved then the offence is absolute and no proof of *mens rea* is required. As we have seen, section 28 of the M.D.A. now ameliorates some of the harshness of the decision in *Warner* by shifting the onus onto the accused to prove that he did not believe, suspect or had reason to suspect that the substance in question was a controlled drug.

It may be thought unrealistic to say that the offence was absolute in 1969 when their Lordships, in *Warner*, stated that the prosecution were required to prove an intention to possess. Perhaps it is a matter of academic debate whether such an intention can properly be termed "mens rea" but, it is submitted that it cannot be so termed. The House of Lords did no more than to exploit what had always been an ingredient of the concept of possession—namely the *animus possidendi*. Had it been held necessary for the accused to know of the nature and quality of the substance then, clearly, this would involve more than proof of an *animus* and would therefore amount to the *mens rea* of the offence.

Bearing in mind that the Prosecution are still required to prove the fact of possession (for the purposes of section 5(2)) it follows that the prosecution must still prove the *corpus* and the *animus* elements in possession. But, in *Wright*[12] the Prosecution argued that the M.D.A. effectively redefined the word "possession," by virtue of the wording of section 28, so as to place the burden of proving a lack of knowledge firmly on the accused. The Court of Appeal did not think that the Crown's contention was correct but the Court was not prepared to make a decision on the point.

Section 28(2) reads as follows:

> "Subject to subsection (3) below, in any proceedings for an offence to which this section applies, it shall be a defence for the accused to prove that he neither knew of nor suspected nor had reason to suspect the existence of some fact alleged by the prosecution which it is necessary for the prosecution to prove if he is to be convicted of the offence charged."

The issue which was raised in *Wright*, is whether the *animus possidendi* amounts to " . . . some fact alleged by the prosecution which it is necessary for the prosecution to prove." If it is, then the burden of proving a lack of knowledge, shifts to the accused. The point was fully considered in *Ashton-Rickardt*.[13] The appellant was found asleep in his car. A cigarette, containing cannabis, was discovered in the vehicle. The trial judge directed the jury that

[12] 65 Crim. App. R. 169, C.A.
[13] [1978] 1 All E.R. 173.

" . . . the 'burden of proof' rests on the defendant . . . that he did not know [the cigarette] was there . . . ." This was a clear misdirection in the light of *Warner* but the Crown contended that section 28(2) altered the position. Roskill L.J., who delivered the judgement of the Court, had no difficulty in rejecting the Crown's argument. He said[13a]:

> "When one construes [sections 28(2) and (3)] in the 1971 Act together with section 5(1) and (2) and one realises that s.5(2) and indeed (3) are each made subject to s.28 of the Act it is apparent that whatever the precise scope of the various subsections of s.28 may be, their manifest purpose is to afford a defence to an accused person where no defence had previously existed . . . It would be very odd indeed if one effect of s.28 which . . . is plainly designed to afford a defence where no defence had previously existed, was at the same time to remove from the shoulders of the Crown the burden of proof by one of the essential elements of the offence as stated by the House of Lords in Warner."

Accordingly, section 28 only adds defences. It was not intended to remove previous defences and, indeed, it does not do so.

What the prosecution must prove

As we have noted, three ingredients are required to be proved, by the Prosecution, before an offence under section 5(2) is made out:

  (i) the thing must be in the physical custody or control of the accused;

  (ii) the accused must know, or at least could reasonably have known, of the existence of the thing;

  (iii) the thing must be a controlled drug.

Ideally, one would prefer to examine the authorities in respect of each ingredient in isolation, but this approach is not appropriate since the first two ingredients heavily overlap. For this reason (although it is essential to keep the three ingredients very much in the forefront of one's mind) a hopefully better approach is to examine seven typical situations, namely, where:

  (1) The Defendant knows of the existence of the thing and he has the custody or control of it.

  (2) The Defendant has no knowledge of the thing, or article, and therefore he is not in a position to exercise control over it.

  (3) The Defendant has the custody of, or general control over a

---

[13a] *Ibid.* at p. 178d.

number of articles but he does not know of the existence of the offending article.

(4) The Defendant knows of the existence of the thing but he does not exert any control over it.

(5) The Defendant knows of the existence of the thing and he has custody or control, but he makes a *mistake as to its quality*.

(6) The Defendant has the custody, or control, of a *container* but he has no knowledge of its *contents*.

(7) The quality is so minute that the presence of the drug indicates no more than previous possession.

(1) Proof of knowledge and control

Few problems are likely to be encountered where an accused is clearly proved to have the custody of a controlled drug or exercises control over it. However, prosecutors have a duty to ensure that the accused is charged appropriately. Thus, in *Muir* v. *Smith*,[14] the defendant was charged with being in possession of "cannabis resin." Police had searched the defendant's flat and found 20 micrograms of cannabis which could have been herbal cannabis or resin. There was no doubt that the defendant was in possession of some kind of cannabis. The Divisional Court held that the conviction had to be quashed since herbal cannabis and resin were two totally different substances.

However, if the Prosecutor had amended the charge to read "a quantity of cannabis or cannabis resin" then it is difficult to see what answer the defendant would have had to the charge. Indeed in *Best*,[15] the Court of Appeal so held when dismissing appeals against conviction by five appellants who had been charged with possession of "cannabis or cannabis resin." The scientific evidence was that the drug found was *either* of those two substances. The charge was held not to be bad for duplicity and reliance on rule 7 of the Indictment Rules 1971 was not necessary.

(2) No knowledge of the thing

Suppose D attends a party at which number of guests are smoking cigarettes. The police raid the premises and a quantity of "joints" containing cannabis are found. If D does not know of the existence of the "joints" he cannot be said to be in possession of the drug contained in them. The position would be different if, upon the arrival of police, the accused unwittingly picked up the offending cigarettes in order to try to "tidy up." In the eyes of the

[14] [1978] Crim. L.R. 293 D.C.
[15] (1979) 70 Crim. App. R. 21.

law, D will now be in possession of the thing—including the drug. Accordingly, D's possession will be unlawful unless he can prove, under section 28, that he neither believed, suspected, nor had reason to suspect that the cigarettes contained a controlled drug. In *Searle* v. *Randolph*,[16] D picked up a number of cigarette ends in a tent used by a number of individuals. One cigarette contained cannabis. He was convicted on the basis that he had the drug in his custody. A mistake as to the quality of the substance was (at that time) no defence. Of course, he now would have a defence under section 28.

The crucial fact in *Searle* v. *Randolph* is that D knew of the existence of the articles—*i.e.* the cigarettes when he picked them up. Had he left then untouched, he would only have had a general interest in the contents of the tent, which would not have been sufficiently specific to amount to control.

Where unsolicited goods, containing drugs are delivered to an individual's address, in the absence of the addressee he is clearly not able to exercise control over them (by reason of his absence) and therefore he cannot be said to have custody or control over them until he returns and becomes aware of their existence. These principles are clearly demonstrated in *Cavendish*[17] case involving the receipt of stolen property, in which it was held that in order to prove possession, something more must be proved in addition to the goods being found on the defendant's premises, namely, that upon his return he became aware of their presence and exercised some control over them, directly or indirectly. The point to note is that *Cavendish* was not responsible for the delivery of the goods. He was not exercising control. But if goods are solicited, having been ordered by D, then the converse is true and the fact that D is absent from the premises at the time of delivery can be no defence. D may not know of the time, or the day of delivery, but it was he who ensured its delivery. He was in control. Accordingly, if the packet contains a controlled drug, D is guilty of unlawful possession.

In *Peaston*,[18] P occupied a bed-sit in a house made up of such accommodation. He received through the post a package containing amphetamine which he had ordered. P was unaware of its arrival. Police arrived shortly after it was delivered and handed the package to P who then opened it. He was charged and convicted of being in unlawful possession of the drugs.

Held, the conviction was right. P had ordered the drugs.

---

[16] [1972] Crim. L.R. 779, D.C.
[17] [1961] 2 All E.R. 856.
[18] (1978) 69 Crim. App. R. 203

(3) General control but no knowledge

There will often be cases where D exercises control over a considerable number of goods, not all of which he necessarily knows to exist. In *Lockyer* v. *Gibb*[19] the defendant was stopped by police. She had in her possession a holdall containing many items including a paper bag which contained a bottle in which white tablets were visible. The tablets were in fact morphine sulphate. The defendant knew of the existence of the tablets but there was a possibility that she did not know that the tablets contained a prohibited substance. Her conviction, for the unlawful possession of amphetamine, was upheld. D was clearly aware of the existence of the tablets. She therefore exercised clear control over them. Her mistake as to the nature of the tablets was purely a mistake as to quality which, at that time, afforded D no defence. Now she would have a defence under section 28. But Lord Parker C.J. took the facts of that case several steps further and remarked:

> "If something were slipped into your basket and you had not the vaguest notion it was there at all, you could not possibly be said to be in possession of it."

It is not difficult to see how such a set of facts might arise in practice. For example, D arrives in the United Kingdom, having travelled from Morocco by air. X, a passenger on the same flight, and fearing detection, slips 2 slabs of cannabis resin into D's wicker basket before D enters the "Green Channel." D certainly has control over the basket and has an interest in the contents. In the ordinary way one would say that D "possesses" the contents. So why should D escape conviction under section 5(2)? The answer is that since possession requires an *animus* (see *Warner*) it follows that custody or control is subject to the knowledge that one has something that is *additional* to those articles which one already knows to exist. Thus, in *Searle* v. *Randolph* the Defendant knew of the existence of cigarette ends (the articles) but only made a mistake as to the quality of the "tobacco." But, in our example, D knew she possessed the wicker basket and certain contents but not the slabs of resin which another person had put there.

The same reasoning probably explains the decision in *Irving*.[20] The defendant was in possession of a bottle of stomach pills but one tablet was heroin. He said that his wife must have put it there. His conviction was quashed since there was no evidence that he knew of its existence. He knew of the existence of the bottle and the stomach pills but that was all.

[19] [1967] 2 Q.B. 243.
[20] [1970] Crim. L.R. 642, C.A.

The same principles apply to all situations in which an individual has general custody of a number of items, some of which he knows to exist and others which he does not. In *Warner*,[21] the House of Lords approved that part of the judgement of Lord Parker C.J., in *Lockyer* v. *Gibb*,[22] when he said:

> " . . . it is quite clear that a person cannot be said to be in possession of some article which he or she does not realise is, or may be, in her handbag, in her room, or in some other place over which she had control . . . "

The classic situation is a house used and occupied by a number of individuals.

> In *Smith*,[23] police found Indian Hemp in a room at a house where S was arrested. The room was used in common by all the people living in the house but the judge directed the jury that they could convict if they concluded that 'she did live in that room and had an interest in it so that she controlled all the things that were in it . . . ."
>
> Held, the direction was defective since such it did not go far enough to demonstrate control and, the judge had not dealt with the issue of knowledge at all. S had a general interest in the room but that was all.

Smith is therefore distinguishable from *Searle* v. *Randolph* (cigarette ends in a tent) where the Defendant, in *Searle* v. *Randolph* knew of the existence of the articles *i.e.* the cigarettes when he picked them up. There is, of course, an apparent conflict between the results in *Irving; Smith* and the dictum of Lord Parker C.J. in *Lockyer* v. *Gibb* on the one hand, and the result of *Searle* v. *Randolph* on the other hand. Thus, if Irving was not in possession of a tablet which he did not know existed then why should D, in *Searle* v. *Randolph* be in possession of the cannabis which, again, he did not know existed in the cigarette? In both cases the offending material was held in a container over which the accused exercised custody and or control. Why, then, was there a different result? The admittedly subtle distinction is that if the drug and the remaining articles are blended to form one substance then that is the commodity or "thing" over which control is exercised. If the accused therefore knows of the existence of the blend (albeit that he may not appreciate its real quality) then he will have the necessary *animus* to put him in possession of it. In *Irving*, and *Smith*, the

[21] [1969] 2 A.C. 256
[22] See *supra*, n. 19.
[23] [1966] Crim. L.R. 558 C.A.

drug had a separate and distinct existence from its neighbouring articles. The issue was whether the defendant knew of the existence of the thing which was, in fact, a controlled drug and, if he did do so, whether he exercised control over it. By contrast, in *Searle* v. *Randolph* the tobacco and cannabis were mixed to form (in reality) one substance. The distinction is capable of producing curious results. If D is given a parcel which, upon examination, is found to contain two bags, one containing flour and the other containing heroin, D will not be guilty of possessing the heroin if he only knows of the existence of the bag of flour. It is for the prosecution to prove that the defendant had the necessary *animus* in respect of each commodity. However, if both drugs had been blended and put into the parcel, D would be in possession of the blend even though he believed the entire substance to be flour: he made a mere mistake as to quality. In these circumstances the burden would therefore be on the defendant to prove, under section 28, that he did not have reason to suspect that the substance included a controlled drug.

The point is again demonstrated in *Marriott*[24]:

> Police searched M's. flat. M was found to be in possession of a penknife. On the blade, forensic scientists detected the presence of cannabis resin. The judge directed the jury that if M was in possession of the knife then even if he did not know of the existence of the material on the blade, he was guilty of possessing what turned out to be cannabis resin. The Court of Appeal held that the judge misdirected the jury. M had to be aware of the existence of some foreign matter on the knife.

It was not enough for M to know of the existence of the knife: he also had to know of the existence of the extra substance as well. If he did know of it's existence but simply thought that the substance was toffee, his mistake would merely be one of quality. Once again, by virtue of section 28, the burden would now be on the accused to prove a lack of knowledge.

The problem of drug traces Section 5(1) makes it unlawful to possess "*any* controlled drug." Strictly interpreted, that phrase means that the actual quantity involved is irrelevant. Unfortunately, the courts got into a terrible muddle as to whether a person can properly be said to be in possession of a drug (for the purposes of section 5) if the quantity involved is so small that it cannot be seen with the naked eye or that it can only be detected by the use of precise scientific equipment. Alternatively, it has been queried

[24] [1971] 1 All E.R. 595.

whether a person can properly be said to be in possession if the drug is capable of being weighed or otherwise measured but is merely too small to be of any practical value to a drug abuser. In a bid to mitigate the strictness of section 5, some courts effectively attempted to add words to section 5(1) in order to give effect to the spirit of the M.D.A. Thus, in *Worsell*[25]

> W was found in possession of a tube which was apparently empty. However a few droplets of heroin were detected under a microscope.
> Held, that the tube was in reality empty and therefore the prosecution could not prove that there was any drug for the defendant to possess at the time of his arrest. But there would have been no defence if the charge was amended to cover possession at an earlier stage.

The conclusion that the tube was in reality empty is, of course, a fiction since the drug exists as a trifling amount. As we shall see the courts refined this approach until they developed a so-called "usability" test. By virtue of this test a person could only be in possession of the drug if it was either usable or sufficiently great to amount to "something." The House of Lords in *Boyesen*[26] later rejected the usability test. But there really was no need to create the fiction in the first instance. In cases where presence of the drug is so minute as to be unusable or even (following *Worsell*) practically "non-existent," the prosecution are unlikely to be able to prove that an accused *knew of the existence of the drugs*. It is the issue of knowledge which would normally be at the heart of the case. In *Worsell*, W knew of the existence of the tube but that was all. He could only be guilty if he knew that he had, or controlled, something else—*i.e.* some substance or matter which in fact turned out to be a controlled drug. But he did not know any such thing. If a scientist would not have known of the presence of a drug without the use of special equipment, it is difficult to understand how can it beproved that the accused would have known of it's existence.

Stinson J., upheld a submission of no case to answer in *Colyer*[27] where C possessed a pipe which was forensically examined. The scientist could not see anything in it but, by an elaborate process, approximately a millionth of an ounce of cannabis was found. There was no evidence the C knew of its existence albeit that he exercised control of the pipe.

---

[25] [1969] 2 All E.R. 1183.
[26] [1982] A.C. 768.
[27] [1974] Crim. L.R. 243.

A similar submission was upheld in *Hierowski*[28] where H admitted that three reefer ends were his. The presence of the drug was only detected by an elaborate chemical process. It could not be presumed that H would have been aware of such small amounts for had that been his state of mind then he would probably have smoked the remainder.

One can only wonder whether the result in *Searle* v. *Randolph*, or *Muir* v. *Smith*[29] (20 micro-grams of cannabis), would have been the same if a similar point had been taken on behalf of the defence.

Whether an amount is so small that the prosecution cannot establish a prima facie case of knowledge is a matter of degree and is to be determined by the trial judge: see *Webb*,[30] (0·4 mg. and 0·6 mg. of cannabis not enough).

It may be thought that, by virtue of section 28, the burden is on the defendant to show that he had no reason to suspect the presence of the trace—but this is not so. It is for the prosecution to establish a prima facie case in respect of all three ingredients required to prove possession. Only when the prosecution succeeds in so doing does section 28 come into play.

Can possession be "lost" by forgetfulness? The point arose in the interesting case of *Buswell*.[31]

> B, a drug addict, was prescribed 70 amphetamine tablets by his doctor. He put the tablets in his jeans. His mother washed the jeans. B, assuming the tablets to have been washed away, obtained a second prescription. He later found the original tablets in a drawer. The police made a search of B's, home and found the drugs.
>
> *Held*, *inter alia*, that where a person in lawful possession of the drugs forgot their existence, he remained in possession of them. They were still in his custody. B's conviction was quashed.

The authorities of *Warner*[32] and *Lockyer* were referred to in the judgement. Phillimore L.J., held that those two cases dealt with something "very different, *i.e.* the question whether an article ever came into the individual's possession at all." The example was given of the drug slipped into somebody's pocket without that person's knowledge. The Court distinguished that situation from

[28] [1978] Crim. L.R. 563.
[29] [1978] Crim. L.R. 293, D.C.
[30] [1979] Crim. L.R. 462.
[31] [1972] 1 All E.R. 75.
[32] (1968) 52 Cr. App. R. 373.

Buswell's Case where the article was "undoubtedly in B's, possession."

At this stage it is worth bearing in mind that two separate considerations arose in *Buswell*. The first concerned the validity of the prescription—*i.e.* whether the legality of the original prescription was destroyed by the obtaining of a second prescription; and secondly, whether the accused continued to possess the drugs. If he did, and if the prescription was no longer valid, then his possession of the drugs would have been unlawful. In respect of the first point the Court found nothing to show that the prescription was not, as it were, still "lawful."

Accordingly, since B had originally been in lawful possession of the drugs by reason of the earlier prescription, his right to possess those drugs under the prescription was not lost by his forgetfulness, or his mistaken belief that they had been destroyed.

That leaves the second point. The prosecution had contended that B had "lost" his original possession when he believed that the drugs were destroyed. Phillimore L.J. questioned whether possession could have been in a state of limbo and added:

> " . . . it is idle to say that if mistakenly you think your mother
> has dissolved the tablets which you put in the pocket of your
> jeans, whereas in fact they are still in the drawer, they have in
> some way passed out of your possession. They have never left
> your care and control accordingly, you are in possession."

The Court of Appeal in *Martindale*,[33] followed the reasoning in *Buswell*, holding that possession did not depend on the alleged possessor's power of memory. In *Martindale*, M was given a piece of cannabis, in Canada, in 1983. Two years later he was arrested in the United Kingdom and searched by police. The officers discovered the cannabis in his wallet. M had forgotten all about it although he admitted that he had put it there some two years previously. Lord Lane C.J., delivered the judgement of the court and said:

> "In our judgement . . . he remained in possession, even
> though his memory of the presence of the drug had faded or
> disappeared altogether. Possession does not depend on the
> alleged possession's powers of memory. Nor does possession
> come and go as memory revives or fails. If it were to do so, a
> man with a poor memory would be acquitted, he with the
> good memory would be convicted."

[33] [1986] 3 All E.R. 25.

The Court of Appeal had been referred to *Russell*[34] which the court declined to follow, and implied that *Russell* was wrongly decided. But, in *Russell*, the Court of Appeal was concerned with a charge of possession an offensive weapon, namely a cosh, which was under the drivers seat of a car driven by the defendant. Jupp J. delivered the judgement of the court saying:

> "It would in our judgement be wrong to hold that a man knowingly has a weapon with him if his forgetfulness of its existence or presence in his car is so complete as to amount to ignorance that it is there at all."

In *Martindale* the Court of Appeal had little doubt that if the court in *Russell* had been referred to *Buswell* the decision " . . . would almost certainly have gone the other way." However, it is submitted that it is difficult to see why that should be, since a charge under section 1(1) of the Prevention of Crimes Act 1953 (which, insofar as it is material, reads "any person . . . who has with him . . . any offensive weapon . . . ") is a very different type of allegation to a charge under s.5(2) of the M.D.A. The words "has with him" for the purposes of section 1(1) of the P.C.A. 1953, clearly denotes that the accused must know of the presence of the weapon at the moment of arrest: see *Cugullere*.[35] The case of *Martindale* serves to demonstrate the dangers of construing the ingredients of possession by reference to another branch of the law.

(4) Knowledge of the substance but no control

Joint possession So far we have been looking at examples where only one person is said to be in physical custody or control of the drug. Not infrequently the suggestion is that a number of people are in joint possession. A typical case is where police raid a dwelling house occupied by a number of residents and a quantity of drug is found. The police may not be in a position to say to whom the drug belongs but, they do find signs of communal living coupled with evidence of communal drug abuse. It may well be that all of the residents know of the existence of the drug on the premises but only two or three of them are active users.

> In *Searle*,[36] drugs were found in a vehicle which was used by the Defendants on a touring holiday. The prosecution could not say which defendant intended to benefit from each type of drug found. The case was put on the basis of joint enterprise.

---

[34] [1985] 81 Crim. App. R. 315.
[35] [1961] 1 W.L.R. 858.
[36] [1971] Crim. L.R. 592, C.A.

The judge told the jury " . . . if they all knew that those drugs were then in the possession of other people and they knew they were drugs then you probably will not have any difficulty in deciding that they are guilty . . . ." It was held that the judge misdirected the jury by equating knowledge with possession. A direction that ought to have been given was to ask the jury to consider whether the drugs formed part of a common pool from which each defendant was entitled to draw.

It was unnecessary for the prosecution to assert joint enterprise. The crucial feature in this case was that each defendant intended to draw from the common pool; each defendant exercised control over the pool and accordingly, each defendant was in possession of the drugs in question. However, to equate mere knowledge of the existence of the pool of drugs was a clear misdirection since such knowledge could not, by itself, amount to proof of control.

A similar problem occurred in *Tansley* v. *Painter*,[37] where two persons were seen sitting in a car but of whom only X sold drugs from the vehicle. The Divisional Court allowed D's appeal on the basis that mere knowledge that X was selling drugs was not evidence that he was in joint possession since, again, mere knowledge of the existence of the drugs could not be equated with custody or control.

Again, in *Irala-Prevost*,[38] D was a passenger in a motor vehicle driven by D2 on a journey from North Africa to England. A large quantity of drug was concealed in the vehicle. The judge directed the jury that if both defendants knew of the existence of the drug, and both intended that it should be taken along in the car, then both were guilty of possessing the drug. The Court of Appeal held that the judge had not said enough to make the jury realise the *degree* of control required. Properly directed a jury would have had abundant evidence upon which to convict each defendant of possession.

It should be noted that on the question of knowledge the prosecution are required to prove a narrower intent in the case of an aider or an abettor, namely, that the accused knew that the confederate was in possession of a controlled drug. It is not necessary that the prosecution prove the type of drug in question; see: *Patel*,[39] and, *Fernandez*.[40]

However, there must be evidence of assistance, active or passive. Passive assistance involves more than mere knowledge that

[37] [1968] Crim. L.R. 139, D.C.
[38] [1965] Crim. L.R. 606.
[39] [1970] Crim. L.R. 274.
[40] [1970] Crim. L.R. 277, C.A.

the confederate possesses or supplies controlled drugs: it requires evidence of encouragement, or some element of control. Thus, a girlfriend who merely co–habits with her boyfriend, whom she knows to be a drug dealer, does not thereby aid or abet his supplying: *Bland*.[40a]

(5) Knowledge is proved but there is a mistake as to quality

It will be remembered that in *Warner* it was held that "ignorance or mistake as to the quality of a substance will not prevent the accused being in possession of it if that substance turns out to be a controlled drug. In *Lockyer* v. *Gibb*,[40b] L was found in possession of a bottle of morphine sulphate. There was doubt as to whether she knew of the nature of the substance. Nevertheless, even if she did not, she merely made a mistake as to quality which afforded her no defence. For the same reason, it would have made no difference in *Marriott*[41] if M believed that the substance on the blade of the knife was toffee. Both cases were, of course, decided before the passing of the M.D.A. Both cases remain relevant to demonstrate when a person will be held to be in possession of the offending article, but the significant difference now is that the accused's possession will not be unlawful if he can bring himself within section 28; section 5(4), or one of the categories exempt from section 5.

(6) The "container" cases

Is a person who knowingly exercises custody or control of a parcel, box or other container thereby deemed to be in possession of its contents, if he has no idea what they are; cannot see inside the container; has no opportunity to examine it or, has no authority to do so? These were the issues that confronted the House of Lords in *Warner*[42]:

> W sold scent as a side line. The proprietor of a cafe told W that there were two boxes for him under the counter. One box contained scent but the other contained 20,000 tablets of amphetamine sulphate. W contended that he believed both boxes contained scent. He was convicted.
>
> Held, W had a defence since he claimed that he believed the contents to be of a wholly different character, but the evidence against him was so strong that the appeal would be dismissed.

[40a] [1988] Crim. L.R. 41.
[40b] [1967] 2 Q.B. 243.
[41] See *supra*, n. 24.
[42] [1969] 2 A.C. 256.

Before going any further, it is as well to consider some of the situations that might reasonably arise in respect of "container cases." First, a person in possession of a container may believe that it is empty: in fact it contains drugs. Second, he may believe that it contains goods of a wholly different description, for example jewellery. Third, he may believe that it contains one type of drug whereas, in fact, it contains another drug. Finally, he may believe that the container holds one commodity whereas he has been the victim of a trick, and drugs have been intermixed with innocent goods.

It may be said that section 28 (which permits a lack of knowledge to be a defence in certain cases) now governs each situation. This is not entirely correct. The first step is for the prosecution to prove that the accused was in possession of the drugs for the purposes of section 5. Only when they have done so does section 28 come into operation. Accordingly, the decision in *Warner*, and other container cases, is relevant to determining whether an accused ever came into possession of the container and its contents in the first place. Although in every case of possession, there must be an *animus possidendi* the question is whether that includes an intention to possess simply the container or the drugs as well. Only if the accused is in possession of the container and its contents is it possible to consider whether a mistake of fact is a defence and, again, section 28 comes into play.

Put shortly, the present position may be summarised as follows. In the ordinary way a person who is in possession of a container will be presumed to possess the contents as well. However, that presumption may be displaced if he shows *either* that he had no right to open the container and had no reason to suspect that its contents were drugs or were in any way illicit; *or* alternatively, that he could have opened the container if he so wanted but, he received it innocently, and did not have a reasonable opportunity to acquaint himself with the actual contents or to discover their illicit nature. At this stage, the only issue is whether the fact of possession is established against an accused. If it is, then one considers whether that possession is lawful or unlawful.

When the above is compared with section 28 then an overlap does appear, but even so, section 28 does not replace the ingredients required to be proved for an offence under section 5.

It will be recalled, that in *Warner*, their Lordships were concerned with section 1(1) of the Drugs (Prevention of Misuse) Act 1964 which provided that " . . . it shall not be lawful for a person to have in his possession [a prohibited substance] . . . ." Section 5(2) of the M.D.A. is worded in similar terms except that it is subject to section 28. The opinions expressed in *Warner* are therefore still relevant and it is on those opinions that the above summary is based.[42a] However, the opinions in *Warner* vary enormously. They are also difficult to reconcile in places and rely on decisions which themselves conflict.

Lord Reid, found great difficulty in accepting that Parliament intended to create an absolute offence but, knowing where to draw the line between *mens rea* and absolute liability, proved to be an equally difficult task:

" . . . suppose that an innkeeper is handed . . . a box or package by a guest for safe-keeping . . . I cannot agree with the contention that if the possessor of a box genuinely believes that there is nothing in the box then he is not in possession of the contents but . . . if he knows there is something in it he is in possession of the contents though they may turn out to be something quite unexpected."

In order to drive the point home Lord Reid added:

"It would, I think, be absurd to say that the innkeeper is not guilty if he genuinely believes that the box is empty but that he is guilty of an offence . . . if he truly believes that it contains jewellery, though it also contains some drugs secreted in it. If he is not guilty in the case where the box contains jewellery as well as drugs, on what rational ground can he become guilty if there is not jewellery in the box but only drugs."

By contrast Lord Guest felt that the words (in section 1 of the 1964 Act) created an absolute offence, while Lord Morris of Borth-y-Guest walked a middle course, holding that possession was established if (a) the accused knew he controlled a container; (b) he had the opportunity to know or to discover the contents; and (c) that the contents were in fact controlled drugs.

However, Lord Pearce (with whom Lord Wilberforce and, reluctantly, Lord Reid concurred) indicated that an appropriate direction to juries would be as follows:

"The Act forbids possession of these drugs . . . If a man has physical control or possession of a thing that is sufficient possession under the Act provided that he knows that he has the thing; but a man does not (within the meaning of the Act of 1964) possess things of whose existence he is unaware."

Accordingly, an accused is not in possession of the contents if he believes the container to be empty. Lord Peace continued:

[42a] See now *McNamara The Times* February 16, 1988, C.A. and *Lewis The Times* February 16, 1988, C.A.

"The prosecution have here proved that he possessed the parcel, but have they proved that he possessed its contents also? There is a very strong inference of fact in any normal case that a man who possesses a parcel also possesses its contents, an inference on which a jury would in a normal case be justified in finding possession."

Thus far the law establishes a presumption of possession of the contents but, it is capable of being rebutted by the accused in the following way:

" . . . by evidence that, although a man was in possession of a parcel, he was completely mistaken as to its contents and would not have accepted possession had he known what kind of thing the contents were. A mistake as to the qualities of the contents, however, does not negative possession . . . If the accused knew that the contents were drugs or were tablets, he was in possession of them, though he was mistaken as to their qualities."

In other words an accused must show that he believed the goods to be of a totally different character. It is always a question of degree whether goods are of a similar character or not. In an earlier passage, Lord Peace thought that sweets would be sufficiently similar, although it is difficult to see why. However, the matter is entirely one for the tribunal of fact to determine.

In *Lockyer* v. *Gibb* Lord Parker C.J., considered that:

" . . . while it is necessary to show that the appellant knew she had the articles which turned out to be a drug, it is not necessary that she should know that in fact it was a drug and a drug of a particular character."

This was not an approach that found favour with Lord Reid who thought that the distinction would not bear critical examination. Nevertheless, he recognised that the appeal in *Warner* would produce that result. It will be recalled that in *Lockyer* v. *Gibb* L was found in possession of a bottle of morphine sulphate but she did not realise that the bottle contained that substance. She made a mere mistake as to its quality but it afforded her no defence. Today, she would still be held to be in possession of the contents, but her possession will not be unlawful if she can prove a defence under, say, section 28 of the M.D.A.

Opportunity to examine the contents. On this aspect the House of Lords in *Warner* made three observations. First, where a person is entitled to open a container, but did not so *at the first opportunity* to ascertain the nature of the contents, then the "proper inference is that he was accepting possession of them" (*per* Lord Pearce). But, (secondly) the converse is true if he had no authority to open the container. Finally, if any person had cause to suspect that there was something wrong with the contents, it was his business to verify them and if he failed to do so, an adverse inference may be drawn that he was accepting possession of them.

Thus, it should not be inferred, in the case of a secretary who receives a bulky letter (containing cocaine) which is addressed to her employer and marked "strictly private and confidential," that she was accepting possession of the contents, providing she did not suspect that there was anything wrong with the letter. If she did, then it would be her responsibility to open it to verify the contents. Consider, on the other hand, the position of a left-luggage attendant, who accepts baggage on the strict understanding that he has a general right to examine it at his discretion. In such a situation, if he is so busy that he chooses not to examine baggage, is it to be inferred that he is accepting possession of the contents of an item of baggage, even if he is unaware that it holds cannabis? Such a conclusion would be unfair on the custodian. But, once he is given that right, such an inference is difficult to resist. In *Warner*, Lord Pearce said:

" . . . a man takes over a package or suit-case at risk as to its contents being unlawful, if he does not immediately examine it (if he is entitled to do so). As soon as may be he should examine it and, if he finds the contents suspicious, reject possession by either throwing them away or by taking immediate sensible steps for their disposal."

Nevertheless, it is still open to the custodian to rely on any defences available to him under section 28.

It is implicit in the decision in *Warner* that a person who fails to take the opportunity to ascertain the contents of a container, only accepts possession of those items that would be discovered by a reasonable examination of the container. Accordingly, if the drug was concealed, say in a false compartment of a suitcase, the attendant who failed to examine the case would not be accepting possession of the drug because (a) a reasonable examination would not have disclosed its existence in any event and (b) even if he had carried out an examination there would be evidence that he knew of the existence of the case and of the visible contents but no evidence at all that he was aware of anything else (see: *Irving*).[43]

The length of time a container remains in the hands of the recipient is also material. If the period of retention is so short that

[43] [1970] Crim. L.R. 642, C.A.

it prevented a reasonable examination of the contents then it could not be inferred that possession of the contents was accepted. In *Wright*,[44] W was a passenger in a motor vehicle. A fellow passenger gave W a tin which he, almost immediately, threw out of the window before he had any idea what it contained. It actually contained cannabis. He therefore had an insufficient opportunity to examine the contents and accordingly he was not in possession of the drug.

More recently, in *McNamara*,[44a] the Court of Appeal has again wrestled with the concept of possession in so far as that concept has been affected by the interplay between section 28 of the M.D.A. and the seemingly conflicting opinions of their Lordships in *Warner*.

> M rode on his motor cycle to an address occupied by a co-defendant. Police found a box, containing cannabis resin on the back of the motor cycle. M denied that he knew the box contained drugs and insisted that he thought the box contained pornography or pirate videos. The trial judge directed the jury that if M was in possession of the box, and that he knew the box contained "something", then M had the burden of proving—on a balance of probabilities—that he did not know, or suspect, or had reason to suspect that the box contained a controlled drug.
>
> *Held*, the direction was correct.

Having regard to the aforementioned principles of law, it may be thought that the result in *McNamara* was inevitable. Nevertheless, the Court took the opportunity to look again at the decision in *Warner* (in the light of section 28) and extracted (*inter alia*) the following propositions:

(1) A man did not have possession of something which had been put into his pocket or house without his knowledge—to use a current vulgarism, "planted" on him.

(2) A mere mistake as to the quality of a thing under the defendant's control was not enough to prevent his being in possession, for example, in possession of heroin believing it to be cannabis or aspirin.

(3) If the defendant believed that the thing was of a wholly different nature from that which in fact it was, then, to use the words of Lord Pearce, in *Warner*, "the result would be otherwise".

(4) In the case of a container or box the defendant's possession

[44] [1975] 62 Crim. App. R. 169, C.A.
[44a] *The Times* February 16, 1988, C.A.

of it led to the strong inference that he was in possession of the contents. But, if the contents were quite different in kind from what he believed, he was not in possession of them. . . .

(5) The draftsmen of the 1971 Act intended that the prosecution should have the initial burden of proving that the defendant had and knew that he had the box in his control and also that the box contained something.

(6) Thereafter, section 28(3) places the burden on the accused to prove that he neither believed, nor suspected, nor had reason to suspect that the thing in question was a controlled drug.

Mixed drugs and goods. A different problem arose in *Irving* where the accused possessed a bottle containing stomach pills. Unbeknown to him one heroin tablet also found its way into the bottle. He contended that his wife must have put it there. His conviction was quashed. At first sight the decision seems to be at variance with the principle that a mistake as to quality does not negative possession (subject to section 28(3)), and seems not to accord with other "container cases," but the reasoning is sound. Irving admitted knowing of the existence of the bottle, *and* the stomach pills. It was those pills over which he intended to exercise control. But he was not aware of the existence of a prohibited substance. The position is therefore identical to that of a lady carrying a wicker basket full of groceries, unaware of the fact that a slab of cannabis has been slipped into it. Only if the Prosecution could prove that Irving knew of the existence of a thing in addition to the stomach pills would a mistake as to its quality not suffice: see *Searle* v. *Randolph*.[45] The tenor of the opinions in *Warner* support the correctness of *Irving* although their Lordships in *Warner* were not then dealing specifically with a case involving a mixture of substances in one container of which only some were controlled drugs. Most interestingly, Lord Reid said:

> "I do not know what the result would be . . . if, in the present case, both the scent and the drugs had been in the same parcel. The appellant, if his story were accepted, would have rightly believed that the parcel contained scent, but would have been ignorant of the fact that drugs had been slipped in with the scent. Could it be right that if the appellant had taken possession of the parcel of scent and thereafter the drugs had been slipped in without his knowledge he would be innocent (which is Lord Parker's view), but that if the drugs had been

[45] [1972] Crim. L.R. 779.

slipped in without his knowledge before he took possession then he would be guilty? That seems to me to be quite unreasonable . . . ''

It may be that in *Irving*, I's wife put the drug into the bottle *before* Irving took hold of it but, if she did then, as Lord Reid pointed out, it would be unreasonable to distinguish between drugs slipped into a container *prior* to possession, and afterwards, if the defendant's state of mind is identical in both instances.

Finally, it may be asked what constitutes a container? In *Searle* v. *Randolph* it was no defence for the accused to deny possession of cannabis in respect of cigarettes which he had picked up, merely because he did not know that they contained the drug. The cigarette paper certainly sealed in the tobacco and cannabis. To that extent the paper "tube" was a container. Nevertheless, the tobacco and cannabis were blended to form one substance. He knew of the existence of that substance (or thing) and therefore made a mere mistake as to quality.

(7) Quantity too minute to possess

In *Worsell*,[46] referred to earlier, the Court of Appeal held that where the presence of a controlled drug is so minute that it cannot be seen with the naked eye, measured or poured, and amounted in reality to nothing, it could not be said that the accused was in possession of the drug. The evidence established no more than proof of an earlier possession.

The principle is, of course, a fiction because section 5(1) prohibits the possession of *"any"* controlled drug including, on a literal interpretation, a trace however slight. Undoubtedly, the principle is sensible, but the very words of section 5(1) indicates just how limited in scope the application of the principle must be. Over the years the courts, perhaps unwittingly, have shifted their ground until eventually, in *Carver*,[47] they departed from the original point enunciated in *Worsell*. This shift can be clearly demonstrated by a brief chronological examination of the authorities. In *Hambleton* v. *Callinan*,[48] C provided a urine sample in which was found a trace of "amphetamine powder." The justices held that C was not in possession because the powder, having been consumed, was now completely changed in its character. Lord Parker C.J. concluded that the justices were right and said:

"It was contended by the prosecution . . . that a man can be

---

[46] See *supra*, n. 25.
[47] [1978] Q.B. 472.
[48] [1968] 2 Q.B. 427.

in possession of a prohibited substance . . . if he has traces of it in his urine, in his intestines, or any other part of his body in which it can be found . . . once you had consumed something and its whole character had altered and no further use could be made of it . . . a man could not be said to be in possession of the prohibited substance."

It is significant that the emphasis was placed on the *changed character* of the substance. Clearly, in that event, it is impossible to hold that a person is in possession of the *original* controlled substance. The trace in the urine could only prove an earlier possession and the consumer should be charged accordingly. Lord Parker C.J. acknowledged that a person who swallows a diamond or a gold ring would still be in possession of it. That much is obvious because neither object would change character. Likewise, in *Worsell* the court was concerned with a minute quantity of a drug which, again, had not changed character. Even so, *Worsell*, it was decided that the courts would equate minute quantities with "nothing." It was at this juncture that the fiction was created. How then was it to be determined whether a drug amounted to "something" or effectively "nothing"? One method is to adopt a principle akin to *de minimis non curat lex*. However, to do so would be to add words to section 5 which prohibits possession of "any" amount of a controlled drug. Another approach is to discover whether the trace is capable of being weighed, measured, poured or seen with the naked eye. Such tests could not be performed in *Worsell*. However, in *Graham*,[49] G had scrapings of cannabis taken out of his pocket; they were very small but were capable of being weighed and measured. Accordingly, it could not be said that the amounts were so small that they amounted to nothing because they had at least been measured. G was accordingly held to be in possession of the cannabis.

In *Frederick*,[50] Police searched F's flat. Traces of cannabis were found on two pipes and a tobacco pouch. But 307 grains of cannabis resin were found in a bag inside a television set. F denied knowledge of the cannabis. The judge directed the jury that if the jury were sure that F possessed the traces but not the 307 grains, then they should convict; and vice versa. The Court of Appeal held that there were logical difficulties in concluding that F was in possession of the traces alone, but the scientific evidence was not explored as to whether the traces were so small as to amount to

---

[49] [1969] 2 All E.R. 1181.
[50] [1969] 3 All E.R. 804.

nothing. Furthermore, the jury could infer from the existence of the traces that F was in possession of the 307 grains.

In *Bocking* v. *Roberts*,[51] Lord Widgery C.J., held that the *de minimis* rule did not apply to offences under section 5(1) but that slight traces merely indicated presence on an earlier occasion. Even 20 micrograms of cannabis resin, found in a pipe, had been measured and therefore amounted to something. Interestingly, the point does not appear to have been taken that the quantity was so small that there was no evidence that the accused knew of its existence—*i.e.* no *animus possidendi*.

A different conclusion was reached by Stinson J. in *Colyer*,[52] who declined to follow *Bocking* v. *Roberts* being, as it was, a decision of the Divisional Court. C was in possession of a pipe which had traces of cannabis measuring 20 micrograms (1 millionth of an ounce). Stinson J. held that to say this amount was "measurable" after a complicated process of extraction, was stretching the meaning of section 5(1). Alternatively, he held that there was no proof of knowledge. Likewise, in *Hierowski*,[53] His Honour Judge Edmonson upheld a submission of no case to answer when not less than 20 micrograms of resin was found by chemical analysis. The judge regarded the amount as being effectively nothing.

By 1977 the principle in *Worsell* had been thoroughly glossed. But in *Bayliss* v. *Oliver*,[54] the courts went even further. The defendants were tried for possession of 0·011 grams and 0·083 grams of cannabis. The Crown had adduced no evidence that the drug was "usable." It was held that there was no evidence that the defendants were in possession of a usable quantity. The learned judge cited Salmon L.J. in *Worsell*, concluding that the appropriate test was one of "usability."

The judgement has two curious features. First, the principle in *Worsell* was not one of usability but whether the drug was capable of amounting to "something." In *Worsell* the drug could not be weighed or measured but in *Bayliss* the quantity of the drug had been ascertained. Secondly, the learned judge included an additional ingredient which the prosecution had to prove, namely that the drug was usable. Such an ingredient is not implicit in the wording of section 5(1). It is true that in *Worsell* and *Hambleton* v. *Calligan*, the Court questioned whether a minute quantity of drug could properly be said to be of "use" to the drug user if it was an

[51] [1974] Q.B. 307.
[52] [1972] Crim. L.R. 243.
[53] See *supra*, n. 28.
[54] [1978] Crim. L.R. 361, D.C.

amount unlikely to produce the desired effect. But in neither case did the Court intend to establish a usability test.

However, in *Carver*,[55] the Court of Appeal did exactly that. The reasoning in *Bocking* v. *Roberts* was accepted but Michael Davies J. added:

> " . . . if the quantity of the drug found is so minute as . . . to amount to nothing or . . . if the evidence be that it is not usable in any manner which the Misuse of Drugs Act 1971 was intended to prohibit, then a conviction for being in possession . . . would not be justified."

On this basis the "usability test" was no longer a mere guide to determine whether a drug amounted to *something* because, even if it did, it must be capable of being used "in any manner which the Misuse of Drugs Act 11971 was intended to prohibit." But what exactly did the M.D.A. intend to prohibit and, secondly, did the "use" of a drug imply obtaining the desired effect from it? These issues resulted in the appeal to the House of Lords in *Boyesen*.[55a]

In *Boyesen*:

> B carried a metal tin which contained a polythene bag. Traces of cannabis resin were found in the bag. The traces were visible to the naked eye and weighed 5 milligrammes. An expert said that it could be picked up and put into a pipe or cigarette.

Lord Scarman, with whom all of their Lordships agreed, held that section 5(1) did not depend upon the test of "usability" but simply whether the drug amounted to something. *Carver* was overruled. *Bocking* v. *Roberts* was approved. Lord Scarman found himself entirely persuaded by the reasoning of the Lord Justice-Clerk (Wheatley) in *Keane* v. *Gallacher*[56]

> "The decision in *R.* v. *Carver* seems to entail the importation into section 5(1) of a qualification to the term 'controlled drug,' namely 'which is capable of being used.' If that be the case, it would add an additional onus on the prosecution to prove that fact. If Parliament had intended that such a qualification should be added it would have been simple to give express effect to it . . . It is the possession of the controlled drug which is made punishable by section 5(1) and (2), not its use or potential use."

However, if the quantity of the drug involved is minute, for

[55] See *supra*, n. 47.
[55a] [1982] A.C. 768.
[56] (1980) J.C. 77 at p. 81–82.

example that it is invisible to the naked eye, it would be farfetched to allege that the person in possession "knew" of the existence of the substance and was therefore in possession. To that extent the quantity of the drug involved is an important factor when considering the accused's knowledge.

Using traces to prove past possession. Even if the prosecution fail to prove possession of the trace, for the purposes of section 5, it is always open to the prosecution to rely on the existence of the trace to show that the accused was in possession of a much larger quantity of the drug on an earlier occasion; see *Worsell* and *Graham*.[57] This is so even if the prosecution cannot specify the amount of drug possessed or when it was acquired. However, prosecutors must display wisdom and not act oppressively. The point is graphically demonstrated in *Pragliola*[58]:

> A pipe belonging to P was taken by police in 1975 and found to contain traces of cannabis. He was not charged in relation to the traces and the pipe was returned to him. Much later P was charged with being in possession of the traces.
> *Held*, the charge was oppressive and could not be justified in the circumstances.

Each case must, of course, be decided on its own facts.

STATUTORY DEFENCES UNDER SECTION 5(4)

In addition to any other defence open to an accused, the M.D.A. provides two statutory defences to a charge of unlawful possession, notwithstanding that he knew or suspected the substance to be a controlled drug. In each case the burden of proving the defence is on the accused. Section 5(4) provides:

> "In any proceedings for an offence under [section 5(2)] above in which it is proved that the accused had a controlled drug in his possession, it shall be a defence for him to prove—
> (a) that, knowing or suspecting it to be a controlled drug, he took possession of it for the purpose of preventing another from committing or continuing to commit an offence in connection with that drug and that as soon as possible after taking possession of it he took all such steps as were reasonably open to him to destroy the

---

[57] See *supra*, n. 49.
[58] [1977] Crim. L.R. 612.

drug or to deliver it into the custody of a person lawfully entitled to take custody of it; or
(b) that, knowing or suspecting it to be a controlled drug,
he took possession of it for the purpose of delivering it
into the custody of a person lawfully entitled to take
custody of it and that as soon as possible after taking
possession of it he took all such steps as were reasonably open to him to deliver it into the custody of such a
person."

Section 5(4)(a)

It follows that an accused must prove:

(i) that he took possession of the drug; and
(ii) that he did so for the purpose of preventing another committing or continuing to commit an offence in connection with
that drug; and
(iii) that, as soon as possible, he took all reasonable steps to:
(a) destroy the drug; or
(b) to deliver it into the custody of a person lawfully
entitled to take custody of it.

The clearest example is that of a parent finding his son or
daughter unlawfully using a controlled drug. The parent is entitled
to take the drug and to destroy it or to hand it over to a person
entitled to receive it, for example a police officer (by virtue of
Regulation 6(6) & (7) of the Misuse of Drug Regulations 1985).
The words "preventing another from committing . . . an
offence . . . " would include the parent who finds, in her child's
absence, a cannabis plant growing in the bedroom and destroys the
plant. However, no protection is afforded by section 5(4)(a) if no
offence is being committed in relation to the drug in question. So,
a parent who destroys heroin found in the son's bedroom, unaware
of the fact that he is a registered heroin addict, and therefore
entitled to possess it, will not be protected under subsection (4)(a).
But protection would have been afforded under subsection (4)(b)
had the drug not been destroyed but given to the police instead.
It is therefore unfortunate that section 5(4)(a) does not protect a
person who has reasonable cause to suspect that an offence is or
may be being committed in relation to that drug.

Section 5(4)(b)

The accused must prove:

(i) that he took possession of the drug; and

(ii) that he did so for the purpose of delivering it into the custody of a person lawfully entitled to take custody of it; and
(iii) that, as soon as possible thereafter, he took all reasonable steps to deliver it into the custody of that person.

It will be noted that subsection (4)(*b*) is not dependent on preventing the commission of a crime and secondly, it is confined to delivery of the drug to a lawful custodian and it does not protect a person who destroys the drug.

In *Dempsey and Dempsey*,[59] MD was a registered drug addict, lawfully entitled to possess ampoules of physeptone. His wife D, held some of the ampoules for safe-keeping while MD went into a lavatory to inject himself with the remainder. It was held that D did not come within section 5(4)(*b*) since she took possession of the drugs for the purpose of removing them from MD albeit temporarily, and not for the purpose of delivering them within the meaning of the sub-paragraph.

It is not clear whether a person "lawfully entitled to take custody" of a drug includes all persons who would be lawfully entitled to possess a controlled drug of a particular description or whether the category of persons is limited to those listed in Regulation 6(6) & (7) of the M.D. Regs. 1985. Parliament's use of the phrase "to take custody" implies a very restricted class and therefore that latter construction was probably intended by Parliament.

POSSESSION WITH INTENT TO SUPPLY

Section 5(3) of the M.D.A. provides that:

"Subject to section 28 of this Act, it is an offence for a person to have a controlled drug in his possession, whether lawfully or not, with intent to supply it to another in contravention of section 4(1) of this Act."

Section 4(1) makes it unlawful to supply or to offer to supply a controlled drug to another.

It has been said that there is a logical difficulty inherent in the wording of section 5(3) in that an intention to supply a controlled drug cannot make the possession of it lawful.[60] If that is true then the words " . . . whether lawfully or not . . . " are redundant.

[59] [1986] Crim. L.R. 171.
[60] See Richard Lord, *Controlled Drugs, Law & Practice* (Butterworths, 1984).

However, there is no general proposition of law that possession is, or becomes, unlawful merely because the purpose for which the drug is intended to be used is unlawful. So where any person, by virtue of a prescription, lawfully and honestly obtains controlled drugs which he subsequently intends to supply, then his simple possession of those drugs remains lawful, even though his subsequent intention now makes him guilty of an offence contrary to section 5(3). In other words, what is being punished in section 5(3), is the guilty intent and it therefore does not matter whether his possession of the drugs was either lawful or unlawful. It is true that *Dunbar*,[61] and Regulation 10(2), of the Misuse of Drugs Regulations 1985, are concerned with rendering unlawful the possession of drugs (which had originally been lawful) in cases of dishonest "double-scripting," or where drugs have been dishonestly obtained from a doctor on prescription. But these are isolated examples expressly catered for by the Regulations.

Proving the offence

The Prosecution must prove (subject to section 28) first, that the accused was in possession of drugs; secondly, that those drugs were controlled by the M.D.A. and thirdly, that the accused intended to supply the drugs to another. Unfortunately, the Act does not define the word "supply" other than to say that "supplying includes distributing"; see section 37(1).

No difficulty arises in the classic and most obvious example of supplying, namely, where a person transfers both custody and total control of a controlled drug to another so that he may do with it as he pleases; see *Mills*.[62] Obviously, a person cannot be supplied with what he already has. In *Harris*,[63] H injected F with F's own heroin. The Court of Appeal held that H was not supplying F since the heroin was already in F's possession and undoubtedly belonged to him. H did no more than to help F administer his own drug. Of course, H did exercise some control over the substance in the sense that she controlled the top of the syringe and thus forced the drug into F's body, but physical control of the drug had not been transferred to H.

Where more than one person has an "interest" in the drug, for example, where one person buys cannabis on behalf of a number of others, then each party exercises some degree of control over the substance once it is acquired by the agent. To that extent each

[61] [1982] 1 All E.R. 188.
[62] [1968] 1 Q.B. 522.
[63] [1968] 2 All E.R. 49.

contributor may be said to be in possession of it. However, if the agent then allows each contributor to draw his share of the drugs from the pool or, if he distributes the drug to the contributors concerned, then he is supplying them because "supplying" is expressed by section 37(1) of the M.D.A. to include "distributing."

"Distributing," in common usage, means to "deal out in portions or to share among others." In *Holmes* v. *Chief Constable of Merseyside*,[64] the Divisional Court held that the word "supply" had to be given its ordinary everyday meaning, so that a person who bought drugs on behalf of himself and others, is to be regarded as supplying those drugs if he thereafter "distributes" them or shares them out. In delivering the judgment of the Court, the Lord Chief Justice said[65]:

> " . . . the question of joint possession can become highly relevant on a charge of possessing, but I do not believe that the question of possession or no, is a satisfactory route to an answer in the type of case we are dealing with at the present time where the charge is of supplying or possession with intent to supply. Section 37 of the Misuse of Drugs Act 1971 in terms says 'supplying' includes distributing, and in my judgment when a Court has to consider an allegation of supply under this Act it must give the word 'supply' its perfectly ordinary natural everyday meaning. I have no doubt at all that a man who goes to market shopping for drugs on behalf of himself and others will often properly be regarded as supplying those drugs when he brings them home and distributes them because distribution is by statute a form of supply and that in itself is enough to cover such a case."

Holmes was approved and applied by the Court of Appeal in *Buckley and Lane*.[66] In that case, B and G agreed to buy cannabis resin in bulk by pooling their money and thereafter, to take their respective share. B, having been put in funds, visited Lane who supplied B with one pound of cannabis. B gave G three-quarters of a pound of the resin, and retained the remainder for himself. At his trial, B pleaded guilty to a charge that he "lawfully supplied to [G] three-quarters of a pound of cannabis resin." Despite his plea of guilty, B appealed on the grounds that since he was G's interme-

---

[64] [1976] Crim. L.R. 125.
[65] See the judgement of Lane L.J. (as he then was) in *Buckley* v. *Lane* [1969] 69 Cr. App. R. 371 at p. 374, who referred to this passage in that case.
[66] [1979] 69 Cr. App. R. 371.

diary, G acquired ownership and legal possession of his share of the drug at the moment B handed the money over to L. On this basis it was argued that B could not be said to be supplying G with what was already his. The Court of Appeal described the argument as "recondite," but found a simple answer to the problem in section 37(1) of the M.D.A. in that "supplying" is expressed to include "distributing." Geoffrey Lane L.J., remarked:

> "Whatever else Buckley may or may not have been doing when he divided up the cannabis and gave three-quarters of a pound to Gilchrist and kept the other quarter pound for himself, he was without any shadow of a doubt—it seems to us— distributing the cannabis whoever may have been the owner or the custodian or in possession of the drug."

As the Court, in *Buckley and Lane* pointed out, had the appellant's contention been correct then any drug-pusher could effectively circumvent the provisions of section 4 by merely collecting monies in advance from all interested purchasers and then buying the controlled drugs so ordered. Such a conclusion would have made a mockery of section 4.

By contrast, in *Searle*[67] the defendants had been on a touring holiday. A motor vehicle used by them for that purpose was searched, as a result of which, controlled drugs were found. The drugs could not been attributed to any particular defendant. Accordingly, the Court of Appeal held that if the drugs represented a common pool from which the defendants were entitled to draw at will and, if there was a joint enterprise to do so, then each defendant who is proved to be a party to that joint enterprise is to be regarded as being in possession of the drugs. Obviously, on the special facts in *Searle,* an intention to distribute drugs to the others could not be established against any of the defendants.

Suppose now that D provides a platter of "reefer" cigarettes for the enjoyment of guests at a party. On these facts D is clearly in possession of the cigarettes with intent to distribute them and thus to supply the drug which they contain.

A more complex problem—which has never been satisfactorily resolved by the courts—arises in connection with the smoking of a "reefer" cigarette which is then passed round a circle of smokers. In *King*,[68] K made reefer cigarettes in the presence of friends. The drug was taken from K's own supply. He would then pass the reefer round. Each person took it in turns to draw a puff from the reefer and then passed the reefer on. His Honour Judge Finlay

---

[67] [1971] Crim. L.R. 592, C.A.
[68] [1978] Crim. L.R. 288.

Q.C., held that K was not guilty of possessing the reefer with intent to supply it, contrary to section 5(3), because the degree of control exercised by each person within the smoking circle was insufficient.

The reasoning of the court is reported, in the Criminal Law Review, to have been as follows:

> " . . . only taking a puff and passing it on does not constitute supplying the material in the cigarette as it exists. It is only a supply if at the beginning the defendant has the material in his possession and at the end it has come into the possession of another in the sense that the other can do with it as he wishes."

This passage is not easy to understand. One supposes that the contention was that only the smoke (a puff) was being supplied and not the drug itself. Smoke was not the material in the cigarette "as it existed." Since only smoke was acquired at the beginning of the defendant's period of possession he did not, and could not, transfer it to another which that other could do with as he wished. Meanwhile the maker of the reefer retained control of the drug.

The strained reasoning adopted in *King*[69] depends on drawing a distinction between the substance and the vapour (if any) which is produced. There is no sound reason for making such a distinction. What was being transferred was the control of the reefer and the drug which it contained. By drawing smoke the user was effectively diminishing the drug-stock in the cigarette. Since the words "supplying" and "distributing" must be given their everyday meaning it follows that the drug was being distributed for use within the circle of smokers.

> In *Moore*[70] M persuaded two girls to "go for a smoke." He rolled a reefer which he intended to share with them. It was submitted to the trial judge that the offer was an offer to supply "smoke" rather than the material in the cigarette.
>
> Held, there was a supply. The court declined to follow *King*.

The court accepted that what was being offered was not only smoke but the custody and temporary control of the reefer from which the two girls could draw smoke. To that extent there had been an offer to distribute the drug by sharing custody of the reefer. The fact that custody was retained for a very short period of time was irrelevant. It is also irrelevant that only a fraction of

[69] *Ibid.*
[70] [1979] Crim. L.R. 789.

the drug would have been consumed. It is submitted that *Moore* is to be preferred and this would seem to be the current thinking of the Court of Appeal.[71]

The problem of "bailment"

So far we have seen examples in which the intention has been to supply the drug for the use or for the benefit of another person. But suppose A intends to give B drugs purely for safe-keeping. Does A intend to supply B contrary to section 5(3)? Furthermore, if B actually receives the drug from A, intending to restore it to A at a later date, does B commit an offence contrary to section 5(3)?

On one interpretation of the term "supplying" it may be thought that all that is required to be proved is a transfer of physical control of the drug to another. On this basis it hardly matters whether A gives drugs to B for safe-keeping or not: either way physical control has been transferred.

However, in order to avert conclusions which would either be regarded as an affront to common sense, or which would seriously weaken an ambition of the Act, the courts have attempted to define the concept of supplying (and thus possession with intent to supply) in the context of the policy of the Act. As a result, various ingredients are said to exist which the prosecution may be required to prove in certain drug-related cases—for example by requiring proof of an intention, on the part of the transferor, to enable the transferee to use the drugs for his own purposes. Unfortunately, the efforts of the Courts, to produce a logical and a consistently applied set of qualifications or refinements to the concept of supplying have largely failed, so that the law produces some strange results. For the moment it is the law that a person who deposits drugs with a custodian for safe-keeping will not ordinarily be guilty of supplying, contrary to section 4 of the M.D.A., whereas the custodian will be guilty of supplying the depositor if he returns the drug to him! This is the effect of the decision of the House of Lords in *Maginnis*,[72] approving *Delgado*,[73] and *Donnelly* v. *HM Advocate*.[74] The conclusion that the custodian is put in a worse position that the depositor is both startling and, it is submitted, grossly illogical.

---

[71] *Chief Constable of Cheshire* v. *Hunt*, April 25, 1983 (unrep.).
[72] [1987] 1 All E.R. 907.
[73] (1984) 1 All E.R. 449.
[74] (1985) S.L.T. 243.

The difficulty of defining "supply"

It is not always easy to state or to define the ordinary natural meaning of a word. "Supply" and "supplying" are two prime examples. Both expressions are not always used precisely and, in any event, not everyone perceives an act of supply in the same terms. The Shorter Oxford English Dictionary devotes almost an entire column to the word "supply" defining it as " . . . fulfilling a want or demand . . . to furnish with . . . to satisfy the wants of . . . provide for . . . to use . . . ," and so on. Accordingly, different instances of supplying may, in fact, possess different characteristics but, the existence (or absence) of a possible characteristic does not necessarily determine whether there has been a supply or not.

As the authorities are examined, it will be seen that different courts seem to focus on different characteristics and treat them as if they were conclusive of an act of supplying. Thus in *Dempsey*,[75] the court looked to see if the transfer was an act designed to benefit the transferee: but not every supply necessarily benefits the recipient. Again, in *Delgado*,[76] the court focussed its attention on the passing of physical control of the article to another. But in *Dempsey* there was a transfer of physical control of a drug and yet the conviction for supplying the drug was quashed.

A delivers the drug to B

Assume that A's intention is that B should act as custodian of the drug so that, upon demand, the drug is returned to A.

> In *Dempsey and Dempsey*,[77] D was a registered drug addict. He lawfully obtained 25 ampoules of physeptone. Maureen held some of the ampoules while D went into the lavatory to inject himself with the remainder. D pleaded guilty to supplying Maureen.
>
> Held, the conviction must be quashed. The mere deposit of an article for safe-keeping and return could not amount to an act of supply.

Lord Lane C.J., giving the judgment of the court, referred to the word "supply" as it appears in the Shorter Oxford English Dictionary and noted that it seems to be an act designed to benefit the recipient, but he added that:

---

[75] [1986] Crim. L.R. 171.
[76] [1984] 78 Crim. App. R. 175.
[77] See *supra*, n. 75.

"It does not seem to us that ["supplying"] is apt to describe the deposit of an article with another person for safe keeping, as was the case here. The example was canvassed in argument of a person who hands his coat to a cloakroom attendant for safe keeping during the show in a theatre or cinema. It could scarcely be said that the person handing the coat supplies it to the cloakroom attendant. Nor do we think it makes any difference that the cloakroom attendant wishes in one sense to get his coat, thinking that he may get a tip at the end of the evening. That is not the sort of wish or need which is envisaged by the definition of the offence."

Clearly, if the transfer of the drug to Maureen was so that she could use the drug for her own purposes, then there would have been a supply of the drug to her.

The Court of Appeal added that the jury had to decide whether the drug was being supplied to Maureen for her own purposes, for example to hand on to someone else, or to use upon her own body, in which case there would have been a supply, or whether it was simply for safe-keeping and return to D " . . . who was lawfully entitled to the drug . . . ." The words quoted are perhaps unnecessary and even a little misleading since they may be thought to imply that a depositor who is not lawfully entitled to possess the drug commits an offence of supplying if he deposits the drug with another for safe-keeping. But this logically cannot be so. Custody and physical control of the drug was given to Maureen but ultimate control was nevertheless retained by D. In ordinary language the drug "belonged" to D and it was not intended that Maureen could deal with it as she pleased. Whether D was lawfully entitled to the drug or not was irrelevant.

In *R. v. Maginnis*,[78] (which is now the leading case on this aspect of the law) Lord Keith said[78a]:

"The word 'supply,' in its ordinary natural meaning, conveys the idea of furnishing or providing to another something which is wanted or required in order to meet the wants or requirements of that other."

The word "supply" does convey such ideas but it can also convey other ideas not dependent on what is either wanted or required by the recipient. Lord Keith, who delivered the majority opinion in the House of Lords, went on to say[78b]:

---

[78] [1987] 1 All E.R. 907, H.L.; [1986] 2 All E.R. 110, C.A.
[78a] [1987] 1 All E.R. 907 at p. 909 f/g.
[78b] *Ibid.* at p. 909g.

"It ['supply'] connotes more than the mere transfer of physical control of some chattel or object from one person to another. No one would ordinarily say that to hand over something to a mere custodian was to supply him with it."

In so holding, their Lordships were clearly approving at least part of the reasoning in *Dempsey and Dempsey*. However, Lord Keith then dealt with the "additional concept" said to be involved in a supply, namely[78c]:

" . . . that of enabling the recipient to apply the thing handed over to purposes for which he desires or has a duty to apply it."

This is not an easy concept to understand. Lord Keith may have meant no more than that a supply connotes the transfer of substantial or complete control over the article handed over. However, construed literally, Lord Keith seems to be saying that the additional concept is satisfied once the recipient is given the opportunity of applying the thing to his own purposes if he so wishes or, if he is under a duty to apply it. But the notion of "enabling" the recipient to so apply the thing handed over is extremely broad. It is difficult to think of any physical transfer of goods to another which does not tend to "enable" the recipient to deal with the goods as he wishes—whether he is entitled to do so or not, and irrespective of the transferor's intentions. On this basis the cloakroom attendant is enabled, or given the opportunity to apply the patron's coat to the purposes for which he desires (lawfully or otherwise), but that fact does not convert the transfer of the coat to the cloakroom attendant, into an act of supply.

Where a custodian is under a "duty to apply" the article in question then he may be said to have been supplied with it. For example, where B is given a power drill by A (while A is on holiday) with a direction that B completes work on A's house in the meantime, then it is difficult to resist the view that B has been supplied with the drill. But this is, of course, a very different case to the custodian who is merely asked to look after the article in question.

B holds the drugs intending to return them to A

In *Maginnis*[79]:

a package of cannabis resin was found by police in M's motor car. He claimed that the package had been left there by a

---

[78c] *Ibid.* at p. 909 g/h.
[79] *Ibid.*

friend who was to collect it from him. He pleaded guilty to an offence under section 5(3) after the trial judge had ruled that the intention to return the package constituted the requisite intent. The Court of Appeal allowed the appeal against that conviction. The Crown appealed to the House of Lords.

Held, the Crown's appeal would be allowed. M intended to return the drug to his friend for that person's benefit.

The majority of their Lordships (Lord Goff dissented) analysed supply in the context of "enabling" the recipient to apply the thing for the recipient's own benefit. Thus, Lord Keith said[79a]:

> "If on a later occasion the defendant had handed the drugs back to his friend, he would have done so in order to enable the friend to apply the drugs for the friend's own purposes."

Lord Keith examined earlier authorities and distinguished them by ascertaining whether the drugs were transferred " . . . so as to enable those persons to apply the drugs to their own purposes . . . ." Of course, a person may, as a fact, enable another to apply the thing in question to his own purposes without actually intending to do so but it is not clear whether the majority of their Lordships were in fact holding that such an intent is required. The tenor of the opinions delivered suggest that proof of such an intent is required although the certified question was amended by their Lordships to read only as follows:

> "Whether a person in unlawful possession of a controlled drug which has been deposited with him for safe-keeping has the intent to supply that drug to another if his intention is to return the drug to the person who deposited it with him."

The majority of their Lordships answered the amended question in the affirmative. Unfortunately, the certified question was not amended to embrace an intention, on the part of the transferor, to enable the transferee to apply the drugs for his own purposes. The amendment to the certified question was considered necessary because the original question was said not to be " . . . in all respects apt to raise the true issue in the case."

The legal position of a custodian, who merely intends to return the drugs to the person who deposited them, has posed a difficult analytical problem for the courts to resolve. The reason is that a custodian of controlled drugs must realise that in almost every case the depositor ultimately intends to either unlawfully use the drugs himself or to unlawfully pass them onto others. It is therefore tempting, for the purposes of section 5(3), to include an ingredient

---

[79a] *Ibid.* at p. 910i.

that the person in possession must know that he is enabling the recipient to use the drugs for the latter's benefit. But the issue is whether the inclusion of such an ingredient gives "supply" an artificial meaning. Take, for example, the cloakroom analogy. The patron who hands a coat to the attendant relinquishes, temporarily, the custody and physical control of the coat but, it is not the attendant's coat to do with as he wishes since ultimate control remains with the depositor. The latter may call for its return. Accordingly, when the attendant returns the coat, he does not as a matter of common sense, "supply" the depositor with it. He knows perfectly well that the coat will be used by the depositor for his own use and has enabled him to use it. But that fact does not, it is submitted, ordinarily convert a return of an article in those circumstances into an act of supply. There is a mere resumption of total possession.

However, a very different view was taken in *Delgado*.[80] In that case the Court of Appeal analysed "supply" in the context of whether or not there had been a transfer of physical control.

> Police arrested D who was carrying 6·31 kilograms of cannabis in a holdall. He said that he was taking them to the persons who had given him the drugs for safe-keeping.
>
> Held, D intended to transfer the drug to another at an agreed time and place and had committed an offence contrary to section 5(3).

The court held that section 5(3) covered a wide range of transactions and that a feature common to all to them is a transfer of physical control of a drug from one person to another. Skinner J. observed[80a] that:

> "In our judgment questions of the transfer of ownership or legal possession of those drugs are irrelevant to the issue whether to supply."

Obviously, every case of supplying involves a transfer of physical control but the converse is not always true. The fact that physical control has been transferred cannot, without more, establish an act of supplying. *Maginnis* is itself authority for that proposition. Yet on the face of it *Delgado* appears to be establishing precisely that. By contrast, in *Dempsey and Dempsey* D gave ampoules (which belonged to him) to Maureen to hold temporarily. D therefore transferred physical control of the ampoules to Maureen, but the Court of Appeal held that D had not supplied her with the

[80] See *supra*, n. 76.
[80a] *Ibid*. 179.

drug: something more was required, namely that there had to be a benefit transferred to the recipient as well.

Not surprisingly the Court of Appeal, in *Maginnis*,[81] believed that a conflict existed between *Delgado* and *Dempsey*. Thus, Mann J., giving judgement for the court, said of those two decisions[81a]:

> "We find it impossible to reconcile the meaning put on the word 'supply' in *R.* v. *Delgado* with the meaning put on that word in *R.* v. *Dempsey*. The decision in *Delgado* is that the word is satisfied if there is a transfer of physical control of the drug in question. However, in *Dempsey* there was a transfer of physical control, yet the conviction was quashed . . . In our judgement the meaning put on the word 'supply' in *Dempsey* is to be preferred."

The Court of Appeal could not accept that the word "supply," as a matter of ordinary language, is apt to mean merely the transfer of physical control. Mann J. said[81b]:

> "We agree with the view of the court in *Dempsey*, that for there to be a supply there must be a transfer of physical control which is for the benefit of the recipient of the article. Counsel for the Crown accepted that this was the correct formulation but agreed that the transferee obtains a benefit when he receives back in article which he has placed in the custody of another."

The only discernible benefit that the Court of Appeal in *Maginnis* could find was the resumption of actual possession which the Court could not accept was sufficient to amount to an act of supply.

But when *Maginnis* went to the House of Lords their Lordships held that both *Dempsey* and *Delgado* are distinguishable on the facts.

Lord Keith explained the distinction in the following terms[82]:

> "In *R.* v. *Delgado* a custodian was found to have the necessary intent to supply because his intention was to hand back controlled drugs to the persons who had deposited them with him so as to enable those persons to apply the drugs to their own purposes, and thus put them back into circulation. In *R.*

[81] See *supra*, n. 78.
[81a] [1986] 2 All E.R. 110 at p. 113–114.
[81b] *Ibid.*
[82] [1987] 1 All E.R. 912d.

v. *Dempsey* there was a mere placing in temporary custody, and no intention of enabling the custodian to use the drugs for her own purposes."

The House of Lords held *Delgado* to have been rightly decided and applied it.

Their Lordships approved, for the most part, the decision of the High Court of Justiciary in Scotland, in *Donnelly* v. *HM Advocate*.[83] In that case, the appellant claimed that a quantity of controlled drugs found in her possession had been put there by another. The court (approving *Delgado*) said (at p. 244) " . . . if the appellant intended to part with all or some of the drugs in her possession to Colin Stewart, even for his own use, she intended to supply Colin Stewart, and it matters not whether his intention was to use them himself or to supply others."

In *Maginnis* their Lordships remarked that if this passage was intended to mean that a mere transfer of physical control of a drug from one person to another may constitute supply then this was not "entirely correct."

The decision of the House of Lords in *Maginnis* is fraught with difficulty and frankly throws up more issues than it settles. Whereas the Court of Appeal in that case looked to see what benefit was conferred on the recipient, the House of Lords by contrast, referred to the intention of the transferor to enable the transferee to use the drugs for his own purposes. The upshot is that the custodian will often be in a worse position than the depositor as the custodian will know that he is enabling the depositor to use the drug, whereas the depositor, does not intend the custodian to do likewise. Lord Goff of Chieveley (who dissented in *Maginnis*) was clearly concerned that the word "supply" would not be given a common sense interpretation if the majority of their Lordships were right. He found himself in agreement with the Court of Appeal in *Dempsey* but he regarded *Delgado* and *Donnelly* v. *HM Advocate* to be wrongly decided.

Lord Goff considered that the primary rule of construction is that the courts should attribute to words their natural and ordinary meaning unless the context otherwise requires but he hesitated to attempt a definition " . . . especially as the word is not always very precisely used"—and thus demonstrated how elusive the ordinary natural meaning, of ordinary words, can be. However, Lord Goff observed that[83a]:

[83] (1985) S.L.T. 243.
[83a] [1987] 1 All E.R. 913 f/g.

" . . . the word [supply], as used in relation to goods, connotes the idea of making goods available to another from resources other than those of the recipient."

In other words, the act of making goods available to a recipient, when those goods already form part of the recipient's own resources, cannot amount to an act of supply. Put another way, a recipient cannot be given what he effectively already has. Thus, Lord Goff said[83b]:

" . . . I would not describe the re-delivery by the depositee to the depositor as a supply of goods, because the goods are simply being returned to him, rather than being made available to him from resources other than his own."

Lord Goff agreed with that part of the judgment of Mann J. when he said[84]:

"In ordinary language the cloakroom attendant, the left luggage officer, the warehouseman and the shoe mender do not 'supply' to their customers the articles which those customers have left with them."

However, Lord Keith pointed to the example of a store-keeper who provided equipment to employees out of the store:

" . . . if an employee draws from his employers store materials or equipment which he requires for purposes of his work, it involves no straining of language to say that the store-keeper supplies him with those materials or equipment, notwithstanding that they do not form part of the store-keeper's own resources and that he is merely the custodian of them . . . "

In this example, however, it was not the employee who deposited the supplies or the equipment with the store-keeper in the first place. That is why the store-keeper could properly be described as a "distributor," and "supplying" of course includes "distributing." Lord Keith therefore gave the additional example of the owner of a business, who obtains tools and materials from his own store-keeper—being articles which formed part of the owner's assets—and concluded that the store-keeper " . . . can be said to be supplying him what he needs . . . ." This was not an illustration

---

[83b] *Ibid.* at p. 913j.
[84] [1986] 2 All E.R. 110 at p. 113–114; [1986] Q.B. 618 at p. 624.

which found favour with Lord Goff who did not think that it would be appropriate to use the word "supply" to describe this situation. He added:

"Even if the word 'supply' were to be used in such a context, I would regard it as a loose or aberrant use of the word which should be regarded as providing any foundation for the proposition that the word can be appropriately used, or is normally used, in every case where a depositee returns the goods to a depositor."

Surprisingly, the majority of their Lordships, in *Maginnis* adopted a highly legalistic approach to justify answering the amended certified question in the affirmative. Lord Keith observed that in *Dempsey* there was no intention of enabling Maureen (the custodian) to use the drugs for her own purposes and, accordingly, a transfer of the drugs to her in those circumstances could not amount to an act of supply. But Lord Keith added:

"One who deposits controlled drugs of which he is in unlawful possession with a temporary custodian has no legal right to require the drugs to be handed back to him. Indeed, it is the duty of the custodian not to hand them back but to destroy them or to deliver them to a police officer so that they may be destroyed. The custodian in choosing to return the drugs to the depositor does something which he is not only not obliged to do, but which he has a duty not to do."

There seems to be no good reason for introducing such legalistic considerations into the concept of "supplying" for the purposes of the M.D.A. If a custodian may be compelled, as a matter of law, to return goods to the depositor, does that mean that the depositor has therefore not been "supplied" with those goods, but that if a custodian cannot be compelled in law to return goods (for example controlled drugs) then he is guilty of supplying them if they are returned? Lord Goff tested the validity of that approach when he said:

"Let us forget about controlled drugs for the moment; and let us suppose that, owing to some technical rule of law, a contract of deposit of goods is unenforceable . . . But the depositee is an honourable man, and returns the goods to the man who deposited them with him. Nobody would, I think, describe him in ordinary language as supplying the goods to the depositor, simply because he was not legally bound to return them. The fact is that the goods came from the deposit-

or's own resources; and all the depositee was doing was
returning them to him.''

The special case of Harris

In *Harris*,[85] H and F were heroin addicts. H was registered as
an addict whereas F was not. At Kingston Railway Station H
and F were seen sitting close together in the waiting room.
Sticking in F's arm was a syringe contained F's heroin. H was
seen injecting F's arm by pushing the top of the syringe. At
the police station H told police "I didn't give him the jack, it
was one of his own. I was only helping him."

This case has sometimes been cited to support the contention
that a transfer of custody or physical control of a drug cannot
amount to a supply even if the transfer was for the benefit of the
recipient. In fact one should approach this case with caution since
the Court of Appeal had to decide the appeal on the basis that the
drug belonged to F and indeed he pleaded guilty to possessing the
drug. In allowing the appeal Lord Parker C.J. said:

> "If B has obtained in some way the possession of the heroin,
> and all that A is doing is to assist in injecting that her heroin
> into B, then A is not supplying heroin contrary to the Regula-
> tion."

In ordinary language, the heroin "belonged" to F and therefore,
as a matter of common sense, F could not be supplied with what he
already had. It would not appear from the facts, as reported in
Harris, that the defendant had been in possession of the drug
(whether jointly or otherwise) moments before she injected F with
"his" drug and, again, there appears to have been no evidence that
H inserted the needle into F's arm—which would otherwise have
meant that she had been in possession of the drug prior to administering it. If H was not in possession of the drug before, or at the
moment of injection, then clearly there was nothing for H to
supply. On one view of the facts F was administering his own
drug—H merely helped him. Accordingly, one may be compelled
to treat *Harris* as having been decided on its own very special facts.
In *Delgado*, Skinner J. seems to have interpreted the facts in *Harris* in this way for he said:

> "The drugs which were injected never left the presence of the
> owner or, as it was strongly argued, his physical control."

[85] [1968] 2 All E.R. 49.

B possesses drugs intending to act jointly with A

Again, in *Maginnis*[86] Lord Keith said:

"If a trafficker in controlled drugs sets up a store of these in the custody of a friend whom he think unlikely to attract the suspicions of the police and later draws on the store for the purposes of his trade, or for his own use, the custodian is in my opinion rightly to be regarded as supplying him with drugs."

In practice the Prosecution may have no difficulty in proving that a custodian (in the circumstances described by Lord Keith) was acting in concert with the depositor and therefore both may be convicted of supplying a third party in accordance with the usual rules of joint enterprise. Thus, the facts of *Delgado* were capable of showing more than just an intention to return the drugs to his friends. There was at least a prima facie case that D was engaged in a joint venture (or a conspiracy) to supply persons unknown; a matter which clearly loomed large during the course of the hearing of the appeal in that case.

But even if the custodian intended to supply the depositor, knowing that the latter would supply the drug to others, that does not mean that the custodian possesses the drug intending to supply those third parties. Thus in *Greenfield*,[87] G was stopped by police in his car. Between the front seats was a plastic bag containing cannabis. G told police that a friend left the bag with him but he knew that his friend was a supplier of cannabis. The judge directed the jury principally on the basis that G held the drug for X knowing that X would supply it. Less emphasis was placed, by the judge in his summing up, on the alternative case, namely, that G himself was engaged on a joint venture with X to supply. G's appeal against conviction for an offence under section 5(3) was allowed on the basis that the intent of somebody else to supply the drugs was not enough.

"The words . . . 'with intent to supply . . . ' predicate that it should be the intent on the part of the person who possesses to supply and not the intent of someone other than that who is in possession of drugs to supply."

A similar point arose in *Downes*,[88] where the trial judge directed the jury that a defendant was guilty under section 5(3) if he knew full well that the depositor was ultimately going to supply

---

[86] [1987] 1 All E.R. 907 at p. 909.
[87] (1983) Crim. L.R. 397.
[88] [1984] Crim. L.R. 552.

the drugs to other even if he, personally, was not going to be involved in the supply. The Court of Appeal quashed the conviction. The prosecution must establish a joint venture with the requisite joint intention. *Greenfield* does not appear to have been cited in *Downes* but both decisions are clearly consistent.[89]

SUPPLYING CONTROLLED DRUGS

Section 4 of the Misuse of Drugs Act 1971 reads as follows:

"(1) Subject to any regulations under section 7 of this Act for the time being in force, it shall not be lawful for a person—
   (*a*) to produce a controlled drug; or
   (*b*) to supply or offer to supply a controlled drug to another.
(2) Subject to section 28 of this Act, it is an offence for a person—
   (*a*) to produce a controlled drug in contravention of subsection (1) above; or
   (*b*) to be concerned in the production of such a drug in contravention of that subsection by another.
(3) Subject to section 28 of this Act, it is an offence for a person—
   (*a*) to supply or offer to supply a controlled drug to another in contravention of subsection (1) above; or
   (*b*) to be concerned in the supplying of such a drug to another in contravention of that subsection; or
   (*c*) to be concerned in the making to another in contravention of that subsection of an offer to supply such a drug."

It will be seen that section 4(1) merely imposes prohibitions on the production or supplying of controlled drugs, (or against the making of an offer to supply such drugs) but offences, arising out of a contravention of any of the prohibitions, are created by subsections (2) and (3).

Unfortunately, the concept of supplying is not straightforward and the M.D.A. offers little assistance. By section 37(1), "supplying" includes "distributing."

In *Mills*,[90] it was suggested by the Court of Appeal, that "supply" involves the passing of possession from one person to another. This statement is plainly an over simplification and not

---

[89] See *Tansley* v. *Painter* [1969] Crim. L.R. 139, D.C.
[90] [1963] 1 Q.B. 522.

apt to cover every situation. In the wake of the decision of the House of Lords in *Maginnis*,[90a] it is now more appropriate to view a supply in the context of a transfer of physical control of a controlled drug, to another, with the intention of enabling the recipient to use that drug for his own purposes. Although many cases of supplying will involve the passing of a benefit, or reward, to the transferee, it is going too far to "gloss" the meaning of "supply" in those terms. So, where a chain of persons are involved in the distribution of controlled drugs, it follows that each member, who transfers the drug to the next person in the chain, will commit a separate act of supply even if each distributor receives no discernible benefit or reward himself.

Many of the authorities, which have considered the meaning of "supplying" and "distributing," are examined in another section ("Possession With Intent To Supply") and the reader is strongly invited to read that section.

DRUGS WHICH MAY LAWFULLY BE SUPPLIED

Bearing in mind that the object of the M.D.A. is to regulate the flow of controlled drugs and their use, and that not all controlled drugs are equally dangerous to use, Parliament had endeavoured to introduce as flexible a system of distribution as it can under a statute. For this reason some drugs may be more freely supplied than others. Indeed, one substance, "Poppy-straw," is not subject to section 4(1) of the M.D.A. at all (see Regulation 4(3) of the Misuse of Drugs Regulations 1985). "Poppy-straw" is defined in Part IV to Schedule 2 of the M.D.A. to mean " . . . all parts, except the seeds, of the opium poppy, after mowing." The extent to which various classes of persons are permitted to supply specified controlled drugs are set out in the Misuse of Drugs Regulations 1985 (S.I. 1985 No. 2066)—as amended by S.I. 1986 No. 2330.

Persons who may lawfully supply any controlled drug

Licensees
    Any person may supply any controlled drug if authorised by Licence so to do: Regulation 5. The licence is issued by the Secretary of State. Obviously, any supply or offer to supply, not in accordance with the terms and conditions attached to the licence,

[90a] [1987] 1 All E.R. 907.

will render such a supply (or offer to supply) unlawful, although it is unlikely to render the licence invalid.

General authority to supply
Regulation 6(1) provides that:

> "Notwithstanding the provisions of section 4(1)(*b*) of the Act, any person who is lawfully in possession of a controlled drug may supply that drug to the person from whom he obtained it."

Regulation 6(1) protects the person who, for example, is prescribed a course of controlled drugs—and is therefore lawfully entitled to possess them—but who then wishes to return all unused drugs back to the prescribing doctor. Regulation 6(1) cannot be used to protect a "bailee," who is given controlled drugs for safekeeping, which are then returned to the "bailor," if the bailee is not a person lawfully entitled to take possession of them in the first instance.

By virtue of Regulation 6(5), and notwithstanding the provisions of section 4(1)(*b*) of the Act, " . . . any of the persons specified in Regulation 6(7) may supply any controlled drug to any person who may lawfully have that drug in his possession." The six classes of persons, listed in Regulation 6(7) are:

> "(*a*) a constable when acting in the course of his duty as such;
>
> (*b*) a person engaged in the business of a carrier when acting in the course of that business;
>
> (*c*) a person engaged in the business of the Post Office when acting in the course of that business;
>
> (*d*) an officer of customs and excise when acting in the course of his duty as such;
>
> (*e*) a person engaged in the work of any laboratory to which the drug has been sent for forensic examination when acting in the course of his duty as a person so engaged;
>
> (*f*) a person engaged in conveying the drug to a person who may lawfully have that drug in his possession."

General authority to supply Schedule 2, 3, 4, & 5 drugs

Drugs returned by patient to practitioner
Regulation 6(2) provides that:

> "Notwithstanding the provisions of section 4(1)(*b*) of the Act,

any person who has in his possession a drug specified in Schedule 2, 3, 4 or 5 which has been supplied by or on the prescription of a practitioner for the treatment of that person, or of a person whom he represents, may supply that drug to any doctor, dentist or pharmacist for the purpose of destruction."

Accordingly, a patient who has been supplied controlled drugs by a "practitioner," and who now wishes to see some or all of those drugs destroyed, may deliver (*i.e.* supply) those drugs to any doctor, dentist or pharmacist for that purpose. It is therefore not necessary to return the drugs only to the person who supplied them. Nor is it necessary for the patient, who was the original recipient, to deliver them up for destruction: he may appoint another person to perform that task. The latter will also be protected by Regulation 6(7). The term "practitioner" is not defined by the Regulations, but is stated in section 37(1) of the 1971 Act to mean " . . . a doctor, dentist, veterinary practitioner or veterinary surgeon."

Drugs returned to veterinary practitioners
It is often forgotten that controlled drugs are also supplied, prescribed and administered in the treatment of animals as well as human beings. Accordingly, persons who have such drugs in their possession will be protected if the drugs are supplied to them in a form authorised by the Regulations. Any person, who intends to deliver them up for destruction, will be protected by Regulation 6(3) if certain conditions are fulfilled. Regulation 6(3) provides that:

"Notwithstanding the provisions of section 4(1)(*b*) of the Act, any person who is lawfully in possession of a drug specified in Schedule 2, 3, 4 or 5 which has been supplied by or on the prescription of a veterinary practitioner or veterinary surgeon for the treatment of animals may supply that drug to any veterinary practitioner, veterinary surgeon or pharmacist for the purposes of destruction."

Administration of drugs
Every act, involving the adminstration of a controlled drug to another, is an act of supply. In respect of drugs specified in Schedule 5 of the 1985 Regulations, any person may administer such drugs to any one else (Regulation 7(1)).

Doctors and dentists may lawfully administer drugs listed in Schedules 2, 3 and 4 to a patient under Regulation 7(2). Indeed, any person may administer such drugs to another *providing* that the drugs are administered in accordance with the directions of a doctor or a dentist: Regulation 7(3).

Persons who may supply *only* Schedule 3 drugs

The drugs which come within Schedule 3 include the following:

"1(*a*)Benzphetamine	Meprobamate
(Cathine)	Methylphenobarbitone
Chlorphentermine	Methyprylone
Diethypropion	Pentazocine
Ethchlorvynol	Phendimetrazine
Ethinamate	Phentermine
Mazindol	Pipradrol
Mephentermine	

(*b*) any 5,5 disubstituted barbituric acid.

2. Any stereoisomeric form of a substance specified in paragraph 1 "not being phenylpropanolamine"—(words added by the Misuse of Drugs (Amendment) Regulations 1986 S.I. 1986/2330).
3. Any salt of a substance specified in paragraph 1 or 2.
4. Any preparation or other product containing a substance specified in any of paragraphs 1 to 3, not being a preparation specified in Schedule 5."

Wildlife licensees
Subject to an appropriate licence being granted under section 16 of the Wildlife and Countryside Act 1981, it is not unlawful to supply or to offer to supply a controlled drug falling within Schedule 3: Regulation 6(4).

Buffering agents in chemical analysis
It is often necessary for laboratory personnel to use a variety of chemicals (some of which may be controlled) in order to carry out chemical analysis. Limited protection is afforded by Regulation 9(6) (as amended by the Misuse of Drugs (Amendment) Regulations 1986 (S.I. 1986 No. 2330) which provides:

"Notwithstanding the provisions of section 4(1)(*b*) of the Act, person in charge of a laboratory may, when acting in his capacity as such, supply or offer to supply any drug specified in Schedule 3 which is required for use as a buffering agent in chemical analysis to any person who may lawfully have that drug in his possession."

Persons who may supply Schedule 2 or 5 drugs

Class of persons lawfully entitled to supply others
Eleven categories of persons may, by Regulation 8(2), lawfully supply or offer to supply Schedule 2 or 5 drugs to any person who may lawfully have that drug in his possession, namely:

"(*a*) a practitioner

(*b*) a pharmacist

(*c*) a person lawfully conducting a retail pharmacy

(*d*) a person in charge or acting person in charge of a hospital or nursing home which is wholly or mainly main- tained by a public authority out of public funds or by a charity or by voluntary subscriptions;

(*e*) in the case of such a drug supplied to her by a person responsible for the dispensing and supply of medicines at the hospital or nursing home, the sister or acting sister for the time being in charge of a ward, theatre, or other department in such a hospital or nursing home as aforesaid;

(*f*) a person who is in charge of a laboratory the recognised activities of which consist in, or include, the conduct of scientific education or research and which is attached to a university, university college or such a hospital as aforesaid or to any other institution approved for the purpose . . . by the Secretary of State.

(*g*) a public analyst appointed under section 76 of the Food Act 1984 or section 27 of the Food and Drugs (Scotland) Act 1956.

(*h*) a sampling officer within the meaning of the Food and Drugs (Scotland) Act 1956.

(*i*) a sampling officer within the meaning of schedule 3 to the Medicines Act 1968.

(*j*) a person employed or engaged in connection with a scheme for testing the quality or amount of the drugs, preparations and appliances supplied under the National Health Service Act 1977 or the National Health Service (Scotland) Act 1978 and the Regulations made thereunder;

(*k*) a person authorised by the Pharmaceutical Society of Great Britain for the purposes of section 108 or 109 of the Medicines Act 1968.

Provided that nothing in this paragraph authorises—

(i) the person in charge or acting person in charge of

a hospital or nursing home, having a pharmacist responsible for the dispensing and supply of medicines, to supply or offer to supply any drug;

(ii) a sister or acting sister for the time being in charge of a ward, theatre or other department to supply any drug otherwise than for administration to a patient in that ward, theatre or department in accordance with the directions of a doctor or dentist."

Group authority

Protection is given to any person who is "authorised as a member of a group" to supply or offer to supply, drugs specified in Schedule 2 or 5, to any person who may lawfully have that drug in his possession: Regulation 8(3). However, such a member must comply (a) with the terms of his group authority, and (b) with any conditions attached to that authority.

By Regulation 2(1), a person is "authorised as a member of a group" if he is:

" . . . authorised by virtue of being a member of a class as respects which the Secretary of State has granted an authority under and for the purposes of Regulations 8(3), 9(3) or 10(3) which is in force, and 'his group authority,' in relation to a person who is a member of such a class, means the authority so granted to that class."

Provisions applicable to non-doctors at sea

By Regulation 8(5):

" . . . (a) the owner of a ship, or the master of a ship which does not carry a doctor among the seamen employed in it;

(b) the installation manager of an offshore installation, may supply or offer to supply any drug specified in Schedule 2 or 5—

(i) for the purposes of compliance with any of the provisions specified in paragraph (6), to any person on that ship or installation;

(ii) to any person who may lawfully supply that drug to him;

(iii) to any constable for the purpose of the destruction of that drug.

By Regulation 8(6):

"The provisions referred to in paragraph (5) are any provision of, or of any instrument which is in force under—

   (*a*) the Merchant Shipping Acts;
   (*b*) the Mineral Workings (Offshore Installations) Act 1971; or
   (*c*) the Health and Safety at Work Act 1974."

Persons who may supply Schedule 3 or 4 drugs

Classes of persons lawfully entitled to supply others
The following nine classes of persons may, by Regulation 9(2), lawfully supply or offer to supply controlled drugs to any person lawfully entitled to have such drugs in his possession, namely,

   "(*a*) a practitioner
   (*b*) a pharmacist
   (*c*) a person lawfully conducting a retail pharmacy[91];
   (*d*) a person in charge of a laboratory the recognised activities of which consist in, or include, the conduct of scientific education or research;
   (*e*) a public analyst appointed under section 76 of the Food Act 1984 or section 27 of the Food and Drugs (Scotland) Act 1956;
   (*f*) a sampling officer within the meaning of the Food and Drugs (Scotland) Act 1956;
   (*g*) a sampling officer within the meaning of schedule 3 to the Medicines Act 1968;
   (*h*) a person employed or engaged in connection with a scheme for testing the quality or amount of the drugs, preparations and appliances supplied under the National Health Service Act 1977 or the National Health Service (Scotland) Act 1978 and the Regulations made thereunder;
   (*i*) a person authorised by the Pharmaceutical Society of Great Britain for the Purposes of section 108 or 109 of the Medicines Act 1968."

As from April 1, 1987 the Misuse of Drugs (Amendment) Regulations 1986 (S.I. 1986 No. 2330) substituted the following paragraph for Regulation 9(3), thus:

---

[91] Not surprisingly, the regulations also permit a retail pharmacist to supply what he is authorised to produce. Thus, by Regulation 9(4)(b) " . . . a person who is authorised under paragraph 9(1)(c) may supply or offer to supply any drug which he may, by virtue of being so authorised, lawfully produce to any person who may lawfully have that drug in his possession."

"(3) Notwithstanding the provisions of section 4(1)(*b*) of the Act—

    (a) a person who is authorised as a member of a group, under and in accordance with the terms of his group authority and in compliance with any conditions attached thereto;

    (b) the person in charge or acting person in charge of a hospital or nursing home;

    (c) in the case of such a drug supplied to her by a person responsible for the dispensing and supply of medicines at that hospital or nursing home, the sister or acting sister for the time being in charge of a ward, theatre or other department in a hospital or nursing home,

may, when acting in his capacity as such, supply or offer to supply any drug specified in Schedule 3, or any drug specified in Schedule 4 which is contained in a medicinal product, to any person who may lawfully have that drug in his possession:

    Provided that nothing in this paragraph authorises—

    (i) the person in charge or acting person in charge of a hospital or nursing home, having a pharmacist responsible for the dispensing and supply of medicines, to supply or offer to supply any drug;

    (ii) a sister or acting sister for the time being in charge of a ward, theatre or other department to supply any drug otherwise than for administration to a patient in that ward, theatre or department in accordance with the directions of a doctor or dentist."

Provisions applicable to non-doctors at sea
By Regulation 9(5):

    " . . . (*a*) the owner of a ship, or the master of a ship which does not carry a doctor among the seamen employed in it;

    (*b*) the installation manager of an offshore installation, may supply or offer to supply any drug specified in Schedule 3, or any drug specified in Schedule 4 which is contained in a medicinal product—

    (i) for the purpose of compliance with any of the provisions specified in Regulation 8(6), to any person on that ship or installation; or

    (ii) to any person who may lawfully supply that drug to him."

Persons who may supply Schedule 5 drugs

We have already seen that any person may administer to another a controlled drug *providing* that it is a drug specified in Schedule 5. The drugs coming within this category are as follows:

"1—(1) Any preparation of one or more of the substances to which this paragraph applies, not being a preparation designed for administration by injection, when compounded with one or more other active or inert ingredients and containing a total of not more than 100 milligrammes of the substance or substances (calculated as base) per dosage unit or with a total concentration of not more than 2·5 per cent. (calculated as base) in undivided preparations.

(2) The substances to which this paragraph applies are acetylihydrocodeine, codeine, dihydrocodeine, ethylmorphine, nicocodine, nicodicodine (6-nicotinoyldihydrocodeine), norcodeine, pholcodine and their respective salts.

2. Any preparation of cocaine containing not more than 0·1 per cent. of cocaine calculated as cocaine base, being a preparation compounded with one or more other active or inert ingredients in such a way that the cocaine cannot be recovered by readily applicable means or in a yield which would constitute a risk to health.

3. Any preparation of medicinal opium or of morphine containing (in either case) not more than 0·2 per cent. of morphine calculated as anhydrous morphine base, being a preparation compounded with one or more other active or inert ingredients in such a way that the opium or, as the case may be, the morphine, cannot be recovered by readily applicable means or in a yield which would constitute a risk to health: and see *R. v. Hunt* [1986] 3 W.L.R. 1115, H.L.

4. Any preparation of dextropropoxyphene, being a preparation designed for oral administration, containing not more than 135 milligrammes of dextropropoxyphene (calculated as base) per dosage unit or with a total concentration of not more than 2·5 per cent. (calculated as base) in individual preparations.

5. Any preparation of difenoxin containing, per dosage unit, not more than 0·5 milligrammes of difenoxin and a quantity of atropine sulphate equivalent to at least 5 per cent. of the dose of difenoxin.

6. Any preparation of diphenoxylate containing, per dosage unit, not more than 2·5 milligrammes of diphenoxylate calculated as base, and a quantity of atropine sulphate equivalent to at least 1 per cent. of the dose of diphenoxylate.

7. Any preparation of propiram containing, per dosage unit, not more than 100 milligrammes of propiram calculated as base and compounded with at least the same amount (by weight) of methylcellulose.

8. Any powder of ipecacuanha and opium comprising—
10 per cent. opium in powder
10 per cent. ipecacuanha root, in powder, well mixed with 80 per cent. of any other powdered ingredient containing no controlled drug.

9. Any mixture containing one or more of the preparations specified in paragraphs 1 to 8, being a mixture of which none of the other ingredients is a controlled drug."

Written authority to supply

" . . . A person who is authorised by a written authority issued by the Secretary of State under . . . [paragraph 8(4)] may, at the premises specified in that authority and in compliance with any conditions . . . supply or offer to supply any drug specified in Schedule 5 to any person who may lawfully have that drug in his possession": see Regulation 8(4).

THE UNLAWFUL SUPPLY OF CONTROLLED DRUGS

Offences arising out of a contravention of section 4(1)(*b*), appear in section 4(3) which reads:

"Subject to section 28 of this Act, it is an offence for a person—
(*a*) to supply or offer to supply a controlled drug to another in contravention of subsection (1) . . . ; or
(*b*) to be concerned in the supplying of such a drug to another in contravention of that subsection; or
(*c*) to be concerned in the making to another in contravention of that subsection of an offer to supply such a drug."

Although the offences of supplying and offering to supply appear together in section 4(3)(*a*) they must be regarded as distinct offences so that charges or counts in the Indictment must clearly specify which offence is being alleged.

It will be seen that section 4(3) creates a total of four offences. The difference between (*b*) and (*c*) is that in (*b*) there must be an actual supply made by an accused whereas, in (*c*), the accused need only be concerned in making an offer to supply. Again, in respect of both (*b*) and (*c*), the word "knowingly" does not appear since both offences are subject to section 28.

In *Hughes*,[92] the Court of Appeal listed the three ingredients which the prosecution must prove, namely;

(1) the supply of a drug to another, or as the case may be the making of an offer to supply the drug to another; and

(2) participation by the accused in an enterprise involving such a supply or, as the case may be, such an offer to supply; and

(3) knowledge by the accused of the nature of the enterprise; either knowledge that it is a venture to supply or to make an offer to supply the drug in question.

It is not apparent from the report whether the Court heard argument as to the effect of section 28 on section 4.

"Supplying" includes "distributing": see section 37(1). In *Holmes* v. *Chief Constable Merseyside Police*,[93] counsel for the defence submitted that a person who held drugs on behalf of himself and others was in joint possession and that a subsequent division of the drugs could not amount to a supply. The Divisional Court rejected that submission, holding that the word "supply" had to be given its ordinary natural meaning (and see *Searle*).[94]

> In *Buckley* and *Lane*,[95] B and G pooled their money intending to buy cannabis in bulk. B took the money to L, the supplier, and bought 1lb of cannabis resin. Thereafter, B gave 3/4 lb of the drug to G representing the latter's contribution to the purchase price. B argued that he could not "supply" to G what he already possessed.
>
> Held, B was guilty of supplying the drug because he distributed it. *Holmes* v. *Chief Constable Merseyside Police* applied.

As the law presently stands, there is a supply upon the transfer of custody and physical control of a controlled drug to another, so as to enable that other to benefit from its use.[96] Many of the authorities relevant to this topic have been considered in the chapter concerning possession with intent to supply.

Making an offer to supply

Because the offence is directed to the making of an offer, it follows that the type of substance actually offered is irrelevant.

---

[92] (1985) 81 Cr. App. R. 344.
[93] [1976] Crim. L.R. 125.
[94] [1971] Crim. L.R. 592.
[95] (1979) 69 Cr. App. R. 371.
[96] See *Maginnis* (1987) 1 All E.R. 907.

Accordingly, where H offered to supply a substance which he mistakenly believed to be L.S.D. but was in fact a totally different substance, H was held (by the Divisional Court) to have been rightly convicted: *Haggard* v. *Mason*.[97]

"Being concerned"

Where a prosecution is brought under section 4(3)(*b*) or (*c*), it is the duty of the trial judge to assist the jury as to the meaning of the word "concerned": see *Hughes*.[98] A failure to do so may result in the conviction being quashed. Given that "concerned" involves some identifiable act of participation, it follows that the assistance given to the jury, by the judge, will vary from case to case. However, any direction must have regard to the relevant evidence of the accused's conduct in the transaction.

There exists, at present, a rather speculative interpretation as to whether the use of the word "concerned" was intended by the Legislature to replace the principles of aiding and abetting. If not then why did Parliament enact (*b*) and (*c*) at all? As Eveleigh L.J. said in *Blake & O'Connor*,[99] section 4(3)(*c*) is very widely drawn so as to include people "who may be at some distance from the actual making of the offer."

> In *Blake*, O made an offer to supply drugs to X in Piccadilly. B was not present but X and O went to B's flat to obtain the drugs. B's, conviction for being concerned in the making of an offer to supply, was upheld.

Supplying to "another"

In cases where defendants were charged with an offence of supplying a controlled drug to another, it was common to find that the "another" was himself a person named in the indictment.

Thus, suppose A supplied heroin to B. Some prosecutors charged both A and B with being concerned in the unlawful supply of heroin to another. Such a charge is misconceived since B cannot be charged with unlawfully supplying drugs to himself: see *Smith*[99a] and *Paolo Ferrara*.[99b]

---

[97] [1975] 1 W.L.R. 187.
[98] See *supra*, n. 92.
[99] [1979] 68 Cr. App. R. 1.
[99a] C.A., February 14, 1983, unreported.
[99b] C.A., July 17, 1984, unreported.

Accordingly, it was common practice for prosecutors to draft separate counts against each defendant so that A was charged with unlawfully supplying heroin to B, whereas the latter was charged merely with unlawfully possessing the drug. It is submitted that such a course is perfectly sensible notwithstanding the fact that both defendants appear on the same indictment. However, the decision of the Court of Appeal in *Adepoju and Lubren*[99c] appears (as the case is presently reported) to hold that the "another", for the purposes of section 4, cannot be a person "in the indictment". If this is truly the *ratio decidendi* of *Adepoju and Lubren* then the decision is surprising to say the least. However, upon a closer examination of *The Times* report, it is submitted that the case was decided on its own special facts and discloses no new law but merely confirms the decisions of the Court of Appeal in *Smith*[99d] and *Paolo Ferrara.*[99e] In *Adepoju and Lubren*, A, L and a Carol Curmi were all charged with being concerned in the unlawful supply of heroin to another (*i.e.* to Curmi) contrary to section 4(3) of the M.D.A. 1971. At the end of the prosecution case Curmi successfully submitted that there was no case for her to answer. She could not supply herself. But the prosecutor successfully applied to the Court for leave to amend the indictment so as to delete Curmi as a defendant from that charge but to name her as the "another" to whom the supply was made.

That amendment prevented the appellants from successfully submitting that there was no case for them to answer on the basis that the prosecution had failed to prove that the appellants had supplied another *i.e.* a person other than a defendant jointly charged in the same count. Even if supply to Carol Curmi could be established she was not "another" so long as she was included in the count on the indictment. The Court of Appeal held that the appellants had been entitled to a ruling in respect of their submission of no case to answer as the indictment stood "at the time". The judge had accordingly been wrong to allow the amendment. As the court remarked " . . . , the trouble had arisen because of careless drafting of the indictment". However, *The Times* law reporter appears to have been under the impression that the court also held that " . . . it was a matter of common sense that 'another' could not be a person in the *indictment*." It is submitted that if the word "count" is substituted for the word "indictment" then the proposition makes sense.

[99c] C.A., January 26, 1988 *The Times*.
[99d] *Supra.*
[99e] *Supra.*

Intoxicating substances

So far we have only been concerned with offences in connection with controlled drugs. However, by the Intoxicating Substances (Supply) Act 1985, Parliament made it an offence to supply or to offer to supply, to a person under 18 years of age, a substance other than a controlled drug, if he knows or has reasonable cause to believe that the substance is, or its fumes, are likely to be inhaled by the recipient for the purpose of intoxication: section 1(1).

However, the substance must be supplied to a person who is under 18 years of age and whom the accused knows, or has reasonable cause to believe, to be under that age: section 1(1)(*a*). Alternatively, the substance must be supplied or offered, to a person who is acting on behalf of a person under 18 years of age, and, whom he knows, or has reasonable cause to believe, to be so acting: section 1(1)(*b*).

If the accused can prove (because the burden is on him) that he was under 18 years of age, at the time when it is alleged that he contravened subsection (1), and that he was acting otherwise than in the course of furtherance of a business, he is entitled to be acquitted: subsection (2).

It follows that an accused aged 18 years or over, commits an offence under the Act whether he supplies an intoxicating substance in the course of a business or not. The Act does not make it an offence for, say, a 17 year old solvent abuser to supply the substance he is abusing, to another 17 year old. However, if a minor regularly sells part of his stock, he may (for the purposes of the Act) be engaged in a "business."

THE PRODUCTION OF CONTROLLED DRUGS

Subject to any regulations which the Secretary of State may make pursuant to section 7 of the M.D.A., it is not lawful for any person to produce a controlled drug: section 4(1)(*a*). Contravention of this subsection is made a criminal offence by section 4(2) of the M.D.A.

What is meant by production of a controlled drug

The legislature has defined the word "produce" to mean:

" . . . producing [a controlled drug] by manufacture, cultivation or any other method, and 'production' has a corresponding meaning" (Section 37(1) of the M.D.A.).

It is worth pointing out at this stage that although "production" includes "cultivating," Parliament (by section 6(2) of the Act) makes it a distinct offence to cultivate plants of the *genus cannabis* unless the grower is authorised to do so by a licence issued by the Secretary of State: see Regulation 12 of the Misuse of Drugs Regulations 1985.[1] It is not immediately apparent why Parliament specifically created this separate offence until one gives "producing" and "production" a narrow meaning. It is clear from section 37(1) that what has to be produced is the controlled drug itself *i.e.* as specified in Schedule 2 to the Misuse of Drugs Act 1971. Some drugs are produced by a process of synthesis, for example LSD. Some drugs are produced by cultivation in the sense that Penicillin, for example, is produced from the mould *Penicillium notatum*. Other drugs are produced after a process of extraction; thus cannabis resin is the resin separated from the cannabis plant.

The word "cultivation" certainly includes the act of nursing plants to fruition; but, not every cultivated plant, in which a drug naturally subsists, is an act of "production," within the meaning of section 37(1), since what is physically produced is not the drug itself—that still subsists in the plant. In 1971, when the Misuse of Drugs Act was passed, "cannabis" was a controlled drug, but the definition of "cannabis" was restricted to the flowering and fruiting tops of the plant: see *Goodchild No. 2*.[2] Accordingly, in 1971, a cannabis plant which had not flowered, or produced fruiting tops, was not a controlled drug, even though the active ingredient subsisted in the plant. Such a plant may have been "cultivated" but a controlled drug had yet to be produced. Accordingly, in order to prohibit persons growing the plant of the *genus cannabis* at all, Parliament enacted section 6.

By contrast, cocaine is a controlled drug. It is extracted from the coca-leaf. Obviously, the process of extraction is an act of production. But the coca-leaf itself, is a controlled drug, and is "produced" by growing it.

In 1977, the definition of "cannabis"—as a controlled drug—was extended to include virtually the entire plant (see section 52 of the Criminal Law Act 1977). As a result, there is now no reason at all why the act of growing the cannabis plant should not be

[1] "Where any person is authorised by a licence of the Secretary of State issued under this Regulation and for the time being in force to cultivate plants of the genus *Cannabis*, it shall not by virtue of section 6 of the Act be unlawful for that person to cultivate any such plant in accordance with the terms of the licence and in compliance with any conditions attached to the licence."
[2] (1978) 2 All E.R. 161.

regarded as an act of "production" for the purposes of section 4 of the M.D.A.

In *Taylor* v. *Chief Constable of Kent*[3]:

> Police found cannabis plants in T's premises but not in a room occupied by him. Nevertheless T knew that the plants were there and that they had been cultivated by X who was convicted under section 6 for so doing. T was charged with permitting or suffering the "production" of the plants in the premises under section 8. The defence argued that the plants had not been produced but only cultivated which was not an activity included in section 8.
>
> Held, the appeal would be dismissed. The 1977 amendment of the term "cannabis," included virtually the whole plant, and now equated production with its cultivation.

However, the so-called "magic mushroom" gives rise to special problems. The mushroom is not a controlled drug although the substance which subsists within it (psilocin) is. Therefore, merely to cultivate the mushroom cannot amount to cultivating the drug.[4]

LAWFUL PRODUCTION

Because many controlled drugs have a medicinal value, the policy of the M.D.A. and the Regulations, is to restrict the category of persons who may lawfully produce controlled drugs so that their activities may be closely monitored and regulated.

Accordingly, if the Secretary of State is of the opinion that it is in the public interest (*inter alia*) for the production, supply and possession of specified controlled drugs to be either totally unlawful, or unlawful except for research purposes, or except under licence, then he may, by Regulation, "designate" the drugs as being so affected: see section 7(4) of the M.D.A. 1971; and the Misuse of Drugs (Designation) Order 1986 (S.I. 1986 No. 2331) which, as from April 1, 1987, revoked earlier orders, namely, S.I. 1977 No. 1379 and S.I. 1984 No. 1144.

The most important drugs which are thus subject to section 7(4) of the M.D.A. appear in Part I of the Schedule to the 1986 Order, and include:

---

[3] (1981) 72 Cr. App. R. 318.
[4] See *Stevens* [1981] Crim. L.R. 568 and *Cunliffe* [1986] Crim. L.R. 547.

Cannabinol	Coca-leaf
Cannabinol derivatives	L.S.D.
Cannabis	Psilocin
Cannabis Resin	Raw Opium

Thus, Regulation 8(1)(a), of the Misuse of Drugs Regulations 1985 (S.I. No. 2066), permits a practitioner or pharmacist to manufacture or compound any drug specified in Schedule 2 or Schedule 5 of the Misuse of Drugs Regulations 1985 providing that they act in their respective capacities. Thus, a pharmacist cannot "produce" a controlled drug merely to demonstrate to family and friends how drugs are made.

Again, by Regulation 8(1)(b) a person who lawfully conducts a retail pharmacy business may manufacture or compound controlled drugs provided (i) that he acts in his capacity as such and (ii) that the production is carried on at the business premises of the registered pharmacy. A person "lawfully conducting a retail pharmacy business" means, by section 37(1) of the M.D.A., (and subject to subsection (5)):

" . . . a person lawfully conducting such a business in accordance with section 69 of the Medicines Act 1968";

Section 37(5) qualifies the above in the following terms:

"So long as sections 8 to 10 of the Pharmacy and Poisons Act 1933 remain in force, this Act in its application to Great Britain shall have effect as if for the definition of 'person lawfully conducting a retail pharmacy business' in subsection (1) above there were substituted—
'a person lawfully conducting a retail pharmacy business' means an authorised seller of poisons within the meaning of the Pharmacy and Poisons Act 1933; . . . "

A similar concession is given to the afore-mentioned persons in respect of drugs listed in schedule 3 and schedule 4 of the regulations: see Regulation 9(1)(a) and Regulation 9(1)(b). Because the controlled drugs in schedules 3 and 4 are considered by the Legislature to be less dangerous to use, a further exemption is given to persons who hold a written authority to produce controlled drugs. Such written authority is granted by the Secretary of State, subject to any conditions which he may provide, see: Regulation 9(1)(c).

A written authority is to be distinguished from a Licence to Produce which may be issued by the Secretary of State in respect of any controlled drug and subject to the terms and conditions attached to the licence: see Reg. 5. But where a person is authorised to produce drugs either by written authority or under licence, he will be obliged to keep a record of each quantity of drug produced by him: Regulation 22(1). Such a record must be preserved for a period of two years (Regulation 23(2)).

In any event any producer of a schedule 3 or 5 drug must keep every invoice (or similar record) in respect of any such drug which is either obtained by him for the purposes of that production or supplied by him: see Regulation 24(1).

Clearly, it is important that the Secretary of State, or an authorised agent, be able to demand the production and inspection of records kept by a drug manufacturer. Such a power is afforded to him by Regulation 25(1)(*a*).

For a multitude of reasons a person entitled to produce drugs under section 4(1)(*a*) may wish to destroy the end product, for example because they are not of the required standard or the stock is getting old. Nevertheless, to ensure that such controlled drugs do not fall into the wrong hands, Parliament has provided that drugs listed in schedules 1–4 are destroyed only in the presence of an authorised person and in accordance with his directions: see Regulation 26(1). The producer is obliged to keep a record of the date of destruction and the quantity of the ·drug destroyed: see Regulation 26(3).

THE UNLAWFUL PRODUCTION OF CONTROLLED DRUGS

Although section 4(1)(*a*) of the Act imposes a general prohibition on the production of controlled drugs, it is section 4(2) which creates offences arising out of a contravention of subsection (1). Thus section 4(2) provides:

"Subject to section 28 of this Act, it is an offence for a person—

(*a*) to produce a controlled drug in contravention of subsection (1) above; or

(*b*) to be concerned in the production of such a drug in contravention of that subsection by another."

In respect of both sections 4(*a*) and (*b*) the prosecution must prove that the accused played some identifiable part in the production process.

In *Farr*,[5] F admitted to police that on one occasion A and C arrived at his house, asking to use his kitchen, which he

[5] [1982] Crim. L.R. 745.

allowed. He knew that A and C produced "pink heroin" there. F was charged with an offence under section 4(2). He had not been charged with an offence of allowing his premises to be used for the production of a drug under section 8.

Held, F's conviction would be quashed. He took no identifiable role in the production although he would have had no answer to a charge under section 8.

It will be noted that section 8 of the M.D.A. prohibits an occupier to suffer or permit premises to be used for the purpose of producing a controlled drug. Sections 4 and 8 are not mutually exclusive since the premises could be made available as part of the act of production for example by a pre-arrangement that the premises would be so used. This had not occurred in *Farr*. Passive conduct would not in itself be enough. It may be said that giving encouragement is a sufficient participation in accordance with the usual principles of aiding and abetting the commission of an offence. The difficulty is that section 4(*b*) also makes it an offence to be "concerned" in the production of a controlled drug. This implies that, once again, some identifiable part in the production of the drug, is required and that accordingly, there is little room for the application for the principles of aiding and abetting: see *Carmichael & Sons (Worcester) Ltd.* v. *Cottle*[6] and *c.f. Blake.*[7]

The word "concerned" in section 4(*b*) is not qualified by the word "knowingly" for the simple reason that section 4(*b*) is subject to section 28. The burden will therefore be on an accused to show that he did not believe, or suspect or had any reason to suspect that what was actually being produced was a controlled drug (section 28(3)(*b*)(i)); or that he did not know, or suspect or had reason to suspect that what he was in fact concerned in, was a production venture (section 28(2)).

THE CULTIVATION OF CANNABIS

Although the word "produce" for the purposes of section 4(1)(*a*) includes "cultivation" (see: section 37(1)), it is the drug which is to be cultivated and not simply the plant in which the drug naturally subsist unless that plant is itself listed as a controlled drug in the Schedules to the M.D.A. Thus, growing the magic mushroom is not an offence merely because a controlled drug (psilocin) naturally subsists within that plant. On the other hand, the entire canna-

[6] [1971] R.T.R. 11.
[7] (1979) 68 Crim. App. R. 1.

bis plant is a controlled drug. Originally, only the flowering and fruiting tops of the plant were controlled by the M.D.A. in 1971, and hence the probable reason why section 6 was enacted. But today there is no good reason why the cultivation of a cannabis plant should not be an offence under section 4(1)(*a*) (production) and section 6. It follows that an occupier, or manager of premises, who permits or suffers the "production" of cannabis will be guilty of an offence under section 8: see *Taylor* v. *Chief Constable of Kent*.[8] Both offences are subject to section 28.

Section 6 provides:

"(1) Subject to any regulation under section 7 of this Act for the time being in force, it shall not be lawful for a person to cultivate any plant of the genus *cannabis*.
(2) Subject to section 28 of this Act, it is an offence to cultivate any such plant in contravention of subsection (1) above."

An exception to section 6(1) applies to plants cultivated under a licence issued by the Secretary of State, and subject to his terms and conditions endorsed on the licence: see Regulation 12 of the Misuse of Drugs Regulations 1985. The principal reason for this exemption is to facilitate research into the drug.

An offence under section 6(2) is made out once the prosecution has proved first, that the accused was cultivating a plant; and, secondly, that the plant was in fact a cannabis plant. It is not necessary for the Prosecution to prove that the accused knew that what was being cultivated was in fact a cannabis plant. Thus, in *Champ*[9]:

C was a herbalist who cultivated a plant in a window box. She believed the plant to be *hemp* which, according to an elderly gypsy, was good for various ailments. The plant was actually cannabis.

Held, the burden was on C to prove, under section 28, that she did not know the plant to be cannabis.

(See chapter dealing with section 28)

Champ has the curious feature that the defendant believed the plant to be hemp: but hemp is another term for cannabis. However, the point does not seem to have been taken either by counsel or by the court.

An offence under section 6 is not absolute since it is expressed to be subject to section 28.

---

[8] (1981) 72 Cr. App. R. 318. The facts of *Taylor* are given in the chapter dealing with Production.
[9] (1981) 73 Cr. App. R. 367.

DRUG ACTIVITIES ON PREMISES

Policing and enforcing the prohibitions imposed by the M.D.A. on the production, supply and use of controlled drugs is an expensive and difficult task particularly as many offences are likely to be committed on premises which are owned, occupied or managed by persons who may not themselves be concerned in the commission of the offences. They may be absent at the material time. Nevertheless, it was clearly Parliament's hope that obligations imposed on occupiers and managers not to permit, or suffer, a limited range of activities to take place on their premises, would encourage them to "police" the Act. Thus, by section 8:

> "A person commits an offence if, being the occupier or con-
> cerned in the management of any premises, he knowingly per-
> mits or suffers any of the following activities to take place on
> those premises, that is to say—
>
>   (a) producing or attempting to produce a controlled drug
>   in contravention of section 4(1) of this Act;
>   (b) supplying or attempting to supply a controlled drug to
>   another in contravention of section 4(1) of this Act, or
>   offering to supply a controlled drug to another in con-
>   travention of section 4(1);
>   (c) preparing opium for smoking;
>   (d) smoking cannabis, cannabis resin or prepared opium.

As a piece of Parliamentary drafting, section 8 represents a quite extraordinary example peppered, as it is, with a host of obvious anomalies. Thus, an occupier is forbidden to permit the smoking of cannabis or prepared opium to take place on his premises but, section 8 does not similarly forbid the smoking or injecting of heroin, or the snorting of cocaine, or the cooking of a "cannabis cake," or the preparation of tablets of LSD to take place. Given that such drug practices must have been well known to the Legislature in 1971, the wording of section 8 is all the more astonishing. Moreover, Parliament made no attempt to define several key words and phrases with which the Courts would obviously require guidance. Thus, the terms "occupier" and persons "concerned in the management of premises" are not defined by the Act.

Premises

Defining "premises" for the purpose of the M.D.A. is not straightforward. Unfortunately, the draftsmen failed on this occasion to provide a "clarifying definition"—a device to state expressly that certain matters are to be treated as coming within a definition.

In tort, we find that the word "premises" has been broadly construed to include real property; appliances and objects upon it, for example ships in dry dock[10]; and also includes movables not in transit such as ships[11]; aircraft[12]; or permanently moored houseboats.[13] If these authorities can be relied upon as being definitive of the word "premises" for the purposes of section 8 then some curious results follow. Thus, the owner of a river cruiser, knowing that cannabis is being smoked on board while the vessel is in motion, will not, it seems, be guilty of an offence contrary to section 8(d). There is no logical reason for excluding movables from the scope of this section providing, of course, that the offence is committed within the jurisdiction of the courts.

There is abundant authority for the proposition that buildings (whether subject to a lease or not) are "premises," but mere land without structures upon it, probably falls outside the definition of "premises."[14]

Who is responsible?

Responsibility is clearly based on occupancy or control and not merely on ownership. Section 8 is expressly aimed at the occupiers or the managers of premises since it is they who may exercise immediate supervision over the activities carried on within them. As the Court of Appeal pointed out in *Tao*[15] the fact that the term "occupier" was not defined in the Act suggests that the intention of the Legislature was to leave it to the tribunal of fact to decide whether an accused exercised "sufficient exclusivity of possession so that he can fairly be said to be 'the occupier' "; (*per* Roskill L.J.).

The court held that a common-sense rather than a legalistic meaning should be given to the term "occupier" so that a person who was in a position to exercise a sufficient degree of control to exclude, say, a cannabis smoker was an occupier for the purposes of section 8.

In *Tao*, the accused, an undergraduate, occupied a room allocated to him by his college. He lived there and held the key to

---

[10] *London Graving Dock* v. *Horton* [1951] A.C. 737.
[11] See *Duncan* v. *Cammell Laird* [1946] A.C. 401.
[12] See *Foxbroke-Hobbes* v. *Airwork Ltd.* [1937] 1 All E.R. 108.
[13] *West Mersea U.D.C.* v. *Framer* [1950] 2 K.B. 119.
[14] See *Bracey* v. *Read* [1963] Ch. 88.
[15] (1976) 63 Cr. App. R. 163.

the room. Police found traces of cannabis resin and they smelt burning cannabis.

Held, T had sufficient exclusivity of possession to be an occupier for the purposes of section 8 of the M.D.A.

The argument advanced by the appellant was that a distinction had to be drawn between "an occupier" and "being in occupation."

There is force in this argument. A number of persons may decide to occupy premises as "squatters." They are certainly in occupation but scarcely enjoy a legal exclusivity of possession. Can they therefore be properly be said to be "occupiers"? Support for the argument was found in *Mogford*,[16] which was then concerned with the word 'occupier' as it appeared in section 5 of the Dangerous Drugs Act 1965. On that occasion, Neild J., held that it must be shown that an accused was in "legal possession" of the premises. He said[16a]:

" . . . the word 'occupier' is not defined in this enactment . . . it is a penal statute . . . the provisions must be construed strictly and favourably to accused persons . . . it seems quite impossible to say here that the word 'occupier' must mean 'owner' . . . the word 'occupier' is used in this Act in its advisory sense . . . in a context which shows clearly that the person . . . is in legal occupation and in control of premises."

Accordingly, where two sisters, aged 20 and 15 years, allowed cannabis to be smoked in their parents house (while their parents were away on holiday) they were not to be regarded as occupiers since they were not in legal possession of the house and therefore, they committed no offence under section 5 of the 1965 Act.

Although, in *Tao*, the Court of Appeal approved the result in *Mogford*, the court did not approve of the reasoning. It was not entirely clear what Neild J., in *Mogford*, meant by "legal possession," given that an individual can be in legal possession of premises without being a tenant or having any estate in land.[17] Furthermore, it is not entirely clear from the report what the facts in *Mogford* really were. It may be that a jury would not have been able to say exactly what the nature of the possession was, so as to amount to occupation of those premises—a matter which evidently troubled the court in *Campbell*[18] as we shall see. But, it is sub-

---

[16] (1970) 63 Cr. App. R. 168.
[16a] *Ibid.* at p. 169.
[17] See *Errington* v. *Errington & Woods* [1952] 1 K.B. 290; and *c.f. Helsop* v. *Burns* [1974] 1 W.L.R. 1241.
[18] [1981] Crim. L.R. 595.

mitted that it is not necessary to embark on an enquiry to determine the exact nature of the proprietary rights (if any) of an
accused. For the purposes of section 8, it is sufficient if the prosecution can show that the accused demonstrably exercised control,
or had the authority of another, to exclude persons from premises
or to prohibit any of the activities referred to in section 8. On the
facts of *Tao* it was held to be enough that the accused had a con-
tractual licence to use the room. He may not have been able to
exclude college staff from entering his room but he could exclude
cannabis smokers or, for that matter, any smoker. In other words
he was in a position to exercise control over the activities that took
place there.

Both *Tao* and *Mogford* were considered by His Honour Judge
Oddie in *Campbell*

> S lived at his mother's address. With her approval, but in her
> absence, S held a party at the address. G, who lived else-
> where, attended. Following a police raid at the party, G & S
> were arrested and both accepted responsibility for the canna-
> bis smoking by other guests at the party.
>
> Held, the facts were undistinguishable from *Mogford* and
> accordingly, G & S were not "occupiers" for the purposes of
> section 8.

The decision is of interest for several reasons but only a brief
report of the case is available (*i.e.* in the Criminal Law Review).
As reported, the court explained *Mogford* in the following terms:

> "Not every transient use of premises or physical ability to
> remove another from the premises would enable the court or
> jury to find the nature, extent and degree of possession suf-
> ficient for finding that the person was the occupier of prem-
> ises . . . "

The court went on to point out that, in *Campbell*, the parents
remained occupiers but had delegated to G & S the task of permitting the guests a licence to enter the premises for the purposes of
the party while their parents were away overnight. For those
reasons G & S were not occupied. However, on its facts, *Campbell*
poses a problem. S arranged the party; he organised it; he decided
who should be invited and, no doubt, decided who should remain.
In short, he was in control. In *Mogford*, Neild J. observed that:

> "Upon the second aspect of the test, namely, control, it was
> no doubt open to these daughters to invite guests and indeed
> to exclude persons from their parents house in the absence of
> those parents but . . . that does [not] amount to the nature

and measure of control which is envisaged in the present statute."

Although the court in *Campbell* felt that the facts were indistinguishable from *Mogford*, in fact, the position in *Mogford* was very different—an aspect which it is now necessary to examine.

The section then being considered was section 5 of the Dangerous Drugs Act 1965 which made it an offence to permit premises " . . . to be used for the purpose of smoking cannabis . . . ." Note the words " . . . for the purpose of . . . ." By contrast, section 8 refers to permitting the activity to take place "on those premises . . . ." Neild J. explained section 5 of the 1965 Act when he said that the words of that section:

" . . . denote a purpose which is or has become a significant one or a recognised one though certainly not necessarily the only one."

Examples were given in *Mogford* of the bowling alley or a hairdressing salon or a cafe. Thus, for the purposes of the 1965 Act, control meant control over premises used for a primary purpose. But in the 1971 Act, section 8 is drafted so as to include a temporary use of the premises for any of the activities referred to in that section.

Accordingly, the decision of *Campbell* should be viewed with caution. It is submitted that *Tao* establishes the correct test for the purposes of section 8 of the 1971 Act.

Liability of one occupier for the acts of a co-occupier

A co-occupier who permits or suffers another co-occupier to do any of the activities referred to in section 8 commits an offence under that section as if the co-occupier had invited a friend to the premises and permitted him to perform the prohibited activity.[19]

In that case, four defendants were charged with an offence under section 5 of the Dangerous Drugs Act 1965 in the following terms, that they "being the occupiers of premises . . . permitted those premises to be used for the purpose of smoking cannabis resin." All four defendants were co-tenants having jointly entered into a tenancy agreement. It was argued that it was not possible in law for one co-tenant knowingly to permit another co-tenant to smoke cannabis on the premises. The Court of Appeal held the argument to be fallacious. Roskill L.J. said[19a]:

"The important point is that the essence of the offence is

[19] *Ashdown, Howard & Others* [1974] 59 Cr. App. R. 193.
[19a] *Ibid.* at p. 194.

knowingly permitting that authority to be carried on . . . why
is there any privilege or immunity attaching to his position of
co-tenant which would prevent him being guilty of an offence
against what was section 5 of the 1965 Act."

Persons in unlawful possession of premises

In *Tao* (1976) the court held that the person charged must be
proved to have had, "whether lawfully or otherwise," sufficient
exclusivity of possession of the premises to be an "occupier."
There is no authority, directly on the point, as to whether or not
trespassers may nevertheless be "occupiers" for the purposes of
section 8. In *Mogford*, and *Tao*, the court was concerned with lawful possession or occupation. Indeed, in *Tao,* the court went so far
as to classify T's right to possession on the basis that he was a "con-
tractual licensee," although Roskill L.J. commented that it would
be "somewhat astonishing" if a squatter could not be an "occupier" under the Act. The matter is not free from difficulty but
there exists no logical reason why "occupier" should be glossed to
mean only a person in lawful possession of premises. One must
also have regard to the mischief which the Act seeks to prevent
and, as the court in *Tao* remarked, the concept of occupation and
possession should not be construed too legalistically.

Persons concerned in the management of premises

"Management" imports the notion of control over the running
of the affairs of an enterprise, venture or business. If a person
therefore controls premises by running them, organising them, or
planning them, then he will be "managing them."[20] in order to be
concerned in the management, it is enough to share, or assist in,
the running of the premises. But there must be something more
than the performance of purely menial or routine duties, see
Abbott v. *Smith*.[21] Thus, the cleaner of a nightclub would not be
assisting in the management of that club even if he knew that the
reason for its existence was primarily the smoking of cannabis.

Although many occupiers may also be concerned in the management of premises the converse need not necessarily follow.
Indeed, there is no reason why a manager should have any proprietary interest in the premises at all. Thus, in *Josephs & Christie*[21a] the appellants were squatters on premises but nevertheless
ran a "card school" in the basement. They were convicted of being

[20] See *Josephs & Christie* [1977] 65 Cr. App. R. 253.
[21] [1965] 2 Q.B. 622.
[21a] [1977] 65 Cr. App. R. 253.

concerned in the management of premises upon which they knowingly permitted the supplying of cannabis, contrary to section 8.
Their appeal against conviction was dismissed. They were managing premises and the fact that they were trespassers was irrelevant.

Knowingly. In *Thomas*,[22] the court was asked to consider whether
the word "knowingly," in section 8, added anything to the section.
The court held that it did not: words "permitting" and "suffering"
clearing implied knowledge of the relevant activity.

The point referred to in *Thomas* is hardly novel given the abundance of authority that exists in respect of similar phrases as they
appear in other statutes.[23]

In *Gray's Haulage* Lord Parker C.J. said:

" . . . knowledge is really of two kinds; actual knowledge and
knowledge which arises either from shutting one's eyes to the
obvious, or what is much the same thing put in another way,
failing to do something or doing something not caring whether
contravention takes place or not."

The next question is whether proof of knowledge necessarily
implies permission or sufference in respect of that activity.

In *Gray's Haulage*, Lord Parker C.J. said:

"Knowledge is not imputed by mere negligence but by something more than negligence, something which one can describe as reckless . . . not caring what happens."

The Court of Appeal in *Thomas* went a little further, observing
that knowledge was not to be implied:

" . . . from neglect to make such inquiries as a reasonable and
prudent person would make, which, generally speaking, has
no place in the criminal law."

It is therefore important to note that section 8 does not impose
on occupiers and persons concerned in the management of premises any duty to exercise vigilance to prevent the activities listed in
section 8. This is particularly important in respect of persons who
do not, for example, live on the premises. They are not required to
investigate the affairs of persons using their premises. However,
shutting ones eyes to the truth is a very different matter.

In *Thomas*, police found cannabis and cannabis smoking

[22] (1976) 634 Cr. App. R. 65.
[23] See *Gray's Haulage Co. Ltd.* v. *Arnold* (1966) 1 W.L.R. 534; *Roper* v.
Taylor Central Garages Ltd. (1951) 2 T.L.R. 284; *Lucas* v. *Peek* (1947)
2 All E.R. 574.

equipment at T's home. T said that it belonged to a friend saying " . . . I have asked him not to smoke in my house but what can you do?"

Held, that the jury were properly directed. Knowledge may include shutting one's eyes to the obvious. The appellant did little to prevent cannabis being smoked on his premises.

A very different conclusion was reached in *Souter*.[24]

S let rooms in his house to drug addicts retaining the living room for his own occupation. He put a notice on the door of that room to the effect that the police would be called immediately if illegal drugs were found on the premises. On several occasions S had turned away illegal drug users from his premises. There was evidence that cannabis had been unlawfully smoked on the premises.

The Court of Appeal *held* that S could do no more to stop the unlawful smoking.

Every case must, of course, be decided on its own facts.

"Permits or suffers"

In *Thomas* it was said that the trial judge was right to direct the jury to disregard the alternative phrase, namely, " . . . or suffers . . . " because, " 'permits' and 'suffers' mean the same thing." In most cases there is no need to draw a distinction but there is in fact a difference which is highlighted by the words of Lord Parker C.J. in *Gray's Haulage*. Thus, "to suffer" an activity involves a failure to act but knowing what is taking place. To "permit" an activity is to do something but not caring whether contravention takes place or not. The distinction is admittedly a fine one but it is safer not to regard these phrases as being synonymous.

It may be asked why the word "knowingly" should be added by the Legislature in the light of the decision of *Sweet* v. *Parsley*.[25] The answer can only be that the draftsman considered the addition necessary to make it plain that (1) *mens rea* is required to be proved by the Crown and (2), constructive knowledge is not enough. In *Sweet* v. *Parsley* the House of Lords considered whether section 5 of the Dangerous Drugs Act 1965 created an absolute offence given that the word "knowingly" did not appear in the section which made it an offence for a person to permit premises to be used for the smoking of cannabis. Their Lordships

[24] (1971) 55 Cr. App. R. 403.
[25] [1969] 53 Cr. App. R. 221.

held that *mens rea* was implied by the use of the word "permits" (and see *Yendel* v. *Fisher*[26]).

Section 8 of the M.D.A. is worded differently to section 5 of the Dangerous Drugs Act 1965 and it is not made subject to section 28. Accordingly, the draftsman was making it plain that nevertheless *mens rea* is required.

PROHIBITING OPIUM SMOKING

Section 9, provides, *inter alia*:

"Subject to section 28 of this Act, it is an offence for a person—

(*a*) to smoke or otherwise use prepared opium[27]; or

(*b*) to frequent a place used for the purpose of opium smoking; or

(*c*) to have in his possession [certain equipment for use in connection with opium smoking]."

Section 9(*c*)(i) and (ii) are considered separately in the next chapter concerning the provision of drug kits as a result of the addition of section 9A to the M.D.A. as enacted by the Drug Trafficking Offences Act 1986.

The section is largely self-explanatory. The words "otherwise use" in subparagraph (*a*) must, it is submitted, refer to other methods of consumption. If the allegation is that opium was being sold by an accused then the proper charge is one alleging the supplying of the drug, for example under section 4(1)(*b*) or a kindred offence.

Opium "dens" have a notorious history. Subparagraph (*b*) is intended to attack their survival by prohibiting opium smokers frequenting such premises. The prosecution must prove that the main use or recognised purpose of the premises is for smoking opium although, of course, that need not be its only one.[28]

The courts have not been asked to define the word "frequent" for the purpose of section 9.

As a matter of natural construction, the word "frequent," in this context, implies a regular course of conduct or, at least, conduct that is repeated more than once. In *Airton* v. *Scott*,[29] the appellant

[26] [1966] 1 Q.B. 440.
[27] Defined by section 37(1) to mean prepared for smoking and includes the dross and other residues after opium has been smoked.
[28] See *Mogford* [1970] 1 W.L.R. 988.
[29] (1909) 100 L.T. 393; 25 T.L.R. 250.

had attended an athletic ground for the purpose of betting. Lord
Alverstone C.J. observed that[30]:

> "As to the word 'frequent,' it was plain that being long
> enough on the premises to effect the particular object aimed
> at was 'frequenting'."

However, in *R.* v. *Clark*,[31] it was held that merely being in a
public place does not amount to "frequenting" and in *Rawlings* v.
Smith,[32] it was held that frequenting involved " . . . the notion of
something which to some degree . . . is continuous or repeated"
(*per* Lord Hewart C.J.). Both *Clark* and *Rawlings* were applied in
R. v. *Nahla*,[33] a decision of the Privy Council. Lord Morris of
Borth-y-Guest considered that "frequents" must be considered in
its context which may require an enquiry as to the reason why a
person is at the premises, the nature of the place, the time spent on
the premises, his movements and continuing or recurrent activities
carried on at the premises.

It is submitted that a similar approach is likely to be adopted if
the issue ever arose in section 9.

DRUG KITS AND ARTICLES
FOR USE IN DRUG MISUSE

Articles for opium smoking

Section 9 of the M.D.A. is directed entirely to prohibiting the
possession of opium smoking equipment. Section 9 reads:

> "Subject to section 28 of this Act, it is an offence for a per-
> son—
>> (*a*) to smoke or otherwise use prepared opium; or
>> (*b*) to frequent a place used for the purpose of opium
>>   smoking; or
>> (*c*) to have in his possession—
>>> (i) any pipes or other utensils made or adapted for
>>>   use in connection with the smoking of opium,
>>>   being pipes or utensils which have been used by
>>>   him or with his knowledge and permission in that
>>>   connection or which he intends to use or permit
>>>   others to use in that connection; or
>>> (ii) any utensils which have been used by him or with

---

[30] 25 T.L.R. at p. 250.
[31] (1884) 14 Q.B.D. 92.
[32] [1938] 1 K.B. 675.
[33] [1976] A.C. 1.

his knowledge and permission in connection with
the preparation of opium smoking."

Opium addiction, notably in the Far East, spans a period of history that is both well known and well recorded. It is therefore not
at all surprising to discover that Parliament, for decades, has forbidden opium smoking in the United Kingdom, and has sought to
punish those who are in possession of opium smoking equipment.
Section 9 of the M.D.A. reflects that established policy. Broadly
speaking, section 9(c)(i) makes it an offence to possess equipment
used in connection with the *smoking* of opium, while section
9(c)(ii) is targeted against those persons who possess articles used
in connection with the *preparation* of opium—for smoking. It will
therefore now be obvious that the ambit of section 9 is incredibly
narrow and presents more interest in terms of what is glaringly
omitted than what is actually included. Thus, Parliament has made
no provision for the possession of equipment used in connection
with opium taken other than by smoking. Furthermore, it is not an
offence to possess articles used in the preparation or administration of other controlled drugs; for example hubble-bubble pipes
used for smoking cannabis. Such omissions are all the more
remarkable when it is remembered that the M.D.A. was passed to
combat a rising tide of drug abuse which then, as now, involves the
misuse of many dangerous substances. Indeed, opium smoking
now represents a very small part of the overall drug problem.
Moreover, Parliament has not sought to broaden section 9. In the
wake of public concern at the number of so-called drug kits hitting
the market, Parliament inserted section 9A into the M.D.A. in
order to prohibit their sale: see section 34A of the Drug Trafficking Offences Act 1986. But, section 9A is only concerned with the
supply of articles used to unlawfully *administer* controlled drugs
and makes no corresponding provision for being *in possession* of
articles supplied in contravention of that section.

Section 9(c)(i)

Section 9(c)(i) applies to "pipes or other utensils." It is not clear
whether "pipes" includes any conduit used in connection with
opium smoking or whether it is restricted to the complete smoking
apparatus including the bowl. If the latter interpretation is to be
preferred then although various parts of the smoking apparatus
such as the mouth piece, or connecting tube, would fall outside the
definition of a "pipe," they may come within the word "utensils."
It is clear from section 9 that the words "pipes or other utensils . . . " are qualified by the words " . . . made of adapted for
use in connection with the smoking of opium . . . ." A typical

tobacco pipe could not be said to be "made" for opium smoking but can it be said to be " . . . adapted for use . . . ," if it is in fact used for that purpose? Certainly, one would normally say that the word "adapt" imparts the requirement of change; adjustment or alteration to the original article. Without more, merely to *adopt* an article for a different purpose would not be sufficient. But section 9(*c*)(i) refers to:

> " . . . pipes or utensils which have been used by him . . . or which he intends to use . . . in that connection . . . "

There is therefore force in the view that those words embrace the adoption of a normally innocent piece of equipment, for example, a tobacco pipe which has been used for the purposes of opium smoking.

Once it has been proved that the article is a "pipe" or "utensil" made or adapted for opium smoking, the prosecution must then prove that the article:

(1) was so used by the accused; *or*
(2) was so used with his knowledge and with his permission; *or*
(3) was intended to be so used by the accused, or (with his permission) by others.

Accordingly, it is not enough that an accused knew that a pipe had been used by another. It must be proved that the accused went further and gave his permission for the article to be used in connection with opium smoking.

Section 9(c)(ii)

It is not necessary for the prosecution to prove that the utensils have been made or adapted for use in connection with the preparation of opium for smoking. Any article which has been used in that regard will come within section 9(*c*)(ii). However, articles merely intended by the accused to be so used fall, outside the section.

Again, if the utensils have been used by a person other than the accused, the Prosecution must prove that the accused knew of that other person's use of those items and that he permitted him to use them. Permission may be granted expressly or by implication, for example conduct.

Drug administration kits generally

In recent years the appearance of so-called "drug-kits" on the legitimate consumer market became prevalent. Some kits were elaborate and did little to hide the fact that they would be of particular interest to drug users but of limited interest to anyone else.

Thus, pouches containing a small mirror; a knife; a fairly broad tube; matches, etc., were handy "kits" for the purpose of snorting cocaine or heroin. Other kits were far less elaborate and, indeed, many of the items sold could not even be described as "kits," for example the sale of a mirror and a packet of wide straws. To the ordinary bystander such a simple sale looked innocent enough but, to the retailer, it may have been apparent that he was selling articles to a drug user whom he believed would use them for that purpose.

To meet this situation, Parliament, by section 34A of the Drug Trafficking Offences Act 1986, inserted section 9A into the M.D.A. which provides:

"(1) A person who supplies or offers to supply any article which may be used or adapted to be used (whether by itself or in combination with another article or other articles) in the administration by any person of a controlled drug to himself or another, believing that the article (or the article as adapted) is to be so used in circumstances where the administration is unlawful, is guilty of an offence.
(2) It is not an offence under subsection (1) above to supply or offer to supply a hypodermic syringe, or any part of one.
(3) A person who supplies or offers to supply any article which may be used to prepare a controlled drug for administration by any person to himself or another believing that the article is to be so used in circumstances where the administration is unlawful is guilty of an offence.
(4) For the purposes of this section, any administration of a controlled drug is unlawful except—
  (a) the administration by any person of a controlled drug to another in circumstances where the administration of the drug is not unlawful under section 4(1) of this Act, or
  (b) the administration by any person of a controlled drug to himself in circumstances where having the controlled drug in his possession is not unlawful under section 5(1) of this Act.
(5) In this section, references to administration by any person of a controlled drug to himself include a reference to his administering it to himself with the assistance of another."

Section 9A(1)

It should be made clear at this stage that section 9A is not concerned with kits sold to abusers of solvents. That matter is dealt with by the Intoxicating Substances (Supply) Act 1985. Section 9A of the M.D.A. is solely concerned with kits supplied in connection with the administration of controlled drugs: solvents are not controlled under the M.D.A.

Section 9A(1) is very widely drawn. Unlike section 9 which refers to "utensils," section 9A(1) applies to any article which *"may* be used" or which may be " . . . adapted *to be used* . . . " in the administration of a controlled drug. In other words any article that has the capability of being used by another to abuse any controlled drug falls within this subsection. Parliament has been careful not to prohibit merely the supply of a collection of articles which may be termed a "kit." Thus, even if only one article is supplied, which by itself, could not be used to facilitate drug abuse but which, if combined with other articles, could be so used, then it falls within section 9A(1).

It is not necessary for the Prosecution to prove that the article has been supplied for any consideration and it is not necessary for the prosecution to prove that the article was supplied to a person who himself intended to use that article for drug abuse. It is enough that the supplier (or the offeror) believes that the article is to be used (not "may be used") " . . . in circumstances where the administration is unlawful . . . ."

Mens Rea under section 9A(1)

Merely to suspect that the supplier would use the article for the unlawful administration of a controlled drug is not enough. However, the prosecution need prove no more than that the accused believed that the article would be so used " . . . in circumstances where the administration is unlawful . . . ."

But what is the position if the supplier's belief is, in fact, erroneous? It is submitted that his mistake affords him no defence. His belief is all important particularly since section 9A(1) prohibits the supplying of (or an offer to supply) any article which may be used or adapted to be used in the administration of a controlled drug. Presumably an accused's belief must be reasonably held having regard to all the circumstances of the case but, it is not clear whether his belief is to be judged subjectively or objectively. Presumably the test is subjective. Section 28 is not expressed to have any application. Therefore, a particularly innocent mirror which is sold in the belief that it will be used in connection with the unlawful snorting of heroin or cocaine is an offence contrary to s.9A(1). Of course some harsh results will flow if, a mistaken belief affords the supplier of an article with no defence in circumstances where the recipient never actually intended to use the mirror for anything other than a perfectly lawful purpose. Suppose X supplies a box of wide straws, to Y knowing that Y regularly snorts cocaine using straws and X believes that all or some of the straws will be so used. In fact Y never intended any such thing but planned to use them for milkshake consumption at a children's party. On a strict interpretation of section 9A(1), X is damned by his own mistaken belief.

Again, suppose Y (weeks later) does in fact use one of the remaining straws to snort cocaine. Is X's fate sealed?

However, it is important that X has more than just a suspicion that the straws will be used for the administration of controlled drugs.

However, nothing in section 9A, prevents the supply or the offer to supply any article for use in connection with the administration of a controlled drug if the drug may be lawfully administered to another by the recipient or may be possessed by him for self-administration: section 9A(4).

The maximum sentence is six months imprisonment and/or a financial penalty on level 5.

Section 9A(2)

It may seem surprising that hypodermic syringes are excluded from subsection (1). As a matter of logic, no doubt they ought to have been included but as a matter of policy one can see reasons why they are not. First, there is the quite considerable problem of regulating the distribution of such syringes if they were to be included. Secondly, it is now well known that serious disease can be readily spread by the use of contaminated needles. The distribution of clean needles and syringes—even from dubious sources—may have been considered by the Legislature as being the lesser of two evils.

Section 9A(3)

Not unlike section 9(c)(ii) of the M.D.A. section 9A(3) is concerned to prohibit the supply—or an offer to supply—any article which may be used to prepare any controlled drug for administration. Again, like section 9 it is not necessary for the prosecution to prove that the article had been "adapted" for use in the preparation of a controlled drug.

SECTION 28 OF THE MISUSE OF DRUGS ACT 1971

Section 28 of the M.D.A. provides a number of statutory defences as follows:

"(1) This section applies to offences under any of the following provisions of this Act, that is to say section 4(2) and (3), section 5(2) and (3), section 6(2) and section 9.

(2) Subject to subsection (3) below, in any proceedings for an offence to which this section applies it shall be a defence for the accused to prove that he neither knew of nor suspected nor had reason to suspect the existence of some fact alleged by the prosecution which it is necessary for the prosecution to prove if he is to be convicted of the offence charged.

(3) Where in any proceedings for an offence to which this section applies it is necessary, if the accused is to be convicted of the offence charged, for the prosecution to prove that some substance or product involved in the alleged offence was the controlled drug which the prosecution alleges it to have been, and it is proved that the substance or product in question was that controlled drug, the accused—

(a) shall not be acquitted of the offence charged by reason only of proving that he neither knew nor suspected nor had reason to suspect that the substance or product in question was the particular controlled drug alleged; but

(b) shall be acquitted thereof—
 (i) if he proves that he neither believed nor suspected nor had reason to suspect that the substance or product in question was a controlled drug; or
 (ii) if he proves that he believed the substance or product in question to be a controlled drug, or a controlled drug of a description, such that, if it had in fact been that controlled drug or a controlled drug of that description, he would not at the material time have been committing any offence to which this section applies.

(4) Nothing in this section shall prejudice any defence which it is open to a person charged with an offence to which this section applies to raise apart from this section."

Without section 28, the offences to which this section relates, would lead to some very harsh results. Thus section 6(2) (cultivation of cannabis) would arguably be an absolute offence. The decision in *Warner* v. *Metropolitan Police Commissioner*[34] produced an unhappy compromise between absolute liability and *mens rea* in cases alleging possession of prohibited drugs. Indeed, section 28 reflects many of the sentiments expressed by Lord

[34] [1969] 2 A.C. 256.

Pearce in *Warner* and the reader is invited to read the speech of Lord Pearce in its entirety. However, section 28(4) makes it plain that nothing in this provision was intended to alter the earlier law but merely runs parallel to establish principles. Furthermore, drug importations or exportations contrary to section 3(1) are not subject to section 28, perhaps for the reasons expressed by Lord Bridge in *Shivpuri*.[35]

Section 28(2)

In respect of each charge to which section 28 applies, the prosecution are required to prove the existence of certain factual ingredients. Thus, for an offence under section 6(2), the prosecution are required to prove that the accused (i) cultivated a plant and (ii) that the plant cultivated was of the *genus cannabis*. Without more the offence would be complete. But, by section 28(2) it is a defence for the accused to prove that he did not know that a plant was being cultivated or, even if he did, that he did not know that the plant was a cannabis plant.

It is sometimes said that there exists a difficulty in understanding the relationship between subsections (2) and (3). The wording is certainly confusing and an over-lap undoubtedly exists. Thus if X did not know that the plant was of the *genus cannabis*, then he has a defence under section 28(3)(*b*)(i) as well as section 28(2).

> In *Champ*,[35a] C had a window box which contained a cannabis plant. Her defence to a charge under section 6(2) was that she thought the plant was "hemp" which she believed was good for alleviating ailments. The trial judge ruled that the burden was on C to prove that she did not know the plant was cannabis.
>
> Held, the judge's ruling was correct. Section 28(2) was subject to subsection (3) " . . . which is not relevant in this case . . . " but subsection (2) placed the burden of proof on C.

The decision, when examined, highlights the confusion that can arise. It is not clear why the court thought that subsection (3) was not relevant since one complaint made by the appellant was that the judge ruled that the burden of proof was on her to show that she did not know that the plant was cannabis by virtue of that very subsection. Another complaint was that the trial judge was wrong to rule that section 28(2) had no application to a charge under section 6(2): yet the court held that the judge directed the jury cor-

[35] [1986] 2 W.L.R. 988.
[35a] (1981) 73 Cr. App. R. 367.

rectly. Clearly, the burden of proof was on the appellant by reason of subsection (2) and/or (3)(*b*)(i). In any event her defence was extraordinarily thin since "hemp" is regarded as another term for cannabis.

The point to note is that subsection (2) is subject to subsection (3) but only in so far as subsection (3) is concerned with knowledge of the "substance or product." To that limited extent there is an overlap between them. Suppose an accused is charged with frequenting premises used for the purposes of smoking opium (section 9(*b*)). The prosecution must prove (a) that the premises were being used for smoking; (b) that opium was being smoked on those premises; and (c) that the accused frequented those premises. If X does not know of the existence of (a) then section 28(2) gives X a defence which he must prove. If X does know of fact (a) but not fact (b) then he has a defence under section 28(2) and section 28(3)(*b*(i).

Does section 28(2) alter the definition of possession?

Whereas in *Warner* the prosecution were held to be required to prove that an accused had the intention to possess the substance which was prohibited, the question arises whether this amounts to "some fact alleged by the prosecution which it is necessary for the prosecution to prove . . . " and therefore, by section 28(2), the onus is now on the accused to prove that he neither knew of, nor suspected, nor had reason to suspect, the existence of this fact.

In *Wright*,[36] the argument was raised but the Court of Appeal did not need to consider it. However, in *Ashton-Rickardt*[37]:

> Police officers found the appellant asleep in his car. A cigarette, containing cannabis, was found in the pocket of the driver's door. The appellant denied knowledge of the reefer or that it contained cannabis. The judge directed the jury that the burden of proving a lack of knowledge fell on the appellant.
>
> Held, section 28(2) had not altered the burden of proof. The burden of proving knowledge of the article rested on the prosecution.

Accordingly, where drugs are planted on an accused, or added to the goods which he knows he controls,[38] the onus of proving knowledge remains on the prosecution. Again, where the accused

[36] (1975) 62 Cr. App. R. 169.
[37] (1978) 1 W.L.R. 37.
[38] See *Irving* [1970] Crim. L.R. 642, C.A.

is in possession of a "trace" the burden of proving knowledge of the trace falls on the prosecution (*per*, Stinson J., in *Colyer*[39]).

What is to be proved by the accused?

When the burden of proof does shift to the accused under section 28, the standard of proof is on a balance of probabilities.[40]

However, the accused is also required to meet a subjective and an objective test if his defence is under s.28(2) or s.28(3)(*b*)(i). Thus, he must prove:
  (i) that he did not know the existence of the relevant fact (subjective); and
  (ii) that he did not suspect the existence of the same (again subjective); and
  (iii) that he had no reason to suspect the existence of that fact.
The last requirement is objective.

> In *Young*,[41] Y who was seriously affected by drink and was almost incapable, sold LSD to W. As Y was about to negotiate a further sale of the drug he was arrested. Y was charged with possessing LSD intending to supply it contrary of section 5(3). Y relied on section 28(3)(*b*)(i). At a District-Court Martial, the assistant Judge Advocate General directed that the test to be applied under s.28(3)(*b*)(i) was that of an "ordinary, reasonable and sober man."
>
> Held, the appeal against conviction would be dismissed. Although it was unnecessary to gloss the direction by referring to the "reasonable, sober man," it was a correct direction since self-induced intoxication did not avail Y. The third limb of s.28(3)(*b*)(i) is objective.

The assistant Judge Advocate General was clearly influenced by *Majewski*,[42] but the Court-Martial Appeals Court had doubts as to whether the same criterion applies when knowledge (as distinct from intent) is under consideration.

Because the third limb to section 28(3)(*b*)(i) is objective, it follows that only to a limited extent can an accused be judged on the basis of what he believed the facts to be; see Lord Diplock in *Sweet* v. *Parsley*.[43] Suppose X possesses "snow" believing this term to be a popular name for "snuff." Snuff is not a controlled substance. "Snow" is in fact a popular name for cocaine which is actually

[39] [1975] Crim. L.R. 243.
[40] See *Carr-Briant* [1943] K.B. 607.
[41] [1984] 2 All E.R. 164.
[42] [1976] 2 All E.R. 142 H.L.
[43] [1970] A.C. 132 H.L.

what X possessed. X may say that he did not believe or suspect that the substance was a controlled drug, but the third limb of s.28(3)(*b*)(i) presents X with colossal difficulties having regard to its " . . . wider concept of objective rationality . . . " (*per* Kilner Brown J., in *Young*).[44] Accordingly, a phrase popularly used to denote a controlled drug is likely to be a sufficient reason to cause a person to suspect that the substance which he possesses, bearing that description, is in fact a controlled drug. (A contrary view is expressed by Richard Lord; see Controlled Drugs, Law & Practice.)

Section 28(3)(b)(ii)

Because the M.D.A. permits the Secretary of State, by regulations, to exempt certain controlled drugs from the activities prohibited by that Act, for example section 4 and section 5, it is conceivable that a person may deal with drug X (which is not exempt) while believing that he is dealing with drug Y (which is exempt). Thus regulation 4(2) of the 1985 Regulations permits any person to possess drugs listed in Schedule 4 of those regulations (for example, Larazepam) notwithstanding section 5(1).

Accordingly, section 28(3)(*b*)(ii) affords a defence to an accused who in fact possesses heroin believing that the drug is Lorazepam. The test is entirely subjective.

[44] [1984] 2 All E.R. 164.

PART IV

CONSPIRACY AND ATTEMPT TO
COMMIT A DRUG OFFENCE

CONSPIRACY TO COMMIT A DRUG OFFENCE

In the last ten years the law of conspiracy and attempt has undergone much change; indeed the common law offences of conspiracy and attempt have been largely abolished by statute. Furthermore, the old offences of inciting the commission of, or attempting to commit, a conspiracy are also abolished (section 5(7) of the Criminal Law Act 1977).

Instead the Criminal Law Act 1977 now creates a statutory offence of conspiracy which, by section 1(1) (as amended by section 5 of the Criminal Attempts Act 1981) provides:

> "Subject to the following provisions of this Part of the Act, if a person agrees with any other person or persons that a course of conduct shall be pursued which, if the agreement is carried out in accordance with their intentions, either—
> (a) will necessarily amount to or involve the commission of any offence or offences by one or more of the parties to the agreement, or
> (b) would do so but for the existence of fact which render the commission of the offence or any of the offences impossible,
> he is guilty of conspiracy to commit the offence or offences in question."

The essence of a conspiracy is the plotting by two or more persons to do an unlawful act or to do a lawful act but by unlawful means, with the intention of carrying out the unlawful purpose: see *Thomson*.[1] But it is not necessary for the prosecution to prove that the conspirators knew the illegality of the course of conduct agreed to be pursued. It follows that an agreement to do any of the acts prohibited by the Misuse of Drugs Act 1971, or the Customs and Excise Management Act 1952, may be charged as a statutory conspiracy.

To be guilty of a conspiracy it is not necessary to prove that the accused was a party to the original scheme. Conspirators may enter and leave a conspiracy at any time during its operation: see *R. v. Simmonds*.[2] The role of each conspirator must be seen in the

---

[1] (1965) 50 Cr. App. R. 1.
[2] [1969] 1 Q.B. 685.

context of the concerted course of conduct: see *Ardalan*[3] and see also *Bailey and Underwood*.[4]

In *Anderson*,[5] the House of Lords examined section 1(1)(*a*) of the Criminal Law Act 1977 and held (*inter alia*) that it is not necessary for the prosecution to prove that each conspirator intended that the material offence or offences should be committed. The expression " . . . if the agreement is carried out in accordance with their intentions . . . " as it appears in the opening words of section 1(1), means that the accused agreed with one or more persons that " . . . a course of conduct shall be pursued." Considerations applicable in civil law have little place in the construction of section 1(1).

In the light of the above it follows that a conspiracy continues until the agreement is performed or abandoned: see *D.P.P.* v. *Doot*.[6] Accordingly, it is not a defence to join the conspiracy and then withdraw from it.

> In *Anderson (W.R.)*,[7] X and A shared a cell. A agreed to help X escape. A was bailed and received £2000 in order to buy equipment in order to facilitate X's escape. At his trial A claimed that he never actually intended to take part in X's escape although he had planned to smuggle equipment into the prison. A's object was primarily to make money out of X.

The House of Lords held that the fact that A did not intend to participate any further in the escape bid, or that A believed the escape to be impossible, afforded A no defence (and see *Gortat* v. *Pirog*).[8]

Furthermore, it is a question of fact in every case as to whether or not the role of the accused amounted to no more than an act preparatory to an agreement.

> In *El Ghazal*,[9] E, T and C were charged with a conspiracy to obtain cocaine. T asked E if he could arrange a meeting between T and C so that both T & C could "make a deal about cocaine." E arranged the meeting and attended it for a short period of time. E complained that the judge misdirected the jury by implying that an agreement to do acts that were

[3] (1972) 56 Cr. App. R. 320; [1972] 2 All E.R. 257.
[4] (1913) 9 Cr. App. R. 94.
[5] [1985] 2 All E.R. 961.
[6] [1973] A.C. 807; [1973] 1 All E.R. 940.
[7] [1984] A.C. 27.
[8] [1973] Crim. L.R. 648.
[9] [1985] Crim. L.R. 52

merely preparatory to commit a crime amounted to a conspiracy under section 1(1).

Held, the appeal would be dismissed. If E introduced T to C knowing of T's intention and knowing that one of them would seek to obtain cocaine, then that was the agreement for the purpose of section 1(1).

At first sight the decision is a little difficult to understand since E on one interpretation of the facts, seems to have done no more than to arrange a meeting between T and C so that a conspiracy to possess cocaine could take place. For this reason the decision—or at least the basis for attaching liability—has been criticised, notably by the learned commentator in the Criminal Law Review[10] and the reader is encouraged to read it. However, it was the prosecution case that E knew from the start that either T or C would obtain the cocaine and therefore E had conspired with T to obtain the drug. C only joined the conspiracy at a later stage. It is submitted that if the jury reached the conclusion that E did know of the object of the meeting right from the start, then it is not illogical to hold that E conspired with T to obtain drugs. The fact that C might have been a necessary link to complete performance (C not having yet been recruited) is not a relevant consideration.

Jurisdiction

Where a person in England, agrees with a person abroad to commit an offence in England, there is a conspiracy triable in England and Wales.

The courts will not look simply to the moment when the agreement was made. Since the offence of conspiracy is a continuing one, an agreement made abroad will nevertheless be indictable in England if acts in furtherance of the conspiracy were performed in England.

In *D.P.P.* v. *Doot*,[11] five American citizens agreed (either in Belgium or Morocco) to smuggle cannabis resin into England and then to re-export it to the United States. The cannabis was concealed in three vans and shipped to England. One van was discovered in Southampton by customs officers and the others were traced. The Court of Appeal quashed their convictions on the basis that the agreement was made, and the offence completed, abroad. The Crown appealed.

Held, the convictions would be restored. An agreement

[10] See [1986] at p. 52.
[11] See *supra*, n. 6.

made abroad was triable in England if acts in furtherance of the agreement was performed in England.

Lord Wilberforce said[11a] that in the normal case of conspiracy carried out, or partly carried out, in this country, " . . . the location of the formation of the agreement is irrelevant." Lord Wilberforce thought that there is "substantial authority," both in England and America, that jurisdiction exists " . . . to try in our courts conspiracies entered into abroad but implemented here." Lord Wilberforce adopted the analysis of Lord Pearson.

For his part, Lord Pearson[11b] observed that a conspiracy involves an agreement, expressed or implied, which has three stages, as follows:

> "(1) making or formation, (2) performance or implementation, (3) discharge of termination. When the conspiratorial agreement has been made, the offence of conspiracy is complete, it has been committed, and the conspirators can be prosecuted even though no performance has taken place: *R. v. Aspinall* (1986) 2 Q.B.D. 48."

Lord Pearson noted that the fact that the conspiracy is complete does not mean that the agreement is dead. "If it is being performed it is very much alive." A conspiracy will be triable in England " . . . if it has been wholly or partly performed in England."

Lord Salmon[11c] felt it unnecessary to consider what the position might be if the conspirators came to England for an entirely innocent purpose unconnected with the conspiracy but acts done in England in furtherance of the conspiracy were triable in England.

Their Lordships applied the decision of *Brisac*.[12]

As Lord Pearson indicated, the legal position is not clear as to whether an offence would be committed in this country if the agreement was made abroad and only lawful acts were committed in this country. The answer probably is that a party to the agreement has committed no offence in this country.

In *Borro and Abdullah*,[13] the appellants agreed abroad to send cannabis from Beruit to Antigua via London. The appellants did no more than to stay overnight in a hotel in London while control over the baggage was retained by the airline. The Court of Appeal dismissed their appeals against their conviction and found no basis upon which *Doot* could be distinguished.

[11a] [1973] 1 All E.R. 940 at p. 943 f/g.
[11b] *Ibid.*, at p. 951.
[11c] *Ibid.*, at p. 956 f/g.
[12] (1803) 4 EAST. 164.
[13] [1973] Crim. L.R. 513.

Where goods have been imported and thereafter two or more persons join the conspiracy to deal with the goods, knowing that the goods were prohibited from importation, a conspiracy to fraudulently evade the prohibition contrary to section 170(2) of the C.E.M.A. will lie against them because a section 170 offence is also a continuing one. In *Ardalan*[14] drugs were posted from Beruit to London and, long after the moment of importation, A arranged to collect them. A's appeal against his conviction for a conspiracy to contravene what is now section 170, was dismissed.

The court in *Ardalan* indicated that terms such as "wheels," "chains," "sub-conspiracies," etc., should be used with care and only to illustrate and to clarify the definition of conspiracy and for no other reason.

In every case the facts must not disclose more than one conspiracy (see *Griffiths*)[15] for if they do the count is bad and may be quashed. Alternatively, a submission of no case can only be upheld: by then it may well be too late for the prosecution to amend the Indictment.

Conspiracy to do the physically impossible

Section 1(1) of the Criminal Law Act 1977 [as amended] now overrules the decision in *D.P.P.* v. *Nock*[16] in so far as section 1 applies to offences committed after August 1981. If two or more persons agree to pursue a course of conduct but, for reasons unknown to them, the object is incapable of performance, a statutory conspiracy will still be committed. In *Nock* the defendants attempted to extract cocaine from powder which was not capable of releasing cocaine and so the object was incapable of performance. The House of Lords held that no offence had been committed. But today section 1(1) covers the position. *Nock* was distinguished in *Harris (K.A.)*.[17]

> H and other persons attempted to make amphetamine. They had the correct formula but incompetently obtained the wrong ingredients and did not fully understand the process of production. They wee convicted of conspiring to produce a controlled drug contrary to section 4(1) of the M.D.A.
>
> Held, the offence was capable of performance but merely ineptly carried out.

[14] See *supra*, n. 3.
[15] (1965) 49 Cr. App. R. 279.
[16] (1978) 67 Cr. App. R. 116.
[17] (1979) 69 Cr. App. R. 122.

ATTEMPTING TO COMMIT A DRUG OFFENCE

Criminal attempts are now given a statutory footing by the Criminal Attempts Act 1981. Section 1(1) of that Act provides:

> "If, with intent to commit an offence to which this section applies, a person does an act which is more than merely preparatory to the commission of the offence, he is guilty of attempting to commit the offence.
>
> (2) A person may be guilty of attempting to commit an offence to which this section applies even though the facts are such that the commission of the offence is impossible.
>
> (3) In any case where—
>
> (a) apart from this subsection a person's intention would not be regarded as having amounted to an intent to commit an offence; but
>
> (b) if the facts of the case had been as he believed them to be, his intention would be so regarded,
>
> then, for the purposes of subsection (1) above, he shall be regarded as having had an intent to commit that offence."

The 1981 Act repealed that part of section 19 of the M.D.A. which was concerned with attempts to commit offences contrary to that Act. Section 19 is now only concerned with "inciting" the commission of any offence under the M.D.A. More radical still, is the effect of section 6, which abolished the offence of attempt at common law. A new statutory law now exists.

However, some of the earlier authorities help to define the limits of the offence under the 1981 Act. Thus, an accused commits an offence contrary to section 1(1) if he does an act that is "more than merely preparatory . . . " to the commission of the offence. The practical significance of these words is not dissimilar to the proximity test laid down in *Eagleton*.[18] In *D.P.P.* v. *Stonehouse*,[19] Lord Diplock provided a neat test to be applied when determining whether or not the facts of a given case amount to an attempt or not, namely:

> " . . . the offender must have crossed the Rubicon and burnt his boats."

The trick is to determine whether the accused has merely reached the Rubicon or crossed it.

---

[18] (1855) Dears. 376.
[19] [1978] A.C. 55.

Turner J., adopted a six-fold classification of attempts in *R.* v. *Donnelly*,[20] thus an accused:

(1) may change his mind before committing any act sufficiently overt to amount to an attempt;

(2) may change his mind, but too late to deny that he had got so far as an attempt;

(3) may be prevented from completing the offence by an outside agency, *e.g.* the arrival of police;

(4) may fail to complete the offence by ineptitude;

(5) may find that commission of the offence is impossible by virtue of some physical fact; and

(6) may find that his course of conduct does not amount to an offence.

An offence is clearly established in cases (2) and (3); and most probably established in cases (4) and (5). No offence is committed in (1).

In 1975 the House of Lords in *Haughton* v. *Smith*[21] held that no offence was committed in respect of case (6).

With the passing of section 1 and 6 of the 1981 Act it was thought that case (6) no longer afforded an accused with a defence. But in *Anderson* v. *Ryan*,[21a] the House of Lords held that an accused, who purchased a video recorder believing it to be stolen (when in fact it was not) was not guilty of an offence of attempting to handle stolen goods. The decision is now overruled by *Shivpuri*.[22]

> While in India S was persuaded by D to receive a suitcase containing drugs which a courier would give to him in Cambridge. S was to deliver the drugs in accordance with D's instructions to third parties. S believed the drugs to be cannabis or heroin but, upon analysis the drugs were found to be either snuff or some such vegetable matter.
>
> Held, a person was guilty of an offence under section 1(1) of the 1981 Act if the steps performed were more than merely preparatory. The fact that such an offence was impossible to commit afford S with no defence.

In *Anderson* v. *Ryan* the House of Lords had tried to distinguish between "guilty acts" and those acts which were "objectively innocent"; in the latter case the mind was said to be guilty but the act was actually innocent (*per* Lord Bridge).

---

[20] [1970] N.Z.L.R. 980.
[21] [1975] A.C. 476.
[21a] (1985) 80 Cr. App. R. 235.
[22] [1986] 2 W.L.R. 988.

But in *Shivpuri*, Lord Bridge reflected on the distinction he drew in *Anderson* v. *Ryan* saying[22a]:

"If we fell into error, it is clear that our concern was to avoid convictions in situations which most people, as a matter of common sense, would not regard as involving criminality."

Later Lord Bridge added[22b]:

"I am satisfied on further consideration that the concept of 'objective innocence' is incapable of sensible application in relation to the law of criminal attempts. The reason for this is that any attempt to commit an offence which involves an 'act which is more than merely preparatory to the commission of the offence' but which for any reason fails, so that in the event no offence is committed, must ex hypothesi, . . . be 'objectively innocent.' What turns what would otherwise . . . be an innocent act into a crime is the intent of the actor to commit an offence."

In other words, every case where the offence is impossible to commit, involves the taking of steps which were only merely preparatory to the commission of the offence. Accordingly, Lord Bridge considered that the distinction sought to be drawn in *Anderson* v. *Ryan* could not be maintained and that " . . . there is no valid ground on which *Anderson* v. *Ryan* can be distinguished."

"If I could extract from the speech of Lord Roskill or from my own speech a clear and coherent principle distinguishing those cases of attempting the impossible which amount to offences under the statute from those which do not, I should have to consider carefully on which side of the line the instant case fell. But I have to confess that I can find no such principle."

Their Lordships therefore overruled *Anderson* v. *Ryan* in accordance with the 1966 Practice Statement.[23]

[22a] *Ibid*. at p. 343 h/j.
[22b] *Ibid*. at p. 344d.
[23] [1966] 3 All E.R. 77.

PART V

ENFORCEMENT

PROOF THAT THE DRUG IS CONTROLLED

All drugs controlled by the M.D.A. are listed in Schedule 2 of the Act and fall into one of three Classes (*i.e.* Classes A to C). Each Class corresponds to Part I to III, of Schedule 2, respectively. Classification depends on the drugs' potential for causing "harm." The list is not closed: the Secretary of State may, by Regulation, add other drugs to the list; or he may re-classify existing controlled drugs; or he may remove some or all of them from Schedule 2 completely.

Since the M.D.A. was passed, Schedule 2 has been extensively modified by a number of Misuse of Drugs Act 1971 (Modification) Orders: S.I. 1973 No. 771; 1975 No. 421; 1977 No. 1243; 1979 No. 299; 1983 No. 765; 1984 No. 859; 1985 No. 1995; and now by S.I. 1986 No. 2230.

It is important to note that the Act also controls (where appropriate) any stereoisomeric form of a controlled drug; or any of their esters, ethers or salts; or certain "preparations" which contains a controlled substance or product.

Determining whether a given substance or product is controlled

In the ordinary way determining whether a substance or product is controlled or not, is a straightforward matter: one simply looks to see if the substance is listed in Schedule 2. But the matter is only made straightforward because Parliament has been careful to ensure that the term "a controlled drug" is narrowly defined so that (except where expressly provided) it is the chemical which is the controlled "substance" or "product" and nothing else.

Accordingly, a drug that naturally subsists in a plant or material, and which has not been extracted, is not a controlled drug unless that plant or substance has itself been expressly controlled by the Act. Thus, in *Goodchild (No. 2)*[1]:

> G was charged with being in possession of cannabis resin after the police found 4 ounces of stalks and leaves of cannabis plants at G's address. At that time the stalks and leaves were not expressly controlled by the Act—just the flowering and fruiting tops of the plant. However, the scientific evidence was that the stalks and leaves would naturally contain cannabis resin. Hence the charge. However, Section 37(1) defines

[1] [1977] 1 W.L.R. 1213.

"cannabis resin" as "separated resin . . . obtained from [a cannabis plant]." This implied some form of extraction which, on the facts, had not occurred. Accordingly, G's conviction had to be quashed.

The definition of cannabis has now been extended to include all of the plant except the mature stalk, fibre and the seeds.

Similarly, cocaine is extracted from the coca-leaf but without further provision the coca-leaf itself would not be a controlled drug. Accordingly, Parliament specifically included the leaf as a Class A substance. "Poppy-straw" (Class A) is yet another example.

Suprisingly, perhaps, the so-called "magic mushroom (*Psilocybe Mexicana*) is not controlled even though it contains psilocin which is a controlled drug (Class A). Accordingly, it is therefore not unlawful to pick the mushroom or to possess it or to supply it.

Ethers, salts, and esters are also controlled

As we have noted, any ethers, esters, salts, or any stereo-isomeric forms of drugs specified in Class A to C are "controlled" substances. These are terms of science. Thus a salt of diamorphine is still heroin (*c.f. Greensmith*[2]).

Meaning of "preparation"

"Preparation" is broadly defined by the Shorter Oxford English Dictionary to mean, *inter alia*, the:

" . . . composition, manufacture of a chemical, medical, or other substance . . . "

The appearance of the word "manufacture" in that definition is of particular interest since it is undoubtedly the case that "preparing" a drug may amount to an act of "production" for the purposes of section 4 of the M.D.A. However, much will depend on the facts of a given case: it would be unsafe to assume that every act of production amounts to an act of preparation or indeed, conversely, that every act of preparation amounts to an act of production. It is submitted that the M.D.A. contemplates a subtle distinction, namely, that an act of "preparation" is calculated to convert a controlled drug into a form suitable for consumption, whereas "producing" a controlled drug is generally confined to the act of creating the drug. It must be remembered that many drugs are synthetically created in a laboratory, for example L.S.D. Steps

[2] [1983] 3 All E.R. 444.

taken to create such drugs are obviously steps taken to "produce" them. However, applying drops of L.S.D. to sugar cubes for human consumption, is an act of "preparation"—not an act of production.

The distinction has practical significance in cases involving the mushroom *Psilocybe Mexicana*. The potency of psilocin (the drug that subsists in that particular mushroom) is considerably increased if the mushroom is dried. In *Stevens*,[3] it was held that the term "preparation" had to be given its natural and ordinary meaning. "Preparation" is not a term of art. So, where S had dried magic mushrooms at a low heat, thereby converting them into a powder, he had accordingly made a "preparation" containing a controlled drug (psilocin). The mushrooms ceased to be in their natural growing state and were now "altered by the hand of man." The intervention of the "hand of man" is the crucial test.

Stevens was applied in *Cunliffe*.[4] In that case C, by the jury's verdict, had subjected a quantity of magic mushrooms to sunlight so that they dried out. He had therefore "prepared" them and he was held to be rightly convicted of possessing a controlled drug.

There is clearly a mental element involved in an act of preparation, namely, an intention to alter the condition of the thing coupled with an intention that the substance should serve as a drug in the future. Accordingly, no offence is committed if the mushrooms in D's possession had dried out of their own accord. The prosecution must show that someone deliberately brought about the change.

In *Walker*,[5] police found between 1000 to 2000 dried magic mushrooms in a cupboard at W's premises. W said that they must have dried out of their own accord. Two-thirds of them had been seized by police in 1982 and then returned. The remainder he had since picked. The jury asked why the mushrooms were returned to W and were they then unlawful for him to possess. The judge directed the jury that they were unlawful to possess in 1982. During the appeal the prosecution argued that picking the mushrooms amounted to an act of "preparation."

Held, that the court was not inclined to accept that merely picking the mushroom amounted to preparation. However, the jury's question, although difficult to understand, was answered incorrectly since it had to be proved that someone

---

[3] [1981] Crim. L.R. 568, C.A.
[4] [1986] Crim. L.R. 547.
[5] (1987) [5640/G3/86]; [1987] Crim. L.R. 565, C.A.

deliberately brought about a change in the condition of the mushrooms.

The court was right not to hold that merely to pick the mushroom was an act of preparation since it does not follow that the mushroom will dehydrate as a result. It could not have been the intention of the Legislature to include, for example, persons who innocently pick the mushrooms which then dry out of their own accord. Obviously, if the mushrooms are picked and deliberately kept in a dry environment so that they dry out, then a process is being adopted to alter their condition "by the hand of man." But deliberate conduct implies the existence of a mental ingredient. However, as yet, the courts have not been asked to examine the nature or the limits of that mental ingredient.

Suppose that a person picks a *Psilocybe Mexicana* mushroom which is then deliberately allowed to dry out so that it may be preserved for botanical study. Is such a person guilty of being in unlawful possession of psilocin? Such a harsh result could be avoided if "preparation" is construed so as to include an ingredient that the accused intended to bring about a chemical change in the condition of the substance or product. It is submitted that such a construction is consistent with the ordinary natural meaning of the word "preparation" in the context of drug use and abuse.

If a substance or product is not expressed in Schedule 2 of the M.D.A. to be a controlled drug, and if the prosecution fail to establish that the substance or product is a "preparation," then it cannot be regarded as a controlled drug. This may seem obvious but consider the case of a person who innocently picks magic mushrooms which dry out naturally. Such a person will not be guilty of unlawful possession if he subsequently learns that the powder is a narcotic and uses it as such. Moreover, if he then shares the substance with others, he cannot be guilty of unlawfully supplying it.

Definition of cannabis

Section 37(1) of the M.D.A., as amended by section 52 of the Criminal Law Act 1977, defines cannabis as:

> "Any plant of the genus cannabis or any part of such a plant (by whatever name designated) except that it does not include cannabis resin or any of the following products after separation from the rest of the plant:
> (a) Mature stalk of any such plant
> (b) Fibre produced from mature stalk of any such plant
> (c) Seed of any such plant."

Cannabis resin means:

" . . . the separated resin, whether crude or purified, obtained from any plant of the genus cannabis."

Both cannabis (herbal) and cannabis resin are class B drugs. However, *cannabinol* and *cannabinol* derivatives are Class A drugs since they are far more potent. *Cannabinol* is not further defined but *Cannabinol Derivatives* are defined in Part IV of Schedule 2 to mean:

" . . . the following substances, except where contained in cannabis or cannabis resin, namely tetrahydro derivatives of cannabinol and 3-alkyl homologues of cannabinol or of its tetrahydro derivatives."

Although all of the above are types of cannabis it would not be right to regard them as generic for the purpose of drafting charges or indictments. Each drug is separately controlled and should be separately particularized in any charge; see *Muir* v. *Smith*,[5a] and c.f. *Best*.[5b]

Since the seeds of the cannabis plant are not controlled it follows that these may be lawfully possessed. But it is an offence to sow them and to cultivate the plant: see section 6.

Although "cannabis resin" means resin that is separated from the plant it does not mean that the prosecution have to show that the resin was separated to the extent that all the cannabis had been removed from the oil-bearing glandular trichomes, since resin includes "crude resin"; see *Thomas*.[6]

The meaning of "cocaine"

In *Greensmith*,[7] G was convicted of possession of 9·04 grams of powder containing 40 per cent. cocaine with intent to supply it. The prosecution called no evidence as to whether the drug was in fact cocaine, or a stereoisomeric form or a salt of cocaine. The expert said whatever it was "it was still cocaine."

Held, G's appeal would be dismissed. "Cocaine" was generic in Paragraph 1 to Part I of Schedule 2 and included a natural substance *e.g.* coca-leaf or a substance resulting from a chemical transformation. Both are cocaine. There was no need for the prosecution to prove the exact form.

[5a] [1978] Crim. L.R. 293, D.C.
[5b] (1979) 70 Cr. App. R. 21.
[6] [1981] Crim. L.R. 496.
[7] [1983] 3 All E.R. 444.

The court attached importance to the words "any substance or product." The word "substance" has a wider meaning than "product." Lawton L.J. noted that "any kind of matter comes within 'substance' whereas 'product' envisages the result of some kind of process."

Two Crown Court cases, *Leaman and Leaman*[8] and *Steeper and Parsons*[9] were referred to in the judgement of the Court of Appeal. Both cases held that the prosecution were bound to specify in the Indictment whether the drug was a form expressed in paragraph 1 of Schedule 2 or whether is was a "ester, ether, salt etc." The Court of Appeal in *Greensmith* advised that neither decision should be followed and indeed this must be right upon a literal reading of the M.D.A. Paragraph 1 of Schedule 2 indicates those substances and products which are controlled. It does not matter for present purposes that neither the word "substance" nor "product" is defined. What does matter, as a matter of science, is that a given substance or product referred to in Schedule 2, may have related to it certain stereoisomeric forms, esters, or ethers, or salts. In other words they are generic. Accordingly, the prosecution are not obliged to particularize which form the drug takes. It is still the same substance or product; (and see: *Watts* [1984][9a]).

Opiate related definitions

"Raw Opium" includes:

" . . . powdered or granulated opium but does not include medicinal opium.": see Part IV of Schedule 2."

"Medicinal Opium" is defined in Part IV of Schedule 2 to mean:

" . . . raw opium which has undergone the process necessary to adapt it for medicinal use in accordance with the requirements of the British Pharmacopoeia, whether it is in the form of powder or is granulated or is in any other form, and whether it is or is not mixed wit neutral substances."

"Prepared Opium," by section 37(1) of the M.D.A., means;

" . . . opium prepared for smoking and includes dross and other residues remaining after opium has been smoked."

"Opium Poppy" means the plant *Papaver somniferum* L."
"Poppy Straw" means, by Part IV:

---

[8] May 17, 1978, unrep.: Maidstone Cr. Ct.
[9] Sept. 27, 1979, unrep.: Inner London Sessions.
[9a] [1984] 1 W.L.R. 757, C.A.

" . . . all parts, except the seeds, of the opium poppy, after mowing";

"Concentrate of Poppy Straw" means, again by Part IV:

" . . . the material produced when poppy-straw has entered into a process for the concentration of its alkaloids";

Using an admission to prove the substance is a drug

Usually, it is the result of scientific analysis which will prove or disprove that the substance is a drug of a particular description. But, occasionally, an accused may equally be in a sound position to express an expert opinion as to the nature of the substance he possesses. In *Bird* v. *Adams*,[10] the defendant was found in possession of 15 tablets. He maintained that they contained L.S.D. and that he had been selling them. The prosecution called no scientific evidence. The Divisional Court held that (1) where an accused was not an expert then an "admission" was in reality no admission at all, and (2) an admission may be valueless where an accused could not have the necessary knowledge, but (3), on the facts, the defendant had sufficient knowledge, having peddled the drug, to make his admission a prima facie case against him.

Each case must of course be decided on its own facts, but a mere belief that a substance is a controlled drug is certainly not sufficient: *Mieras* v. *Rees*.[11]

By contrast, in *Wells*[12] where W admitted taking cannabis and amphetamine sulphate. She pleaded guilty to possessing those drugs. The Court of Appeal held that her pleas were good since "in the last analysis all evidence as to the nature of the substance was an expression of opinion, though scientists might be able to express more reliable opinions than others." The court distinguished *Mieras* v. *Rees* on the basis that there was a plea of not guilty in which the circumstances required proof of the nature of the substances.

To describe the results of chemical analysis as an expression of "opinion" is an understatement to say the least. However, most users will have their own method of ascertaining the nature of the substance they have acquired in order to avoid being "ripped-off" by receiving a substance of a totally different description. Consuming the drug and noting its effects, is one method. Once *Wells* had consumed the substance and thereafter pleaded guilty to possessing drugs of a type specified by the prosecution, the court was

[10] [1972] Crim. L.R. 174, D.C.
[11] [1975] Crim. L.R. 224, D.C.
[12] [1976] Crim. L.R. 518, C.A.

entitled to act on the basis that she knew perfectly well what the drugs were. Her pleas were the best evidence.[13]

Again, a person who admits injecting himself with heroin but later retracts that admission by asserting that he in fact used flour has at least a case to answer.[14] The original admission is a declaration against interest in circumstances in which, as a user of the drug, he is likely to know the effects of heroin consumption. But his subsequent assertion is self-serving: it does not neutralise the admission, still less does it prove innocence.[15]

POWERS OF POLICE AND CUSTOMS OFFICERS

Recognising that much has been written by others concerning the powers of the police (but comparatively little concerning the powers of customs officers) what follows is intended only to be a summary of the most important powers, rights and duties conferred on officers in so far as they affect the investigation and prosecution of drug offences. The Police and Criminal Evidence Act 1984 ("P.A.C.E.") and the Drug Trafficking Offences Act 1986 ("D.T.O.A.") have radically altered much of the earlier law and therefore earlier authorities, to the extent that they may appear to be relevant, must be considered and applied with care. However both P.A.C.E. and the D.T.O.A. do little to affect the powers exercisable under the Customs and Excise Management Act 1979 (C.E.M.A.).

Section 24 of the M.D.A. (previously concerned with the powers of arrest under that enactment), has been totally repealed.

Accordingly, the duties, rights, powers, and privileges conferred on police and customs officers are chiefly to be found in four statutes, namely;

   (i) The Police and Criminal Evidence Act 1984
  (ii) The Misuse of Drugs Act 1971
 (iii) The Customs and Excise Management Act 1979
 (iv) The Drug Trafficking Offences Act 1986.

Citizens may also take certain steps in the prevention of crime—but very much at their peril. The over-riding principle of our constitutional law is that no one in the United Kingdom may lay hands on another, or on his property, without his permission and without lawful justification. For this reason greater powers are given to police and to customs officers than to anyone else.

[13] *C.f. Porter* [1976] C.L.R. 58.
[14] See *Chatwood* [1980] 1 All E.R. 467.
[15] See *Storey* and *Anwar* (1968) 52 Cr. App. R. 334.

POWERS OF THE CITIZEN

Seizing a controlled drug

A citizen possesses no inherent right at common law to seize property under the control of another, but, section 5(4) of the M.D.A. provides a defence to a person charged with the unlawful possession of a controlled drug if he proves that he took possession of it for the purpose of preventing another from committing an offence in connection with the drug (section 5(4)(a)), or that he took it for the purpose of giving it to a person lawfully entitled to take custody of it, for example a police officer or customs officer (see: section 5(4)(b) of the M.D.A.).

A citizen's arrest

Under section 24(4) of P.A.C.E. any person may arrest, without a warrant, anyone who is in the act of committing an arrestable offence or, anyone whom he has reasonable grounds for suspecting to be committing such an offence. Again, he may arrest, without a warrant, anyone who is guilty of the offence or, whom he has reasonable grounds for suspecting to be guilty of it: see section 24(5) of P.A.C.E.

Both section 24(4) and (5) follows the earlier law so, where no arrestable offence has in fact been committed, a private person who performs an arrest faces an action for false imprisonment: see *Walters* v. *Smith (W.H.) & Son Ltd.*[16] and *Beckwith* v. *Philby*.[17]

An individual once arrested by another must be taken to a police station, by a constable, as soon as practicable: section 30(1).

There is no general power conferred by the law on a private person to effect a search of another.

POWERS OF THE POLICE

Arrests

Powers of arrest are conferred on constables by section 24 of P.A.C.E. and include offences arising under the Customs and Excise Acts; see: section 24(2) of P.A.C.E and section 1(1) of the C.E.M.A.

No warrant is needed where a constable has reasonable grounds for suspecting that an arrestable offence has been committed (section 24(6) of P.A.C.E.). He may also arrest anyone who is, or is

---

[16] [1914] 1 K.B. 595.
[17] (1872) 6 B. & C. 635.

reasonably suspected to be, about to commit an arrestable offence
(section 24(7)). An arrest involves an act of compulsion so that a
mere invitation to a person to accompany an officer to a police
station is not an arrest: see *Alderson* v. *Booth*[18] and see *Wheatley*
v. *Lodge*[19] and *R.* v. *Inwood.*[20]

Reasonable suspicion is not the same as prima facie proof and
may be based on the receipt of information which, at the trial,
would in fact be inadmissible; see *Hussain* v. *Chong Fook Kam*[21]
and see *Dumbell* v. *Roberts.*[22]

A person is to be told of the reason for the arrest at the time, or
as soon as is practicable after the arrest; see section 28(3) and
Christie v. *Leachinsky.*[23]

Searches without a warrant

A constable who has reasonable grounds to suspect that any person is in possession of controlled drugs may stop and search that
person, and detain him for that purpose (section 23(2)(*a*) of the
M.D.A.), or to search a vehicle or vessel in which the drug may be
found (section 23(2)(*b*) of the M.D.A.). Section 23(2)(*a*) expressly
authorises detention for the purpose of searching a suspect; it does
not give the officer a general right to question him. But in *Geen*,[24]
the Court of Appeal considered that a right to detain involved the
right to ask questions which were at least incidental to the exercise
of that statutory power.

Furthermore, an officer has no right to stop a vehicle, or to
search it simply because he suspects that the vehicle (and not the
occupants) has been used in connection with a drugs offence.

> In *Littleford*[25] an officer stopped a vehicle and searched it and
> the occupants. The officer had been informed by radio that
> the car was suspected of being involved in drug trafficking.
>
> Held, the searches were illegal. The officers suspicion was
> in connection with the vehicle and not the occupant.

By section 2(2) of P.A.C.E. if a constable contemplates a search
he must take reasonable steps to bring to the attention of the
appropriate person the fact that he is a constable (if not in

[18] [1969] 2 Q.B. 216.
[19] [1971] 1 W.L.R. 29.
[20] [1973] 1 W.L.R. 647.
[21] [1970] A.C. 492.
[22] [1944] 1 All E.R. 326.
[23] [1984] A.C. 573.
[24] (1982) 605.
[25] [1978] Crim. L.R. 48.

uniform) and, in any event, he must give his name, the name of the police station to which he is attached, the object of the search and the constable's grounds for making the search (see section 2(3) of P.A.C.E.) and *c.f. Brazil* v. *Chief Constable of Surrey*[26] and *c.f. Lindley* v. *Rutter.*[27]

An officer may also search an unattended vehicle but he must leave a notice inside the vehicle (if possible) of the fact that he has searched it and stating that an application for compensation may be made at the constable's police station: section 2(6) and (7) of P.A.C.E. The officer shall record details of a search: section 3(1) of P.A.C.E.

Where a person has been arrested a constable may then search that person for anything which might be evidence relating to an offence (section 32(2)(*a*)(ii) of P.A.C.E.) providing that the constable has reasonable grounds to believe that the person may have concealed something on him relevant to an offence (section 32(5)).

Search of premises without a warrant

At common law there was no right vested in the police or anyone else to enter a private house, without a warrant, no matter how serious the crime being investigated was. The one exception was following a culprit in "hot pursuit" see *McLori* v. *Oxford.*[28]

If a person is arrested by police, in any premises, and that person is a danger to himself or to others, the police are perfectly within their rights to search those premises but only for evidence relating to the offence for which he has been arrested (section 32(2)(*b*) of P.A.C.E.) and only to the extent that the search is reasonably required (section 32(3)) but, there must be reasonable grounds to believe that there is relevant evidence on the premises (section 32(6)).

Irrespective of whether or not a person arrested is a danger to himself or to others, a constable, under section 18 of P.A.C.E., may enter and search any premises occupied or controlled by the person arrested if he has reasonable grounds for suspecting that on the premises there is evidence relating to that offence or indeed another similar offence. However, before invoking section 18, the constable needs the written authorisation of an officer of at least the rank of inspector unless, (and this seems a curious addition to the section) the presence of the arrested party, at the premises is "necessary for the effective investigation of the offence . . . " (sec-

---

[26] [1983] 3 All E.R. 537.
[27] [1981] 72 Cr. App. R. 1.
[28] (1982).

tion 18(5)). This would presumably include a person who had stashed drugs, and items relevant to the offence, and who would therefore be able to assist the police (if he wishes to do so) to find them.

Searching for an individual

In addition to these powers, a constable in uniform (section 17(3) of P.A.C.E.) may enter and search any premises—without a warrant—if the object of gaining entry is (*inter alia*) to execute a warrant of arrest, or to arrest a person for an arrestable offence (section 17), providing there are reasonable grounds to believe that the person is on the premises (section 17(2)(*a*)) and only if it is reasonably required for the purpose of finding the person concerned.

All former rules of common law which emerged to give a constable power to enter premises without a warrant are now abolished: section 17(5). It follows that section 17 is a codifying provision (*c.f. Thomas* v. *Sawkins*[29]; *Davis* v. *Lisle*[30]; *Robson* v. *Hallett*.[31] Parliament has now empowered officers not merely to enter premises in order to prevent the commission of an offence therein, but also to investigate crime generally.

Intimate searches and searches at police stations

Previous statutes and rules at common law affecting the ability of the police to search suspects at police stations and to carry out intimate searches, have been abolished (section 53 of P.A.C.E.).

Instead, a new set of principles have been enacted by section 55 of P.A.C.E. Thus, an intimate search is restricted to certain purposes only; for example where a Class A drug is concealed on the suspect and he "was in possession of it with the appropriate criminal intent before his arrest"—a passage which may present some difficulties of application and construction (see section 55(1)(*b*)). In any event an intimate search must be authorised in writing by an officer of at least the rank of superintendent (section 55(1) and (3)) providing that he has reasonable grounds to believe that the class A drug cannot be found without such a search (section 55(2)) and that it is carried out by a registered medical practitioner or registered nurse (unless the superintendent thinks this impracticable): see section 55(4) and (5) and (17) of P.A.C.E. An intimate search for a class A drug must not be carried out at a police station but at

[29] 11935] 2 K.B. 249.
[30] [1936] 2 K.B. 434.
[31] [1967] 2 Q.B. 939.

a hospital; or at the surgery of a General Practitioner, or some other place used for medical purposes (see section 55(9) and (8)).

Again, intimate samples (for example, blood, saliva, urine) may not be taken unless a person is reasonably suspected of having committed a "serious arrestable offence"—a term which is narrowly defined by the Act (see section 116 and schedule 5 of P.A.C.E.) but which includes an arrestable offence aggravated by the happening of certain events listed in section 116(6) for example, substantial financial gain to any person. Therefore, a person reasonably suspected of being a major drugs supplier who has substantially benefited from the proceeds of drug trafficking is likely to be a person from whom intimate samples may be taken subject to the requirements of section 62. Other samples may be taken with the accused's consent.

Searches with a warrant

Warrants may be obtained under a number of different enactments but three principal statutes are dealt with here. The first is section 23 of the M.D.A.; the second is section 8 of P.A.C.E. and the third is section 28 of the D.T.O.A.

Warrants under section 23 of the M.D.A.

A Justice of the Peace is authorised by this section to grant a warrant authorising a constable to search premises at "any time or times" within one month from the date of the warrant. But there must be reasonable cause to suspect that controlled drugs are in the possession of a person on any premises, or that documents exist in relation to a drugs transaction.

In *Adams*,[32] the Court of Appeal considered whether a warrant issued under section 3(1) of the Obscene Publications Act 1959 authorised officers to search premises on more than one occasion. During the course of legal argument section 3(1) was contrasted with section 23(3) of the M.D.A. where the words "at any time or times within one month" might imply authorisation of a number of quite separate searches within that time. The Court considered section 23(3) of the M.D.A. 1971 to "fortify, rather than found" their conclusion that the wording of section 3(1) of the O.P.A. 1959 authorised only one search per warrant.[33]

However, it is unlikely that Parliament intended to give police blanket authorisation to enter premises as often as they wish

---

[32] (1980) 1 All E.R. 473.

[33] See *Dickinson* v. *Brown* (1794) 1 Esp. 218, 170 E.R. 334. And see s.152(1) of the Licensing Act 1953.

within the relevant time merely upon the grant of a warrant under section 23(3) of the M.D.A. 1971.

In the absence of authority to the contrary, the words "time or times" may mean no more than that a justice of the peace is empowered to grant a warrant specifying multiple searches if the evidence given to him on oath justifies such a course. Any other construction would result in the total inability of the court, granting the warrant, to prevent a subsequent entry, search, and seizure within the operational period which is not, on its merits, actually warranted.

By contrast, a search warrant granted under section 8 of P.A.C.E. authorises an entry on one occasion only.[34]

If the main or only reason for being on premises is to detect offences under the M.D.A. it is not essential that a warrant be obtained under section 23(3) of the M.D.A. if entry is gained by virtue of another enactment.[35] *Foster* v. *Attarde*.

Once a constable is authorised to enter premises by virtue of section 23 of the M.D.A., he may use such force as is reasonably necessary to gain admission and to search the premises and any occupants but, in *King* v. *R*.[36] the Privy Council held that a warrant, granted under similar Jamaican legislation, was unlawful if it did not expressly authorise the search of persons as well as premises.

Any drugs or relevant documents found during the course of a search under section 23 of the M.D.A. may be seized and retained by the police.

Warrants granted under section 8 of P.A.C.E.

The police also have power to apply to a justice of the peace for a search warrant in respect of premises under section 8 of P.A.C.E. Although the granting of a warrant under this section is confined to cases where there is reasonable cause to believe that a "serious arrestable offence" has been committed, nevertheless, as has been said already, this may include a major drugs supplier or a person concerned in the unlawful importation/exportation of controlled drugs where substantial gains are suspected to have been made.

Warrants granted under section 8 above may be executed by a constable (section 16(1) P.A.C.E.). Again, entry may be effected within one month from the date of its issue (section 16(2)

[34] See Rule B: 5, 3 of the Codes of Practice (S.I. 1985 No. 1937).
[35] *Foster* v. *Attarde* (1986) 83 Cr. App. R. 214.
[36] [1969] 1 A.C. 304.

P.A.C.E.) but with the qualification that the entry and search must be carried out at a reasonable hour unless the purpose of the search would be frustrated as a result.

Warrants issued under section 28 of the D.T.O.A.

By section 28(1) a constable (or, in Scotland, the Procurator Fiscal) may for the purpose of an investigation into drug trafficking, apply to a Circuit Judge (or, in Scotland, the Sheriff) for a warrant in respect of specified premises authorising (by virtue of section 28(2)) a constable to enter and search the premises if an order for the disclosure of material on premises under section 27 of that Act has not been complied with, or certain conditions stipulated in section 28(3) or section 28(4) are fulfilled. Where a constable has entered premises in the execution of a warrant issued under section 28, he may seize and retain any material, other than "items subject to legal privilege" (as defined by section 10 of P.A.C.E.) and "excluded material" (as defined by section 11 of P.A.C.E.) which is likely to be of substantial value to the investigation for the purpose for which the warrant was issued: see section 28(5) of the D.T.O.A.

References in the D.T.O.A. to a "constable" includes a person commissioned by the Commissioners of Customs and Excise: see section 28(1) of the D.T.O.A.

Generally

Although it is obviously desirable that warrants should be correctly drafted, nevertheless, an inconsequential error or misspelling is unlikely to vitiate the warrant.

> In *Atkinson*[37] police wished to search the defendant's flat. They thought that the number of the flat was "45" and accordingly, obtained a warrant to search "Flat 45." In fact the defendant lived at "Flat 30." Police entered Flat 30 and searched it.
>
> Held, the search could not be justified since a highly material particular, concerning the identity of the premises, had been misdescribed.

It follows from the above, (and there is abundant authority, for the proposition) that a general warrant expressing insufficient particulars is illegal at common law.[38]

---

[37] (1976) Crim. L.R. 307.
[38] See *Leach* v. *Money* (1765) 19 St. Tr. 1002; *Wilkes* v. *Wood* (1763) 19 St. Tr. 1153; *Entick* v. *Carrington* (1765) 19 St. Tr. 1030.

But a suggestion that a court had insufficient grounds to justify granting a warrant will not be lightly entertained: see *Wyatt* v. *White*.[39]

One object of present legislation seems to be to avoid putting goods into a more sacred category than persons: see Lord Denning M.R. in *Chic Fashions* v. *Jones*[40] and *Ghani* v. *Jones*.[41]

Seizure of articles

Where Parliament has given a right to police to search persons and premises in connection with the purposes for which they have been authorised to carry out the search, there exists a corresponding right to seize relevant materials (see sections 8, 18, 32, 54 and 55 of P.A.C.E.; and section 23 of the M.D.A.). But there now exists general powers of seizure conferred, on the police, by section 19(1) of P.A.C.E. which are exercisable by a constable who is lawfully on any premises. These powers are to seize anything which:

  (i) has been obtained in consequence of the commission of an offence and which is in danger of being concealed, lost, damaged, altered, or destroyed; or

  (ii) is evidence in respect of any offence; or

  (iii) is evidence held by computer in respect of any offence and which may be destroyed, etc., if not seized.

The powers conferred by section 19 are additional to any other powers conferred under P.A.C.E.: section 19(5). Items seized under section 19 may be retained for as long as it is necessary in the circumstances: section 22(1).

In *Ghani* v. *Jones*[42] Lord Denning M.R. said, *obiter*, that seizure was not justified unless the police have reasonable grounds to believe that "the person in possession of it has himself committed the crime, or is an accessory or at any rate, his refusal [to deliver up property] must be quite unreasonable." But, an unreasonable refusal is not a sufficient reason for seizure under P.A.C.E.

POWERS OF CUSTOMS AND EXCISE

The powers conferred on customs officials are extensive and deliberately widely drawn in response to the tasks that the Commissioners of Customs and Excise are expected to undertake. Most of the powers are conferred by the C.E.M.A.

[39] (1860) 5 H. & N. 371.
[40] [1960] 2 Q.B. 299.
[41] [1970] 1 Q.B.
[42] *Ibid.*

Section 1(1) of that Act, defines an "officer" as a person commissioned by the Commissioner of Customs and Excise to be an officer. However, there is another class of "officer" who, by section 8(2), includes " . . . any person, whether an officer or not . . ." who is engaged in carrying out an "assigned matter" (see s.1(1)), and shall therefore be deemed to be the " . . . the proper officer . . . ." An officer falling within the latter category may be engaged by order of the Commissioners or simply engaged with their concurrence. Irrespective as to whether an officer is a "commissioned" officer or "engaged" under section 8(2), his powers are nevertheless identical: section 8(3).

Powers of search

The powers of stop and search under the C.E.M.A. are set out in Annex "A" to the Police and Criminal Evidence Act 1984 (Codes of Practice) (No. 1) Order 1985 (S.I. 1985 No. 1937):

POWER	OBJECT OF SEARCH	EXTENT OF SEARCH	WHERE EXERCISABLE
CEMA s.163	Goods: (a) on which duty has not been paid; (b) being unlawfully removed, imported or exported; (c) otherwise liable to forfeiture to HM Customs and Excise.	Vehicles and vessels	Anywhere
CEMA	Goods: (a) on which duty has been paid; (b) the importation or exportation of which is restricted or prohibited by law.	Persons only	At entry to departure from UK; on board or at landing from ships or aircraft; in dock areas or Customs and excise airports; at entry to, departure from or within approved wharves, transit sheds or free zones; or when travelling to or from any place beyond the N. Ireland boundary.

There are a large number of activities, carried out in respect of certain goods, which would entitle an officer to treat the goods as being liable to forfeiture. Controlled drugs unlawfully imported, or intended for export, fall into this category. Once liability to forfeiture arises a number of different powers come into effect.

Thus by section 161(1) of the C.E.M.A., an officer having a "Writ of Assistance" may enter any building or place where there are reasonable grounds to suspect that anything liable to forfeiture is kept or concealed. Entry may be made by day or by night. If the entry is to be made at night, the officer must be accompanied by a constable (section 161(2)). Articles liable to forfeiture may be seized and detailed (section 161(1)(a)). In the exercise of these powers an officer may break open any window, door or container. He may forcefully remove any impediment (section 161(1)(b)).

Additionally, the officer may apply to a Justice of the Peace for a *search warrant*, under section 161(3) of the C.E.M.A. (as amended by clause 6 of Schedule 6 to P.A.C.E.), which will entitle him to the same powers as if he had a Writ of Assistance. But whereas a Writ of Assistance runs for the duration of that Writ and for a period of six months thereafter, a warrant must be executed within one month (see s.161(6) and clause 38 of Schedule 6).

Where a person comes within a category of persons listed in section 164(4), for example, any person who is within the dock area of a port, or who has landed from any ship or aircraft, he may be searched, providing that there are reasonable grounds to suspect that he is carrying any article (not just drugs) with respect to the importation or exportation of prohibited goods. A person who is to be searched under section 164, may complain to the officer's superior or to a justice of the peace, who will decide whether or not a search is to take place: section 164(2) of the C.E.M.A.

No woman or girl may be searched by a man (section 164(3)) although there is nothing in section 164 to say that a male cannot be searched by a woman!

Any vehicle or vessel may be stopped and searched by an officer, constable, coastguard or a member of the armed forces, if there are reasonable grounds to suspect that the vehicle or vessel is carrying, *inter alia*, a controlled drug: section 163.

Searching at will

Many of the powers conferred by the C.E.M.A. do not require an officer to have reasonable grounds to suspect the commission of any offence before he exercises those powers. Thus, by section 27 any officer, and " . . . any other officer duly engaged in the prevention of smuggling . . . " may board any ship which is within the limits of a port, or any aircraft at a customs and excise airport, or a vehicle on an approved route, so that he may search it.

It is not clear which categories of person Parliament had in mind when referring to " . . . any other person duly engaged in the prevention of smuggling . . . " but presumably includes a coastguard or police officers assigned to such a task.

Officers once on board are entitled to free access to every part of the ship, aircraft or vessel and may break open any place or container which is locked and of which the keys are withheld: section 28(1) of the C.E.M.A. Any goods found concealed on board shall be liable to forfeiture: section 28(2).

A commander of an aircraft must allow an officer to board an aircraft and to inspect goods and documents therein: section 33. If an officer or a constable considers that an aircraft is likely to leave the United Kingdom from a place other than a customs and excise airport, then he may take such steps as appear to him to be necessary in order to prevent the fight: section 34. This seems to permit all manner of dramatic measures to be adopted (seemingly with impunity) if the officer sees fit.

An officer or constable who has reasonable cause to suspect that signals or messages in connection with a smuggling operation are being made or transmitted from a ship; aircraft; vehicle; house or place he may board or enter, as the case may be, and take such steps as are reasonably necessary to stop and prevent the sending of the signal or message: section 84(5).

Seizure of articles and the taking of samples

An officer, constable, coastguard or any member of the armed forces may seize and detain anything liable to forfeiture under the customs and excise Acts: section 139(1).

Samples may be taken of any goods which an officer is empowered to examine under the C.E.M.A.: section 160(1).

Detention of persons

An officer, coastguard, or a member of the armed forces may arrest a person whom he has reasonable grounds to suspect has committed a drugs related importation/exportation: section 138. The power of arrest may be exercised within three years of the offence being committed: section 138(1).

ILLEGALLY OBTAINED EVIDENCE

It has long been a rule of law, although much criticised, that evidence adduced by unlawful or improper means (save in relation to involuntary confessions and generally with regard to evidence obtained from the accused after the commission of the offence) is admissible in evidence.[43] The principle safeguard has always been the courts inherent discretion to exclude such evidence if its prejudicial effect outweighs its probative value.[44] A similar discretion has now been given statutory effect by section 78 of P.A.C.E. which enables a court to disallow Prosecution evidence if, having regard to the circumstances in which the evidence was obtained, its admissibility "would have such an adverse effect on the fairness of the proceedings." It is not yet clear whether section 78 has altered the earlier position, but is of interest that the section makes reference to the effect on the fairness of the proceedings.[44a] In other words it would seem that the court is not restricted to assessing whether the introduction of the evidence complained of would be unfair to the accused, or whether the evidence is so grossly prejudicial that it would be unreasonable to admit it. Accordingly, it is submitted that the words " . . . fairness of the proceedings . . . " was the draftsman's way of rewording the cliché that "Justice must not only be done, but also be seen to be done." If, then, a reasonable bystander viewing the proceedings were heard to say that the evidence was obtained in circumstances so patently unfair, that it would be an affront to our system of justice to admit it, then the judge (fulfilling the role of the bystander) ought to exclude it.

OBSTRUCTION OF OFFICERS

Obstruction of police officers under the M.D.A.

Section 23(4) of the M.D.A. provides:

"A person commits an offence if he—
(a) intentionally obstructs a person in the exercise of his powers under this section; or
(b) conceals from a person acting in the exercise of his powers under subsection (1) above any such books, documents, stocks or drugs as are mentioned in that subsection; or
(c) without reasonable excuse (proof of which shall lie on him) fails to produce any such books or documents as are so mentioned where their production is demanded by a person in the exercise of his powers under that subsection."

Subsection (4)(b) and 4(c) apply only to commercial concerns who carry on business as producers or suppliers of controlled drugs.

---

[43] See *Kuruma* [1955] A.C. 197; *Maqsood Ali* (1966).
[44] See *Sang* [1979] 2 All E.R. 1222; *Jeffery* v. *Black* [1979] 3 W.L.R. 895.
[44a] Also see *O'Leary*, *The Times*, May 18, 1988.

Constables, or other persons, authorised by the Secretary of State may enter the business premises and inspect the companies paperwork, stock or drugs. Accordingly, an offence will be committed if the relevant items are either concealed or not produced upon demand without a reasonable excuse.

The wording of section 24(4)(*b*) implies that an accused need only know that the documents, stock or drugs concealed relate to drug transactions and that an officer might wish to see them. However, an allegation made under section 23(4)(*c*) is to be objectively determined so that the accused must provide a reasonable excuse to explain why the documents concerned could not be physically produced when demanded, (for example, destroyed in a fire, or retained by a court for the purposes of pending litigation). The motives of the accused are immaterial. Thus, merely to protect the identity of a confidential client who is lawfully entitled to buy and possess the drugs, would not be a defence or a reasonable excuse.

Defining an intentional obstruction

In *Forde (J)*,[45] the Court of Appeal held that an offence is committed once an act is done which when viewed objectively, obstructed the officer in the execution of his powers under section 24 and was intended by an accused to obstruct.

It would therefore appear that the words "intentionally obstructs" has the same meaning as "wilfully obstructs" found in other enactments and notably section 51(3) of the Police Act 1964. In *Hills* v. *Ellis*[46] the Divisional Court, when considering section 51(3) of that Act, asked " . . . what is meant by an intention to obstruct?" and gave the following reply (*per* McCullough J.):

> "I would construe 'wilfully obstructs' as doing deliberate actions with the intention of bringing about a state of affairs which, objectively regarded, amount to an obstruction . . . the fact that the defendant might not have called that state of affairs an obstruction is . . . immaterial."

But what is an obstruction? The answer is an act calculated to make it more difficult for the police to carry out their duties.[47] See *Rice* v. *Connolly*. Thus, to throw drugs away before the police can seize them is a classic example of obstruction under section 23. It is

---

[45] (1985) 81 Cr. App. R. 19.
[46] [1983] Q.B. 680.
[47] See *Rice* v. *Connolly* [1966] 2 Q.B. 414.

not necessary to prove a "hostile" motive in obstructing the officer: see *Willmott* v. *Atack*[48] and *Green* v. *Moore*.[49]

In *Kelly*,[50] the Court of Appeal held that an offence is committed under section 23(4)(*a*) if D knows that the officer is detaining, or trying to detain him, in order to search D for drugs. D's conduct when viewed objectively did obstruct the detention and search. D's conduct, viewed subjectively, was intended to obstruct.

The court, in *Kelly*, accepted that there may be occasions when the obstructing act was performed before the constable had the opportunity to explain what he was doing. However, the existence of such a feature would not automatically excuse a defendant in circumstances where the reasons for the constable's conduct must have been obvious to the defendant.

OBSTRUCTING CUSTOMS OFFICERS

By section 16(1) of the C.E.M.A. 1979:

"Any person who—
   (*a*) obstructs,[51] hinders, molests or assaults any person duly engaged in the performance of any duty or the exercise of any power imposed or conferred on him by or under any enactment relating to an assigned matter, or any person acting in his aid; or
   (*b*) does anything which impedes or is calculated to impede the carrying out of any search for any thing liable to forfeiture under any such enactment or the detention, seizure or removal of any such thing; or
   (*c*) rescues, damages or destroys any thing so liable to forfeiture or does anything calculated to prevent the procuring or giving of evidence as to whether or not any thing is so liable to forfeiture; or
   (*d*) prevents the detention of any person by a person duly engaged or acting as aforesaid or rescues any person so detained,
or who attempts to do any of the aforementioned things, shall be guilty of an offence under this section."

These provisions are really self-explanatory but go a great deal further than section 23 of the M.D.A.

[48] [1976] 3 W.L.R. 753.
[49] [1982] Q.B. 1044.
[50] (1984) unrep. November 19, 1984 5624883.
[51] See *George and Davies* (1980) Crim. L.R. 185.

THE DRUG TRAFFICKING ACT 1986

On the July 8, 1986, by virtue of the Drug Trafficking Offences Act 1986 (the "D.T.O.A."), Parliament introduced sweeping and radical changes in the law to enable the Courts to recover the proceeds of drug trafficking.[52] Previously, the courts were equipped only with the statutory powers of forfeiture; the making of "deprivation" orders or "criminal bankruptcy" orders, and/or the imposition of fines. All these powers continue to exist, but they are very limited in scope. Thus, by section 27 of the M.D.A. 1971 only those assets which directly relate to an offence committed by the accused, under that Act, may be forfeited.[53] *Choses* in action and intangibles are not usually capable of being forfeited.[54] Drug profits, originally received by the accused, but which were then transferred to a third party could not be seized. The imposition of a substantial fine on the accused, coupled with an order that he pay the costs of the trial (either wholly or in part) is a crude method of recouping drug profits and rightly regarded as bad sentencing policy being a "back-door" approach. In any event, the bold defendant who simply refused to pay the fine would sometimes prefer to "sit-it-out" and serve a sentence of imprisonment in default of payment, knowing that the court was powerless to enforce the sale of his assets in order to satisfy the fine or other fiscal orders. It was to meet such weaknesses in the law that the D.T.O.A. 1986 was enacted.

By section 1 of the Act the moment an accused appears before the Crown Court to be sentenced in respect of a "drugs trafficking offence,"[55] the court is obliged to embark upon an enquiry to recover, under a "Confiscation Order," the proceeds of drug trafficking received by him. Note that the D.T.O.A. aims to confiscate the proceeds of drug trafficking and not merely the profits made by the offender. Thus, where D unlawfully earns £1,000

---

[52] S.1(3), 2(1), 24, 34, 38 and 40 came into force on September 30, 1986; see Drug Trafficking Offences Act (Commencement No. 1) Order 1986 (S.I. 1986 No. 1488). Sections 27 to 29, 31 and 33 in force on December 30, 1986 and the remainder in force on January 1, 1987; see Drug Trafficking Offences Act 1986 (Commencement No. 3) Order 1986 (S.I. 1986 No. 2145) In Scotland, see Drug Trafficking Offences Act 1986 (Commencement No. 2) (Scotland) Order 1986 (S.I. 1986 No. 1456) and the Drug Trafficking Offences Act 1986 (Commencement No. 4) (Scotland) Order 1986 (S.I. 1986 No. 2266).

[53] See *R.* v. *Morgan* [1977] Crim. L.R. 488, C.A.

[54] See *R.* v. *Khan (S.A.)* [1982] 3 All E.R. 969, C.A.

[55] Defined by s.3(1).

which he then expends on the purchase of cannabis resin and which he then re-sells for £1,500, the Court is entitled to confiscate the full £1,500 and not merely the profit of £500. Unlike any other sentence, a Confiscation Order need not mark the extent of a defendant's criminality because the Act catches all drug proceeds whether they represent his drug trafficking or not, and irrespective as to whether the trafficking took place in the United Kingdom or abroad. The Act applies to property held in England and Wales or elsewhere: section 38(3).

The method by which a court may assess the value of the proceeds of drug trafficking is one of the most controversial features of the Act. There will often be cases where an accused can be shown to have received property over a period of years but there exists little or no evidence to prove that the property represents the proceeds of drug trafficking. Accordingly, the Act creates a number of far reaching assumptions—all totally adverse to the defendant's interests—which the court is entitled (but not compelled) to make. Inevitably, in complicated and hotly contested confiscation proceedings, much court time will be spent tracing funds and ascertaining their origin.

There are clear signs that the Act is beginning to bite. On September 22, 1987 the *Independent* Newspaper reported that some seven million pounds sterling had been seized from suspected drug dealers under 104 "Restraint Orders" granted under the D.T.O.A. In fact this figure is of limited significance. As we shall see, a Restraint Order merely prevents an accused from wasting his assets long before the court gets to the stage of being able to consider making a Confiscation Order. What will be of particular significance, is the proportion of that seven million pounds which is ultimately confiscated, an not merely restrained.[55a]

Persons to whom section 1 of the D.T.O.A. applies

Confiscation Orders may only be made against persons who appear before the *Crown Court* to be sentenced in respect of one or more "drug trafficking offences"—a classification which, by section 38(1) of the D.T.O.A. includes:

"(*a*) an offence under section 4(2) or (3) or 5(3) of the Misuse of Drugs Act 1971 (production, supply and possession for supply of controlled drugs);

(*b*) an offence under section 20 of that Act (assisting in or induc-

---

[55a] See: the case of *George Bradley*, *The Guardian*, Friday, November 6, 1987.

ing commission outside United Kingdom of offence punishable under a corresponding law);

(c) an offence under—
  (i) section 50(2) or (3) of the Customs and Excise Management Act 1979 (improper importation),
  (ii) section 68(2) of that Act (exportation), or
  (iii) section 170 of that Act (fraudulent evasion), in connection with a prohibition or restriction on importation or exportation having effect by virtue of section 3 of the Misuse of Drugs Act 1971;

(d) an offence under section 24 of this Act;

(e) an offence under section 1 of the Criminal Law Act 1977 of conspiracy to commit any of the offences in paragraphs (a) to (d) above;

(f) an offence under section 1 of the Criminal Attempts Act 1981 of attempting to commit any of those offences;

(g) an offence of inciting another to commit any of those offences, whether under section 19 of the Misuse of Drugs Act 1971 or at common law; and

(h) aiding, abetting, counselling or procuring the commission of any of those offences."

It has been emphasised that only the Crown Court is empowered to make a Confiscation Order under section 1 of the Act. Although the section will apply in cases where the defendant is committed by the Magistrates Court to the Crown Court for sentence pursuant to section 38 of the Magistrates Court Act 1980, it will not apply to juveniles who are committed to the Crown Court with a view to being sentenced to Youth Custody under *section 37* of the Magistrates Court Act 1980,[56] or where the powers of the court are limited to dealing with the defendant in a way which a Magistrates Court might have dealt with him in connection with the offence charged.[57] Accordingly, section 1 does not apply to defendants who appeal to the Crown Court against their conviction and/or sentence in the Magistrates Court. Furthermore, section 1 has no application where a defendant has been " . . . peviously . . . sentenced or otherwise dealt with in respect of his conviction for the offence or . . . any of the offences concerned": section 1(1). Section 1 therefore does not apply to persons who are in breach of a Community Service Order or a suspended sentence of imprisonment.

---

[56] See s.1(7)(a) of the D.T.O.A.
[57] See s.1(7)(b) of the D.T.O.A.

Summarising the mechanics of the act

Whenever a defendant appears before the Crown Court to be sentenced in respect of one or more "drug trafficking offences," the court has no alternative[58] but to make a Confiscation Order, if it can do so, by following the steps set out in section 1 of the Act. Broadly speaking, the relevant steps (and those which result from an application of section 1) may be briefly summarised as follows:

(1) the court must determine whether the accused has benefited from drug trafficking: section 1(2)

(2) if he has, the court must then assess the value of the proceeds of drug trafficking received; section 1(4) and section 4,

(3) thereafter the court must: determine the amount to be actually recovered in the defendant's case before sentencing or otherwise dealing with him; section 1(4) and section 4

(4) the court must order the defendant, by way of a Confiscation Order, to pay that amount: section 1(5),

(5) the court must treat the Confiscation Order as a fine, and impose sentence of imprisonment in default: section 6

(6) Finally in a proper case, the court may vary or discharge the Confiscation Order: section 14

If the court is minded to make a Confiscation Order then it must determine the amount to be recovered from the defendant before sentencing him (section 1(4)) and, furthermore, the court is obliged to take account of the order before imposing a fine (section 1(5)(b(i)) or before making an order under section 27 of the M.D.A. 1971 (forfeiture orders), or section 39 of the Powers of the Criminal Courts Act 1973 (criminal bankruptcy orders), or section 43 of that Act (deprivation orders): see section 1(5)(b)(ii) and (iii).

By section 1(5)(c) the court is also obliged to leave the Confiscation Order out of account in deciding the appropriate sentence to be passed on the defendant.

It would therefore seem that the safest course is for the court not to sentence the defendant at all until after it has made a Confiscation Order. Unfortunately, the Act does not make it clear whether

---

[58] Section 1(1) reads: "Subject to subsection (7) below, where a person appears before the Crown Court to be sentenced in respect of one or more drug trafficking offences (and has not previously been sentenced or otherwise dealt with in respect of his conviction for the offence or, as the case may be, any of the offences concerned), the court shall act as follows . . . [set out below]." Note the words " . . . *the court shall act* . . . ."

the court is prevented from passing a sentence in respect of non drug-trafficking offences until such an Order is made or (at least) until the amount to be recovered from the defendant is ascertained. However, in the absence of express language in the Act to the contrary, it is submitted that the court is not bound to wait until the procedural steps in section 1 are fulfilled before sentencing an offender in respect of non drug-trafficking offences.

It seems implicit from the wording of the Act[59] that a Confiscation Order is "a sentence" for the purposes of section 11 of the Criminal Appeal Act 1968. Accordingly, a defendant may appeal to the Court of Appeal (Criminal Division) against the making of such an order.

Where a defendant defaults in the payment of the Confiscation Order, the prosecution may ask the High Court to appoint a Receiver to realise assets that are held either by the defendant, or by persons whom the defendant has directly or indirectly made a "gift" for the purposes of the Act: see *section 11* and *section 5*. Property realised by the Receiver may then be applied towards satisfying the Order: see *section 12* and *section 13*. Special rules will apply in the case of *any* person (not just the defendant) who is adjudged to be bankrupt but who nevertheless holds "realisable property": see *section 15* and *section 16*. Special rules also apply to companies which are in the process of being wound up but which possess realisable property: *section 17*.

In order to avoid the risk that a defendant may be tempted to dispose of his assets before a court can confiscate them, the High Court is empowered, upon the application of the prosecutor, to grant a "Restraint Order" prohibiting *any* person from dealing with "realisable property" except as directed by the Court: section 7 and 8. Furthermore, a Receiver may be appointed to take possession of any realisable property and to manage or to otherwise deal with that property: section 8(6).

Since much realisable property will consist of land or other securities it is desirable, in cases where a Confiscation Order has not yet been made, to impose a Charge on the property to secure the payment of monies to the Crown. The D.T.O.A. provides the necessary machinery for doing so by virtue of section 9. Accordingly, the High Court may, upon the application of the prosecutor, grant a "Charging Order" (*ex parte* if necessary) and may appoint a Receiver to take possession of the property: section 11.

Obviously, a defendant, against whom the proceedings do not result in his conviction for a drug-trafficking offence, may feel aggrieved that the prosecution have detrimentally meddled in his

---

[59] See, *e.g.* s.6(6).

financial affairs. His assets, having been realised, means that he was unable to liquidate them and to re-invest the proceeds as he wished. In certain cases the financial loss might be considerable. Third parties, from whose hands property had been realised by a court under the D.T.O.A., may also be similarly affected. Parliament therefore took (at first sight) a robust course and enabled persons so affected to apply to the High Court for an order of compensation to be paid to them: *section 19*. In reality, the hurdles put in the path of an Applicant are considerable. Not only must there be "serious default" on the part of a police officer, or a customs officer, or a member of the Crown Prosecution Service concerning the investigation or prosecution, but there must also be proof that the proceedings would not have been instituted or continued but for that default: *section 19(2)(a)*. Furthermore, it must be shown that the loss is "substantial"—whatever that may mean. Even when an Applicant succeeds in meeting those requirements it does not follow that he will be fully compensated: the "amount of compensation . . . shall be such as the High Court thinks just in all the circumstances of the case": *section 19(3)*.

Finally, the Act creates a number of offences. For example, where A retains, or controls, the proceeds of B's drug-trafficking, or uses those proceeds to secure funds for B's disposal or to acquire (for B) investment property, then A shall be guilty of the offence of "Assisting a Drug Trafficker" if A knows or suspects that B is, or has been, a drug-trafficker, or has benefited from drug-trafficking: *section 24*.

THE MAKING OF A CONFISCATION ORDER

It will be recalled that the court must determine whether the defendant has benefited from drug-trafficking[60] and if he has to determine the amount to be recovered.[61] Realistically, each element must be examined in the context of the other, since an amount can only be recovered if it represents a benefit of drug-trafficking and vice versa.

Thus by section 1(3):

> "For the purposes of this Act, a person who has at any time (whether before or after the commencement of this section) received any payment or other reward in connection with drug-trafficking carried on by him or another has benefited from drug-trafficking."

Accordingly, one cannot divorce the method by which the court

[60] Section 1(2).
[61] See s.1(4) and s.4.

must determine whether the defendant has benefited from drug-trafficking, from the procedure laid down in the Act for assessing the value of the defendant's proceeds of that trade.

Section 1(4) provides that:

> "If the court determines that he has so benefited, the court shall, before sentencing or otherwise dealing with him in respect of the offence or, as the case may be, any of the offences concerned, determine in accordance with section 4 of this Act the amount to be recovered in his case by virtue of this section."

When one therefore looks at section 4(1), we see that the " . . . amount to be recovered . . . " is to be equated with:

> " . . . the amount the Crown Court assesses to be the value of the defendant's proceeds of *drug-trafficking.*"

Note the words in italics. Obviously, there will often be cases where an accused no longer holds capital and/or savings to meet the amount the court assesses to be the value of the defendant's proceeds of drug trafficking. The Act does not seek to make him bankrupt in those circumstances but, on the contrary, the Act provides by section 4(3) that the "amount to be recovered" shall therefore be the amount that can be "realised."[62]

Quantifying the defendant's proceeds of drug-trafficking

Section 2(1) provides that:

> "For the purposes of this Act—
> (a) any payments or other rewards received by a person at any time (whether before or after the commencement of section 1 of this Act) in connection with drug-trafficking carried on by him or another are his proceeds of drug-trafficking, and
> (b) the value of his proceeds of drug-trafficking is the aggregate of the values of the payments or other rewards."

Several points should be carefully noted. First, the proceeds of drug-trafficking will include any "payment" or other "reward" be

---

[62] Section 4(3) provides "If the court is satisfied that the amount that might be realised at the time the confiscation order is made is less than the amount the court assesses to be the value of his proceeds of drug-trafficking, the amount to be recovered in the defendant's case under the confiscation order shall be the amount appearing to the court to be the amount that might be realised."

it cash, a "gift," a chose in action, or another intangible. Secondly, it does not matter *when* the payment or reward was received by the defendant. There is no time limit as to how far back the prosecution may scan. Thus, payments made *before* the commencement of the Act are included. Thirdly, the payment must be actually received by the defendant: presumably an offer to advance a payment or reward cannot be taken into account; and similarly a payment, which has been misdirected, (*i.e.* forwarded to another individual in error) cannot feature in the calculation. Fourthly, it does not matter whether the payment is in connection with the defendant's drug-trafficking or someone elses'.

The practical effect of *section 2(1)* may be summarised as follows. If the prosecution can prove that a payment or reward was received by the defendant at any time *and* if it can be proved to be connected with drug-trafficking, then such payments represent the "proceeds" of drug-trafficking for the purposes of the Act. Obviously, there will be many occasions when the prosecution cannot prove the link between a payment and a drug-trafficking offence—however suspicious the circumstances of its receipt may seem. Parliament has therefore permitted the court to make certain "assumptions" concerning the origin of property received by the accused in specified circumstances. Thus, section 2(2) provides:

> "The Court may, for the purpose of determining whether the defendant has benefited from drug-trafficking and, if he has, of assessing the value of his proceeds of drug-trafficking, make the following assumptions, except to the extent that any of the assumptions are shown to be incorrect in the defendant's case."

By section 2(3) those assumptions are:
> "(*a*) that any property appearing to the court—
> > (i) to have been held by him at any time since his conviction, or
> > (ii) to have been transferred to him at any time since the beginning of the period of six years ending when the proceedings were instituted against him,
>
> was received by him, at the earliest time at which he appears to the court to have held it, as a payment or reward in connection with drug-trafficking carried on by him,
> (*b*) that any expenditure of his since the beginning of that period was met out of payments received by him in connection with drug-trafficking carried on by him, and

(c) that, for the purpose of valuing any property received or assumed to have been received by him at any time as such a reward, he received the property free of any other interests in it."

Both subsection (2) and (3) pose difficult problems of construction, but if more thought and a little imagination had been applied to their effect, many of the problems could largely have been avoided. As it is, the courts will no doubt be compelled to construe the two subsections in the context of the policy of the Act, and subject to the fact that the making of a Confiscation Order is a penal sanction.

If the court chooses to make any of the assumptions specified in section 2(3) then (as is apparent from the wording of subsection (3)) they will be made on the basis that the defendant has received a payment or reward in connection with drug-trafficking carried on *by him* and by no-one else.

It is plain from the opening words of subsection (2) that the court is not *obliged* to make the assumptions in question. Subsection (2) is therefore permissive and not mandatory. Although the court must not invoke any of the assumptions capriciously, the circumstances in which the Court of Appeal would be prepared to interfere with the decision of the trial judge in this regard is by no means clear or obvious.

However, by virtue of subsection (2), the trial judge should not make any of the assumptions specified in subsection (3) to the extent that " . . . any of the assumptions are shown to be incorrect in the defendant's case."[63]

These words are not easy to understand. At first sight they seem to imply that the burden of proving an assumption to be incorrect falls on the defendant but, a closer reading of subsection (2) suggests that this need not necessarily be so if the words " . . . the defendant's case"—as the appear in subsection (2)—are treated as being synonymous in meaning with the words "in the case against the defendant." In the ordinary way, a reference to "the defendant's case" may mean one of two things. It may refer to the case presented on behalf of the defendant—for example, by calling evidence as part of the defence case. But, secondly, it may also refer to the entire proceedings against a named defendant. We see an example of the latter employed in section 4(1).[64] Accordingly, it is to be regretted that if Parliament intended to cast the evidential burden on the accused, that the draftsman did not use plainer

---

[63] See s.2(2).

[64] " . . . the amount to be recovered in the defendant's case . . . shall be . . . the value of the defendant's proceeds of drug-trafficking."

language. As it is, when Parliament (in subsection (2)) speaks of an assumption being " . . . shown to be incorrect in the defendant's case" one is left asking "shown by whom"? If Parliament intended to place the burden of proof on the defendant then it would have been very easy for the draftsman simply to have used the words " . . . shown to be incorrect *by the defendant.*" The fact that he did not do so may suggest that it was not Parliament's wish to put a burden of proof upon any particular party at all. This is because the court is *obliged* to follow the steps set out in section 1. Accordingly, unlike any other order, or relief which is made on the application of the party seeking it, the making of a Confiscation Order (in theory) should normally be initiated by the court: see the opening words to section 1(1). If the evidence in the case—no matter who adduces it—shows an assumption to be incorrect, then the court may not make it.

Of course, in practice, it will often be the case that the defendant has no alternative but to shoulder the responsibility of rebutting an assumption if the court is minded, or likely, to make one. Unfortunately, it is not apparent, from the wording of the Act, whether the court is duty bound to indicate, during the proceedings, that it proposes to rely on any of the statutory assumptions or whether it may simply invoke them at the moment of adjudication.

Just as the Act does not expressly deal with the *burden* of proof, so it does not deal with the *standard* of proof. However, given that the making of a Confiscation Order is a penal sanction, and that any assumption made is on the basis that the defendant received a payment or reward in connection with *his* own drug-trafficking, it is reasonable to presume (in the absence of an express provision to the contrary) that the "usual rules" apply, so that a defendant need only prove an issue on the balance of probabilities whereas the Crown must prove any allegation it makes to the much higher standard, namely, that the court feels sure that the allegation is made out.

Unfortunately, the D.T.O.A. does not provide the Crown Court with any statutory guidance or directions as to the form the hearing should take when following the procedural steps in section 1. One presumes that the court must conduct a form of trial, giving both the Prosecution and the defendant an opportunity to call evidence in the traditional, adversarial, way. Because a Confiscation Order is presumably to be treated as a sentence for the purposes of *section 11* of the Criminal Appeal Act 1968 (the Act does not expressly say so) one therefore supposes that the hearing should take the form, (including order of speeches), familiar to criminal law practitioners. Again, it is to be regretted that greater attention was not paid to this aspect of the legislation.

Periods of time embraced by section 2(3)

It was plainly the intention of Parliament that subsection (3) should embrace two very different periods of time. Obviously subsection (3)(a)(ii) relates to the six years ending when the proceedings were "instituted" against the defendant. By section 38(11) proceedings for an offence are instituted in England and Wales:

(a) when a justice of the peace issues a summons or warrant under section 1 of the Magistrates Courts Act 1980 in respect of the offence,

(b) when a person is charged with the offence after being taken into custody without a warrant,

(c) when a bill of indictment is preferred under section 2 of the Administration of Justice (Miscellaneous Provisions) Act 1933 in a case falling within that paragraph (b) or subsection (2) of that section;

and where the application of this subsection would result in there being more than one time for the institution of proceedings, they shall be taken to have been instituted at the earliest of those times.

By contrast, section 2(3)(a)(i) relates to any property appearing to the court " . . . to have been held by him since his conviction . . . ." However, subsection 3(a)(i) is so ambiguously drafted that it may be construed so as to apply either to payments received by the defendant *at any time* in his life, and which he continues to hold since his conviction, or, it only relates to payments received and held by the defendant *after* his conviction.

The ambiguity arises by virtue of the words " . . . held by him . . . " as they appear in subsection (3)(a)(i). In support of the first construction, the argument is that the draftsman did not (as he did in 3(a)(ii)) use the words " . . . transferred to him," or "received by him." Accordingly, it is said that section 2(3)(a)(i) was designed to apply to all property which was received by the defendant, at some time in his life, and which he held at the time of his conviction and subsequently. The prosecution may not be able to show when the defendant actually received the property in question but it may be possible to show when he "held" it and therefore, by section 2(3)(a), the court may assume that the property was received " . . . at the earliest time at which he appears to the court to have held it . . . " and—having made that assumption—that it was a payment or reward in connection with drug-trafficking.

However, if section 2(3)(a)(i) really does catch property received by the defendant at any time, then why did the draftsman use the words " . . . at any time since his conviction . . . "?

The second interpretation of section 2(3)(*a*)(i) is that the court is only entitled to look to property received and held by the defendant literally *since* his conviction. Any assumption made by the court will be on the basis that the proceeds resulted from the defendant's drug-trafficking. As a matter of common sense it will be far more difficult—if not impossible—to rebut an assumption appertaining to payments received or paid before the six year period. Records relating to a business, etc., which would otherwise support the defendant's contention that it was a payment or reward lawfully earnt, may be lost or destroyed. Furthermore, witnesses may no longer be traceable or capable of supporting the legality of a given transaction. Arguably, the statutory assumptions in subsection (3) were therefore intended to embrace only a relatively short period of the defendant's career. Furthermore, the proceeds of drug-trafficking may be invested (for example, abroad) and payments made to the defendant after his conviction for a drug-trafficking offence. For a variety of reasons there may be an appreciable delay between conviction and the making of a Confiscation Order. Since section 2(3)(*a*)(ii) only relates to payments received for a period of six years *ending* when the proceedings were instituted against the defendant, it follows that payments received after conviction would not be caught by that provision. Accordingly, section 2(3)(*a*)(i) was enacted.

Incidentally, for reasons that are inexplicable, payments received and held by the accused while awaiting trial, do not seem to be embraced by any of the assumptions listed in section 2(3).

It is important to remember that the court *must not* make any of the assumptions in section 2(3) if the only offence for which the defendant is to be sentenced is that of assisting a drug trafficker contrary to section 24 of the Act.

Some ramifications of section 2(3)

It will now be evident that the implications of *section 2(3)* are enormous. Even if a defendant is convicted of, say, supplying drugs over a very short period of time the court is entitled (in appropriate cases) to assume that all property transferred to the defendant over the preceding six years (prior to the moment when proceedings were instituted against him) was a payment or reward made in connection with drug-trafficking carried on by the defendant and moreover, that any expenditure made by the defendant over that period, came out of the proceeds of drug-trafficking. It may seem harsh that the courts powers of confiscation run way beyond the limits within which the prosecution are obliged to put their case in relation to any drug-trafficking offence for which the defendant appears to be sentenced. However, where property is proved to have been received by an accused, and where there is no evidence at all to suggest that when he received it, the accused (or the transferor) were engaged in drug-trafficking, then such a lack of evidence may of itself be the best evidence to show that the "assumptions," which the court can make under *section 2(2)*, are incorrect.

Finally, it is important that legal advisers, acting on behalf of defendants accused of drug trafficking offences, should take detailed instructions from their clients in anticipation of proceedings being pursued under the D.T.O.A. 1986.

Statements tendered

Putting the relevant party to "strict proof" of their case will often result in the contents of any statement tendered to the other side not being admitted for a variety of reasons, for example, the statement infringes the hearsay rule. So, where, for example, a prosecutor is in possession of information alleging that on certain dates valuable property was given to the accused, he may seek to embody those allegations in a statement which he can then serve on the defence by way of *section 9* of the Criminal Justice Act 1967, in the hope that the statement will be accepted. In fact, if put to strict proof, the prosecutor might find that he cannot prove the contents at all.

To meet this problem and for the purposes of the D.T.O.A., Parliament has endeavoured to make life a little easier for the prosecutor by imposing certain obligations on the defendant in order to see if a certain amount of "common ground" can be established. Thus, by section 3(1) of the D.T.O.A., where:

"(*a*) there is tendered to the Crown Court by the prosecutor a statement as to any matters relevant to the determination whether the defendant has benefited from the drug-trafficking or to the assessment of the value of his proceeds of drug-trafficking, and

(*b*) the defendant accepts to any extent any allegation in the statement,

the court may, for the purposes of the determination and assessment, treat his acceptance as conclusive of the matters to which it relates."

So far, so good. There is nothing in section 3(1) that is particularly controversial. But where a defendant declines to accept, to any extent, any allegation in the statement then one looks to section 3(2) which provides:

"(2) Where—
  (a) a statement is tendered under subsection (1)(a) above, and
  (b) the court is satisfied that a copy of the statement has been served on the defendant,
the court may require the defendant to indicate to what extent he accepts each allegation in the statement and, so far as he does not accept any such allegation, to indicate any matters he proposes to rely on."

Section 3(2) now asks the court to adopt an inquisitorial role. The defendant may therefore be asked to state those matters (if any) which he proposes to rely on to refute an allegation contained in the statement tendered. The penalty, for a failure to comply with section 3(2), is set out in section 3(3) which provides as follows:

"(3) If the defendant fails in any respect to comply, with a requirement under subsection (2) above he may be treated for the purposes of this section as accepting every allegation in the statement apart from—
  (a) any allegation in respect of which he has complied with the requirement, and
  (b) any allegation that he has benefited from drug trafficking or that any payment or other reward was "received by him in connection with drug trafficking" carried on by him or another."

Although it is obvious from the wording of section 3(3)(b) that the Legislature was not prepared to go so far as to say that a defendant's non-compliance with the requirements of *subsection 2* should be construed as *an admission* that he either benefited from drug-trafficking, or that any payment or reward received by him represents the proceeds of that activity, nevertheless the reality of the situation is that once the prosecution have established that the defendant has received property, it is open to the court to see if it may assume that the payment was received in connection with drug-trafficking by virtue of *section 2(2) and (3)*. The burden of showing that assumption to be incorrect may very well fall upon the defendant: section 2(2).

Suppose that a defendant indicates to the court that he does not accept a particular allegation in a statement tendered and served on him under section 3(2), and suppose that the defendant indicates to the court a number of matters upon which he proposes to rely. Is the court then bound to accept that he has complied with section 3(2) or, may the court (believing that the accused could indicate a great deal more) treat him as having failed to meet the requirements of that subsection? Although any court must be very slow to conclude that an accused has failed to comply with subsection 2, nevertheless, where a defendant is clearly demonstrated to be obstructive or less than forthcoming there exists no good reason why the court should be prevented from treating his conduct as a constructive failure to meet the requirements of subsection 2.

Statement tendered by the defence

Section 3(4) provides where:

"(*a*) there is tendered to the Crown Court by the defendant a statement as to any matters relevant to determining the amount that might be realised at the time the confiscation order is made, and

(*b*) the prosecutor accepts to any extent any allegation in the statement,
the court may, for the purposes of that determination, treat the acceptance by the prosecutor as conclusive of the matters to which it relates."

It will be seen that subsection 4 is limited purely to matters relevant to determining the amount that "might be realised" at the time the confiscation order is made. Unlike section 3(1) to (3) it is not expressed to include matters that are relevant to determining whether the defendant has benefited from drug-trafficking or assessing the value of his proceeds as a result.

So far as both the prosecution and the defence are concerned, an allegation may be accepted or matters may be indicated or relied upon in rebuttal, for the purposes of *section 3*, either "(*a*) orally before the court, or (*b*) in writing in accordance with Crown Court Rules": section 3(5).

Use of admissions in the trial for the offence

Section 3(6) provides an accused with a crucial safeguard, namely that:

"No acceptance by the defendant under this section that any payment or other reward was received by him in connection with drug trafficking carried on by him or another shall be admissible in evidence in any proceedings for an offence."

Thus where, for example, a defendant is accused of supplying drugs over a period of two weeks but he accepts (for the purposes of proceedings under the D.T.O.A.) that he has received property in connection with drug-trafficking over the preceding six years, it is not open to the prosecutor to use that admission to initiate fresh proceedings, or to support the charge alleged, or to support an application to add a count alleging the supplying of drugs over the longer period to which the admission relates.

"Proceeds of drug-trafficking" versus "realisable property"

The amount to be recovered in the defendant's case under a Confiscation Order should (ideally) be the full value of the defendant's proceeds of drug-trafficking: section 4(1). But, where the amount of realisable property is less than the value of his proceeds, then *section 4(3)* imposes an obligation on the curt to confiscate the lesser amount and to issue a certificate giving the court's opinion as to the matters taken into account when determining the amount that might be realised at the time the confiscation order is made *(section 4(2))*. This means that in every case the court is obliged to assess the value of a accused's "realisable property" and to compare that value with the value of the defendant's proceeds of drug-trafficking. After all, in practice, it is only "realisable property" which may effectively be seized and managed by a Receiver appointed under the Act. Accordingly, section 5(3) of the Act provides:

> "For the purposes of sections 3 and 4 of this Act the amount that might be realised at the time of confiscation order is made against the defendant is—
> (a) the total of the values at that time of all the realisable property held by the defendant, less
> (b) where there are obligations having priority at that time, the total amounts payable in pursuance of such obligations,
> together with the total of the values at that time of all gifts caught by this Act."

It follows that the court must add together two distinct valuations. First, the net value of "realistic property" held by the defendant himself and secondly, the total values of all *"gifts"* caught by the Act.

In calculating the defendant's realisable property there must be deducted amounts payable in respect of "obligations having priority." Such obligations are specified in section 5(7):

> "For the purposes of subsection (3) above, an obligation has priority at any time if it is an obligation of the defendant to—
> (a) pay an amount due in respect of a fine, or other order

of a court, imposed or made on conviction or an offence, where the fine was imposed or order made before the confiscation order, or

(b) pay any sum which would be included among the preferential debts (within the meaning given by section 386 of the Insolvency Act 1986) in the defendant's bankruptcy commencing on the date of the confiscation order or winding up under an order of the court made on that date."

What is meant by "realisable property"

Section 5(1) defines "realisable property" in the following terms:

"In this Act, 'realisable property' means, subject to subsection (2) below:

(a) any property held by the defendant and

(b) any property held by a person to whom the defendant has directly or indirectly made a gift caught by this Act."

However, by section 5(2) property is not realisable if:

"(a) an order under section 43 of the Powers of Criminal Courts Act 1973 (deprivation orders),

(b) an order under section 27 of the Misuse of Drugs Act 1971 (forfeiture orders) or,

(c) an order under section 223 or 436 of the Criminal Procedure (Scotland) Act 1975 (forfeiture of property),

is in force in respect of the property."

Section 5(2) enacts the obvious in that property already seized by an order of the Court, albeit under a different enactment, can hardly be seized twice and made the subject of a Confiscation Order.

Property is said to be "held" by any person if he holds any interest in it (section 38(7)) and includes "a reference to property vested in his trustee in bankruptcy; permanent or interim trustee within the meaning of the Bankruptcy (Scotland) Act 1985 or liquidator": see section 38(8).

It would seem that, for the purposes of section 5(1)(a), it is immaterial whether the property was received by the defendant in connection with drug-trafficking or not. This makes good sense since the object of the Act, at this stage of the proceedings is to assess the extent of the defendant's assets and thereby enable the court to recoup illgotten gains even if some or all of those gains had originally been squandered.

Gifts

Different considerations apply in relation to "gifts" as is apparent from the wording of section 5(9)—particularly (9)(b).

Section 5(9) reads:

> "A gift (including a gift made before the commencement of section 1 of this Act) is caught by this Act if:
> (a) it was made by the defendant at any time since the beginning of the period of six years ending when the proceedings were instituted against him, or
> (b) it was made by the defendant at any time and was a gift of property:
> (i) received by the defendant in connection with drug trafficking carried on by him or another, or
> (ii) which in whole or in part directly or indirectly represented in the defendant's hands property received by him in that connection."

It is therefore plain that where it can be shown that the defendant made a gift at *any time* in his career then it will be caught by the Act *if* it was received by him in connection with, or represents the proceeds of, drug-trafficking. No such qualifications or restrictions operate in respect of gifts made by the defendant during the six year period ending when proceedings were instituted against him: see section 5(9)(a). Accordingly, it is submitted that all gifts made by the defendant during the relevant six year period are caught by the Act and it is immaterial whether they represent the proceeds of drug trafficking or not.

It is tempting to construe, section 5(9) in conjunction with the assumptions the court may make pursuant to section 2(2) and (3), but such an approach is liable only to mislead, not least because section 2 and section 5 are concerned with two very different stages in the determination of the making of a Confiscation Order. Section 5 applies only after the court has assessed the value of the defendant's proceeds of drug-trafficking by making, if necessary, any of the statutory assumptions for that purpose.

Most unhelpfully the Act makes no provision for the incidence of the burden or standard of proof for the purposes of section 5(9)(b).

A gift is expressly caught by the Act if it is made by the defendant, but it is not clear what the position would be if the gift was in fact made by a person other than the defendant—for example, by his wife. Presumably where a person can be demonstrated to have acted on behalf of the defendant, then the courts would have little difficulty in holding that the acts performed were in reality those of the defendant himself.

In the ordinary way a "gift" of property relates to a transfer of property, to another, free of any consideration. But the Act anticipated cases where the defendant transfers property to another for a consideration far less than the actual value of the property. Accordingly, section 5(1) provides:

> "For the purposes of this Act—
>
> (a) the circumstances in which the defendant is to be treated as making a gift include those where he transfers property to another person directly or indirectly for a consideration the value of which is significantly less than the value of the consideration provided by the defendant, and
>
> (b) in those circumstances, the preceding provisions of this section shall apply as if the defendant had made a gift of such share in the property as bears to the whole property the same proportion as the difference between the values referred to in paragraph (a) above bears to the value of the consideration provided by the defendant."

It follows that where property is sold to another for a consideration which substantially reflects its true value then the property sold is not realisable. Instead, the Court will look to the payment received by the defendant, as a result of the sale, and confiscate that sum (or the property it represents if it has been converted). Obviously, if the defendant does not invest or re-invest the proceeds of sale but chose to squander the proceeds instead, then the extent of the defendant's "realisable property" is diminished as a result.

By section 38(1), property is transferred by one person to another " . . . if the person transfers or grants to the other any interest in the property."

Valuing the property

The value of property, other than cash, is based on the market value of the property less any debt payable in connection with it, for example, a mortgage. Thus, section 5(4) provides:

> "Subject to the following provisions of this section, for the

purposes of this Act the value of property (other than cash) in relation to any person holding the property:

> (*a*) where any other person holds an interest in the property, is:
>> (i) the market value of the first mentioned person's beneficial interest in the property less
>> (ii) the amount required to discharge any incumbrance (other than a charging order) on that interest, and
> (*b*) in any other case, is its market value."

The Act makes special provision in connection with the valuation of gifts. Obviously, a gift of property made by a defendant in say, 1978, may today cost a great deal more once inflation is taken into account. Accordingly, section 5(5) provides for an adjustment of the value of a gift as follows:

> "Subject to subsection (1) below, references in this Act to the value at any time (referred to in subsection (6) below as "the material time") of a gift caught by this Act or of any payment or reward are references to:
>> (*a*) the value of the gift, payment or reward to the recipient when he received it adjusted to take account of subsequent changes in the value of money, or
>> (*b*) where subsection (6) below applies, the value there mentioned,
> whichever is the greater."

Section 5(6) is concerned with the value of the gift as assessed by the recipient himself. For example, if an antique vase (being the proceeds of drug-trafficking) is sold to the recipient for £1,200 when, in fact, according to expert opinion it was only worth £800, the Act takes the higher figure as representing the value of the gift. Section 5(6) reads as follows:

> "Subject to subsection (10) below, if at the material time the recipient holds:
>> (*a*) the property which received (not being cash) or
>> (*b*) property which, in whole or in part, directly or indirectly represents in his hands the property which he received,
> the value referred to in subsection (5)(*b*) above is the value to him at the material time of the property mentioned in paragraph (*a*) above or, as the case may be, of the property mentioned in paragraph (*b*) above so far as it so represents the property which he received, but disregarding in either case any charging order."

As we have seen, the defendant may transfer property for a consideration significantly less than its actual value. The Act will treat that transfer as a gift: section 5(10)(*a*). Obviously the property, once in the hands of the recipient may increase in value. Therefore, by section 5(10)(*b*) the value of the property so transferred is calculated as follows:

> "In those circumstances, the preceding provisions of this section shall apply as if the defendant had made a gift of such share in the property as bears to the whole property the same proportion as the difference between the values referred to in paragraph (*a*) above bears to the value of the consideration provided by the defendant."

Suppose for example that D transfers property to X for a consideration of £1,000. The property was actually worth £10,000. By section 5(10)(*b*) the original value of the gift transferred was £9,000 in the ratio of 1:9. If, when the confiscation order is made, the property is then worth £100,000 the value of the gift is in the proportion of 1:9 *i.e.* £90,000.

ENFORCING A CONFISCATION ORDER

Broadly stated there are two ways in which a Confiscation Order may be enforced. The first method is by treating such an order as a fine. A defendant who is tempted not to pay the fine faces the prospect of facing a consecutive sentence of imprisonment in default. The second method is by the appointment of a Receiver who will (if necessary) seize, realise and manage the defendant's realisable property.

Treating the confiscation order as a fine

Section 6(1) clearly sets out the general principles to be applied and lists the terms of imprisonment to be served in default of payment (in excess of £10,000) as follows:

> "Where the Crown Court orders the defendant to pay any amount under section 1 of this Act, sections 31(1) to (3C) and 32(1) and (2) of the Powers of Criminal Courts Act 1973 (powers of Crown Court in relation to fines and enforcement of Crown Court fines) shall have effect as if—
> > (*a*) that amount were a fine imposed on him by the Crown Court, and
> > (*b*) in the Table in section 31(3A) (imprisonment in

default), for entry relating to an amount exceeding
£10,000 there were substituted—

"An amount exceeding £10,000
but not exceeding £20,000 .... 12 months
An amount exceeding £20,000
but not exceeding £50,000 .... 18 months
An amount exceeding £50,000
but not exceeding £100,000 .... 2 years
An amount exceeding £100,000
but not exceeding £250,000 .... 3 years
An amount exceeding £250,000
but not exceeding £1 million .... 5 years
An amount exceeding £1 million .... 10 years."

By *section 6(2)*, a term of imprisonment (or detention) ordered
to be served in default of payment, shall run *after* the defendant
has served any sentences of imprisonment which were imposed in
respect of the offences for which he appeared for sentence at the
Crown Court.

Thus, section 6(2) provides:

"Where:
    (*a*) a warrant of commitment is issued for a default in pay-
        ment of an amount ordered to be paid under section 1
        of this Act in respect of an offence or offences, and
    (*b*) at the time the warrant is issued, the defendant is liable
        to serve a term of custody in respect of the offence or
        offences,
the term of imprisonment or of detention under section 9 of
the Criminal Justice Act 1982 (detention of persons aged 17 to
20 for default) to be served in default of payment of the
amount shall not begin to run until after the term mentioned
in paragraph (*b*) above."

By section 6(3):

"The reference in subsection (2) above to the term of custody
which the defendant is liable to serve in respect of the offence
or offences is a reference to the term of imprisonment, youth
custody or detention under section 4 or 9 of the said Act of
1982 which he is liable to serve in respect of the offence or
offences; and for the purposes of this subsection:
    (*a*) consecutive terms and terms which are wholly or partly
        concurrent shall be treated as a single term, and
    (*b*) there shall be disregarded:
        (i) any sentence suspended under section 22(1) of the

said Act of 1973 which has not taken effect at the time the warrant is issued,

(ii) in the case of a sentence of imprisonment passed with an order under section 47(1) of the Criminal Law Act 1977, any part of the sentence which the defendant has not at that time been required to serve in prison, and

(iii) any term of imprisonment or detention fixed under section 31(2) of the said Act of 1973 for which a warrant of commitment has not been issued at that time."

One interesting point is whether the words "offence or offences" in *section 6(2)* refers only to "drug-trafficking offences." Suppose D appears before the Crown Court to be sentenced in respect of an offence of supplying drugs over a period of one month (count 1) and an offence of robbery (count 2). He is sentenced to three years imprisonment on count 1 and six years imprisonment on count 2; both sentences to run concurrently. A Confiscation Order is made in the sum of £12,000. By *section 6(1)*, a term of 12 months imprisonment is ordered to be served in default. D does default. Does the term of 12 months imprisonment run after the sentence in respect of count 1 is served (being a "drug-trafficking offence"), or, after the total sentence of six years imprisonment, in respect of both offences, is served?

The point is not free from difficulty but when section 6(2) and (3) speak of "the offence" or "offences" this can only be a reference to the offence or offences in respect of which the Confiscation Order is made under section 1, *i.e.* "drug-trafficking offences" (and see section 6(2)(*a*)). Accordingly, it is submitted that a sentence in default must run consecutively to any term of imprisonment imposed in respect of the drug-trafficking offence or offences.

Appointment and powers of a receiver

In summary, once a Confiscation Order has been made which is not subject to appeal and which has not been satisfied, the High Court may, on the application of the Prosecutor, appoint a receiver[65] to realise any realisable property[66] with a view of satisfying the Confiscation Order[67] and to apply the property so realised

[65] Section 11(2).
[66] Section 11(5).
[67] Section 13(2).

on the defendant's behalf towards the satisfaction of the order.[68]
A reasonable opportunity must be given for persons holding any
interest in the property to make representations to the court.[69]
Sums remaining in the hands of the receiver after the satisfaction
of a Confiscation Order must be distributed among the holders of
property in such proportions as the court shall direct.[70]

Powers conferred on a Receiver are set out (in so far as they are
material) in section 12 of the Act which provides:

"(1) Where:
    (a) in proceedings instituted for a drug-trafficking offence,
        a confiscation order is made,
    (b) the order is not subject to appeal, and
    (c) the proceedings have not been concluded,
the High Court may, on an application by the prosecutor, exercise the powers conferred by subsections (2) and (6) below.
(2) The court may appoint a receiver in respect of realisable
property.
(4) The court may order any person having possession of realisable property to give possession of it to any such receiver.
(5) The court may empower any such receiver to realise any
realisable property in such manner as the court may direct.
(6) The court may order any person holding an interest in realisable property to make such payment of the receiver in respect of
any beneficial interest held by the defendant or, as the case may
be, the recipient of a gift caught by this Act as the court may
direct and the court may, on the payment being made, by order
transfer, grant or extinguish any interest in the property.
(7) Subsections (4) to (6) above do not apply to property for the
time being subject to a charge under section 9 of this Act.
(8) The court shall not in respect of any property exercise the
powers conferred by subsection (3)(a), (5) or (6) above unless a
reasonable opportunity has been given for persons holding any
interest in the property to make representations to the court."

It must be noted that the section 11(1)(b) a Receiver cannot be
appointed if the order is subject to appeal. An order is expressed,
pursuant to section 38(13), to be subject to appeal:

" . . . so long as an appeal or further appeal is pending against
the order or (if it was made on a conviction) against the conviction; and for this purpose an appeal or further appeal shall
be treated as pending (where one is competent but has not

---

[68] Section 12(1).
[69] Section 11(8).
[70] Section 12(2).

been brought) until the expiration of the time for bringing that appeal."

Again, by section 11(*c*), a Receiver can only be appointed if "proceedings have not been concluded." By section 38(12) proceedings in England and Wales for an offence are concluded on the occurrence of one of the following events:

"(*a*) the discontinuance of the proceedings;
(*b*) the acquittal of the defendant;
(*c*) the quashing of his conviction for the offence;
(*d*) the grant of Her Majesty's pardon in respect of his conviction for the offence;
(*e*) the court sentencing or otherwise dealing with him in respect of his conviction for the offence without having made a confiscation order; and
(*f*) the satisfaction of a confiscation order made in the proceedings (whether by payment of the amount due under the order or by the defendant serving imprisonment in default)."

The Powers of the High Court or the Receiver must be exercised within the framework set out in section 13 which (in so far as it is material) provides:

"(2) Subject to the following provisions of this section, the powers shall be exercised with a view to making available for satisfying the confiscation order or, as the case may be, any confiscation order that may be made in the defendant's case the value for the time being of realisable property, held by any person by the realisation of such property.
(3) In the case of realisable property held by a person to whom the defendant has directly or indirectly made a gift caught by this Act, the powers shall be exercised with a view to realising no more than the value for the time being of the gift.
(4) The powers shall be exercised with a view to allowing any person other than the defendant or the recipient of any such gift to retain or recover the value of any property held by him.
(5) An order may be made or other action taken in respect of a debt owed by the Crown.
(6) In exercising those powers, no account shall be taken of any obligations of the defendant or of the recipient of any such gift which conflict with the obligation to satisfy the confiscation order."

It will be seen that the principal object is to satisfy the Confiscation Order notwithstanding any obligation which the defendant or the recipient may have which conflicts with the satisfaction of the order.[70a]

The application of proceeds of realisation

The Application of proceeds of realisation and other sums is explained in section 12 which provides:

"(1) Subject to subsection (2) below, the following sums in the hands of a receiver appointed under section 8 or 11 of this Act or in pursuance of a charging order, that is
- (a) the proceeds of the enforcement of any charge imposed under section 9 of this Act,
- (b) the proceeds of the realisation, other than by the enforcement of such a charge, of any property under section 8 or 11 of this Act, and
- (c) any other sums, being property held by the defendant, shall, after such payments (if any) as the High Court may direct have been made out of those sums, be applied on the defendant's behalf towards the satisfaction of the confiscation order.

(2) If, after the amount payable under the confiscation order has been fully paid, any such sums remain in the hands of such a receiver, the receiver shall distribute those sums:
- (a) among such of those who held property which has been realised under this Act, and
- (b) in such proportions,

as the High Court may direct after giving a reasonable opportunity for such persons to make representations to the court.

(3) The receipt of any sum by a justices' clerk on account of an amount payable under a confiscation order shall reduce the amount so payable, but the sum shall be applied as follows:
- (a) if paid by a receiver under subsection (1) above, it shall first be applied in payment of his remuneration and expenses,
- (b) subject to paragraph (a) above, it shall be applied in reimbursement of any sums paid by the prosecutor under section 18(2) of this Act,

and the balance shall be treated for the purposes of section 61 of the Justices of the Peace Act 1979 (application of fines, etc.) as if it were a fine imposed by a magistrate's court.

In this subsection, 'justices' clerk' has the same meaning as in the Justices of the Peace Act 1979."

The provisions of section 12 are largely self explanatory.

[70a] See *In Re P*, *The Times*, April 26, 1988.

Expenses incurred by the Receiver will be met out of realised property.

Variation of a confiscation order

A variation of a Confiscation Order is to be carefully distinguished from an appeal against the making of an order. Where a defendant complains that the court erred in the determination of the order, for example, in the assessment of his proceeds of drug-trafficking, then his appropriate course is to appeal against the making of the order because such an order is a sentence for the purposes of section 11 of the Criminal Appeal Act 1968.

However, a variation of a Confiscation Order under the Act, is confined to a reduction in the amount of the order in cases where the defendant's realisable property is inadequate to satisfy the making of an order. Thus section 14(1) provides:

> "If, on an application by the defendant in respect of a confiscation order, the High Court is satisfied that the realisable property is inadequate for the payment of any amount remaining to be recovered under the order the court shall issue a certificate to that effect, giving the court's reasons."

Note that the High Court can do no more than to issue a Certificate and to give its reasons for so doing. It cannot vary the order under section 14. Clearly if the defendant has been adjudged bankrupt then the court must take into account the extent to which his property will be distributed among his creditors. The court must also guard against the manipulative defendant who has taken steps to prevent the court seizing his assets. To this end, section 14(2) provides:

> "For the purposes of subsection (1) above:
> (a) in the case of realisable property held by a person who has been adjudged bankrupt or whose estate has been sequestrated the court shall take into account the extent to which any property held by him may be distributed among creditors, and
> (b) the court may disregard any inadequacy in the realisable property which appears to the court to be attributable wholly or partly to anything done by the defendant for the purpose of preserving any property held by a person to whom the defendant had directly or indirectly made a gift caught by this Act from any risk of realisation under this Act."

By section 14(3), where a Certificate has been issued under sub-section (1), the defendant " . . . may apply to the Crown Court for the amount to be recovered under the order to be reduced."

The powers of the Crown Court are expressed, by section 14(4) to be as follows:

> "The Crown Court shall, on an application under section (3) above:
> (a) substitute for the amount to be recovered under the order such lesser amount as the court thinks just in all the circumstances of the case, and
> (b) substitute for the term of imprisonment or of detention fixed under subsection (2) of section 31 of the Powers of Criminal Courts Act 1973 in respect of the amount to be recovered under the order a shorter term determined in accordance with that section (as it has effect by virtue of section 6 of this Act) in respect of the lesser amount."

It would seem that the Crown Court is obliged to substitute a lesser amount although the actual figure is entirely a matter for the court to decide. Even if the High Court were to quantify the amount by which the realisable property is inadequate to satisfy the order, the Crown Court is not obliged to vary the order to that extent but must substitute a lesser amount " . . . as the court thinks just in all the circumstances of the case . . . "

Nothing in section 14 requires the prosecution to be put on notice of an application under that section which, presumably, may therefore be made *ex parte*. However, it is difficult to imagine many applications proceeding on that basis and it is submitted that the appropriate course is for the prosecutor to be notified.

RESTRAINT ORDERS

In order to prevent any person (not just the defendant) dealing with, or disposing of property, which may be made the subject of a Confiscation Order when the defendant appears before the Crown Court to be sentenced in respect of one or more drug-trafficking offences, the Prosecutor may apply to the High Court (*ex parte* if necessary) for a "Restraint Order" under section 8(1) as follows:

> "The High Court may by order (in this Act referred to as a 'restraint order') prohibit any person from dealing with any realisable property, subject to such conditions and exceptions as may be specified in the order."

By section 8(7) "dealing with property held by any person includes":

> "For the purposes of this section, dealing with property held by any person includes (without prejudice to the generality of the expression):
> (*a*) where a debt is owed to that person, making a payment to any person in reduction of the amount of the debt, and
> (*b*) removing the property from Great Britain."

Powers conferred on the High Court in connection with the making of a Restraint Order (or Charging Order) are exercisable under section 7(1) if:

> "(*a*) proceedings have been instituted in England and Wales against the defendant for a drug-trafficking offence,
> (*b*) the proceedings have not been concluded,
> (*c*) the court is satisfied that there is reasonable cause to believe that the defendant has benefited from drug-trafficking."

The same powers are exercisable even if proceedings have not yet been instituted against a person but the court is satisfied, by section 7(2) that:

> "Those powers are also exercisable where the court is satisfied:
> (*a*) that an information is to be laid under section 1 of the Magistrates' Courts Act 1980 that a person has or is suspected of having committed a drug-trafficking offence, and
> (*b*) that there is reasonable cause to believe that he has benefited from drug-trafficking."

Where a Restraint Order (or Charging Order under section 9) has been made by virtue of section 7(2), the Court shall discharge the order if " . . . the proposed proceedings are not instituted within such time as the court considers reasonable": *per* section 7(4). In all other cases where a Restraint Order is made, the High Court may discharge it, or vary it, in respect to any property and it must be discharged when the "proceedings for the offences are concluded": see section 8(5). By section 38(12)(*b*) this would include the acquittal of the defendant, but the wording of section 8 makes it clear that the Crown Court has no power to discharge the Restraint Order upon his acquittal—only the High Court may do so.

By section 8(4) a Restraint Order may be made only on an application by the prosecutor[71] and although it may be made by an *ex parte* application to a judge in chambers[72] notice must be given to persons affected by the order.[73]

A Restraint Order may apply to all realisable property held by a "specified person" whether the property is described in the order or not.[74] Furthermore, a Restraint Order may apply to realisable property held by a person specified in the order being property which has been transferred to him after the making of the order.[75]

Once the High Court has made a Restraint Order a police constable may seize the property in order to prevent any realisable property being removed from Great Britain[76] and it shall be dealt with in accordance with the court's directions.[77]

Clearly, it will often be desirable—particularly in complicated cases where assets are not easily seized—to employ the services of a Receiver. Accordingly, section 8(6) provides:

> "Where the High Court has made a restraint order, the court may at any time appoint a receiver:
> (*a*) to take possession of any realisable property, and
> (*b*) in accordance with the court's directions, to manage or otherwise deal with any property in respect of which he is appointed,
> subject to such exceptions and conditions as may be specified by the court; and may require any person having possession of property in respect of which a receiver is appointed under this section to give possession of it to the receiver."

In cases where a Receiver has been appointed under this section, the court must exercise its powers in accordance with the provisions of section 11 (Realisation of Property); and section 12 (Application of Proceeds of Realisation), and section 13 (Exercise of powers of High Court or Receiver). Each of those sections have been quoted above (in so far as they are material) save for section 11(3) which provides:

> "The court may empower a receiver appointed under subsection (2) above, under section 8 of this Act or in pursuance of a charging order:

[71] Section 8(4)(*a*).
[72] Section 8(4)(*b*).
[73] Section 8(4)(*c*).
[74] Section 8(2)(*a*).
[75] Section 8(2)(*b*).
[76] Section 8(8).
[77] Section 8(9).

(*a*) to enforce any charge imposed under section 9 of this Act on realisable property or on interest or dividends payable in respect of such property, and

(*b*) in relation to any realisable property other than property for the time being subject to a charge under section 9 of this Act, to take possession of the property subject to such conditions or exceptions as may be specified by the court."

CHARGING ORDERS

Where a person is about to be charged, or has been charged, in connection with a drugs trafficking offence, the High Court upon the application of the prosecutor (*ex parte* if necessary) may make a Charging Order under section 9 in respect of certain assets (chiefly land, securities and trusts) held by, or on behalf of that person. The powers exercisable by the Court, under section 9 must comply with the requirements of sections 11, 12 and 13 cited above.

By section 9(2), a "Charging Order" is defined as:

" . . . an order made under this section imposing on any such realisable property as may be specified in the order a charge for securing the payment of money to the Crown."

It may only be made on an application by the prosecutor[78] and may be made as an *ex parte* application to a judge in chambers.[79]

Not all assets may be the subject of a Charging Order. Indeed by section 9(4) and subject to subsection (6), a charge may be imposed by a charging order only on:

"(*a*) any interest in realisable property, being an interest held beneficially by the defendant or by a person to whom the defendant has directly or indirectly made a gift caught by this Act

(i) in any asset of a kind mentioned in subsection (5) below, or

(ii) under any trust, or

(*b*) any interest in realisable property held by a person as trustee of a trust if the interest is in such an asset or is an interest under another trust and a charge may by virtue of paragraph (*a*) above be imposed by a charging order on the whole beneficial interest under the first-mentioned trust."

[78] Section 9(3)(*a*).
[79] Section 9(3)(*b*).

The assets referred to in subsection (4) are expressed by section 9(5) to be

"(a) land in England and Wales, or
(b) securities of any of the following kinds:
    (i) government stock,
    (ii) stock of any body (other than a building society) incorporated within England Wales,
    (iii) stock of any body incorporated outside England and Wales or of any country or territory outside the United Kingdom, being stock registered in a register of the unit holders is kept at any place within England and Wales,
    (iv) units of any unit trust in respect of which a register of the unit holders is kept at any place within England and Wales."

The Secretary of State may amend this list: see section 10(6).

Section 9(6) allows the High Court to extend the charge to include any interest or dividend payable in respect of the assets listed in subsection 5(b).

A Charging Order may be made absolutely or it may be made subject to various conditions of notification so that a person who holds an interest in the affected property is notified that the property is subject to a Charging Order, or he is notified as to the time when the charge is to become enforceable see section 10(1).

The High Court may discharge or vary the Charging Order and it must do so if either the proceedings for the offence are concluded or if the value of the amount secured by the charge is paid into court: section 9(7). Where a Charging Order has been protected by an entry registered under the Land Charges Act 1972 or the Land Registration Act 1925 an order, discharging the Charging Order under section 9(7), may direct that the registered entry be cancelled: section 10(5).

Protection of receivers

Section 18 provides:

"Where a receiver appointed under section 8 or 11 of this Act or in pursuance of a charging order takes any action:
    (a) in relation to property which is not realisable property, being action which he would be entitled to take if it were such property,
    (b) believing, and having reasonable grounds for believing, that he is entitled to take that action in relation to that property,

he shall not be liable to any person in respect of any loss or damage resulting from his action except in so far as the loss or damage is caused by his negligence.

(2) Any amount due in respect of the remuneration and expenses of a receiver so appointed shall, if no sum is available to be applied in payment of it under section 12(3)(*a*) of this Act, be paid by the prosecutor or, in a case where proceedings for a drug-trafficking offence are not instituted, by the person on whose application the receiver was appointed."

Compensation

Where persons hold realisable property in connection with proceedings instituted against any person which do not result in his conviction, it is open to them to apply for compensation under section 19 which, by subsection (1) provides:

"(1) If proceedings are instituted against a person for a drug-trafficking offence or offences and either:
  (*a*) the proceedings do not result in his conviction for any drug trafficking offence, or
  (*b*) where he is convicted of one or more drug-trafficking offences:
      (i) the conviction or convictions concerned are quashed (and no conviction for any drug-trafficking offence is substituted), or
      (ii) he is pardoned by Her Majesty in respect of the conviction or convictions concerned,
the High Court may, on an application by a person who held property which was realisable property, order compensation to be paid to the applicant."

However, quite considerable hurdles are placed in the path of the party seeking compensation under this section. Thus, by section 19(2):

"The High Court shall not order compensation to be paid in any case unless the court is satisfied:
  (*a*) that there has been some serious default on the part of a person concerned in the investigation or prosecution of the offence or offences concerned, being a person mentioned in subsection (4) below, and that, but for that default, the proceedings would not have been instituted or continued, and
  (*b*) that the applicant has suffered substantial loss in consequence of anything done in relation to the property by or in pursuance or:

  (i) an order of the High Court under section 8 to 11 of this Act, or

  (ii) an order of the Court of Session under section 20, 21 or 22 of this Act."

The persons, mentioned in subsection (2)(*a*), are mentioned in section 19(4):

"Compensation payable under this section shall be paid:

 (*a*) where the person in default was or was acting as a member of a police force out of the police fund out of which the expenses of that police force are met,

 (*b*) where the person in default was a member of the Crown Prosecution Service or acting on behalf of the service, by the Director of Prosecutions, and

 (*c*) where the person in default was an officer within the meaning of the Customs and Excise Management Act 1979 by the Commissioners of Customs and Excise."

By subsection (3) the amount of compensation payable under section 19 "shall be such as the High Court thinks just in all the circumstances of the case."

Given the wording of subsection (2) it follows that very few cases are likely to succeed under this section. Proving some serious default on the part of a person concerned in the investigation, or prosecution, is difficult enough but establishing that the proceedings would not have been instituted or continued had it not been for that default, is unlikely to be successful in all but the rarest and clearest of cases. Furthermore, the Act provides no guidance as to what is meant by "substantial loss."

OFFENCES UNDER THE ACT

Assisting drug traffickers

By section 24(1) and (2):

"(1) Subject to subsection (3) below, if a person enters into or is otherwise concerned in an arrangement whereby:

 (*a*) the retention or control by or on behalf of another (call him "A") of A's proceeds of drug trafficking is facilitated (whether by concealment removal from the jurisdiction, transfer to nominees or otherwise), or

 (*b*) A's proceeds of drug trafficking:

  (i) are used to secure that funds are placed at A's disposal, or

  (ii) are used for A's benefit to acquire property by way of investment, knowing or suspecting that A is a person who carries on or has carried on drug-trafficking or has benefited from drug-trafficking, he is guilty of an offence.

(2) In this section, references to any person's proceeds of drug-trafficking include a reference to any property which in whole or in part directly or indirectly represented in his hands his proceeds of drug-trafficking."

The offence is designed to prohibit the "laundering" of drug money. It is triable either way and punishable on conviction on Indictment, to imprisonment for a term not exceeding 14 years or to a fine or to both (section 24(5)(*a*)) and, on summary conviction, to a term of imprisonment not exceeding six months or to a fine not exceeding the statutory maximum or to both (section 24(5)(*b*)). An offence under section 24 is expressed, by subsection (6), to fall within Part II of Schedule 1 to the Criminal Justice Act 1982 so that offenders will not be eligible for early release. It is also a "serious arrestable offence" for the purposes of section 116 of P.A.C.E. 1984: see section 36.

The *mens rea* of the offence is either knowing or suspecting that "A" is a person who carries on, or has carried on drug-trafficking, or has benefited from someone elses drug-trafficking. However, it is not necessary for the prosecution to prove that the defendant knew or suspected that he had entered into, or was otherwise concerned in, any of the arrangements specified in subsection (1). Instead, the Legislature has shifted the burden of proof to the accused to prove, by section 24(4):

"(*a*) that he did not know or suspect that the arrangement related to any person's proceeds of drug-trafficking, or

(*b*) that he did not know or suspect that by the arrangement the retention or control by or on behalf of A of any property was facilitated or, as the case may be, that by the arrangement any property was used as mentioned in subsection (1) above, or

(*c*) that:

    (i) he intended to disclose to a constable such a suspicion, belief or matter as is mentioned in subsection (3) above in relation to the arrangement, but

    (ii) there is reasonable excuse for his failure to make disclosure in accordance with subsection (3)(*b*) above."

Not only does the Act prohibit the laundering of drug monies, it also seeks to encourage the relaying of information to the police concerning the movement of monies even if that information was originally given to a party who was contractually bound to treat is as confidential.

Thus, section 24(3) provides:

> "Where a person discloses to a constable a suspicion or belief that any funds or investments are derived from or used in connection with drug-trafficking or any matter on which such a suspicion or belief is based:
>
> (a) the disclosure shall not be treated as a breach of any restriction upon the disclosure of information imposed by contract, and
>
> (b) if he does any act in contravention of subsection (1) above and the disclosure relates to the arrangement concerned, he does not commit an offence under this section if the disclosure is made in accordance with this paragraph that is:
>
> > (i) it is made before he does the act concerned, being an act done with the consent of the constable, or
> >
> > (ii) it is made after he does the act, but is made on his initiative and as soon as it is reasonable for him to make it."

Accordingly, a banker who holds money on behalf of A, suspecting that A has benefited from drug-trafficking will not be in breach of contract if he disclosure his suspicion to a constable[80] and he will be protected by the provisions of subsection (3)(b)(i) or (3)(b)(ii). Solicitors representing alleged drugtraffickers may find that they are put in a similarly difficult position.

It should be noted that the expression "drug-trafficking" is a term of art defined by section 38(1) to mean:

> "doing or being concerned in any of the following, whether in England and Wales or elsewhere:
>
> (a) producing or supplying a controlled drug where the production or supply contravenes section 4(1) of the Misuse of Drugs Act 1971 or a corresponding law;
>
> (b) transporting or storing a controlled drug where possession of the drug contravenes section 5(1) of that Act or a corresponding law;
>
> (c) importing or exporting a controlled drug where the importation or exportation is prohibited by section 3(1) of that Act or a corresponding law;
>
> and includes a person doing the following, whether in England and Wales or elsewhere, that is entering into or being otherwise concerned in an arrangement whereby:

[80] Section 24(3)(a).

(i) the retention or control by or on behalf of another person of the other person's proceeds of drug-trafficking is facilitated, or

(ii) the proceeds of drug trafficking by another person are used to secure that funds are placed at the other person's disposal or are used for the other person's benefit to acquire property by way of investment."

Accordingly, "drug-trafficking" is to be carefully distinguished from a "drug-trafficking offence" which is as defined in section 38(1).

Offence of prejudicing an investigation

Section 32(1) provides:

"(1) Where, in relation to an investigation into drug-trafficking, an order under section 27 of this Act has been made or has been applied for and has not been refused or a warrant under section 28 of this Act has been issued, a person who, knowing or suspecting that the investigation is taking place, makes any disclosure which is likely to prejudice the investigation is guilty of an offence."

Section 27 (considered below) is concerned with the making of material available to a constable or an officer of customs and excise relevant to an investigation into drug-trafficking.

An offence under section 31 can only be committed if an order under section 27 has been made or applied for, or a warrant (authorising a search) under section 28 has been issued. The prosecution must prove that the accused knew or suspected that the investigation is taking place, but it is not necessary for the prosecution to prove either that he knew or suspected that any of the steps mentioned in section 31(1) had in fact been taken, or that he knew or suspected that the disclosure was likely to prejudice the investigation.

By section 31(2):

"In proceedings against a person for an offence under this section, it is a defence to prove:

(a) that he did not know or suspect that the disclosure was likely to prejudice the investigation, or

(b) that he had lawful authority or reasonable excuse for making the disclosure."

An offence under section 31 is triable either way and punishable on indictment to imprisonment for a term not exceeding five years or to a fine or to both (section 31(3)(*a*)) and, on summary conviction, to a term of imprisonment not exceeding six months or to a fine not exceeding the statutory maximum or to both (section 31(3)(*b*)). The offence is not a "drug-trafficking offence" within the meaning of section 38(1) but is an arrestable offence for the purposes of the Police and Criminal Evidence Act 1984.

INVESTIGATIONS INTO DRUG-TRAFFICKING

Notwithstanding the fact that the police or the customs and excise may have insufficient evidence to arrest (let alone charge) an individual in connection with a drugs trafficking offence, nevertheless, by section 27(1) a constable (or, in Scotland, the procurator fiscal) may for the purpose of an investigation into drug-trafficking, apply to a Circuit Judge (or, in Scotland, the sheriff) for an order under section 27(2) requiring the person who appears to be in possession of particular material, or material of a particular description, to *either* produce it to a constable for him to take away, *or* to give a constable access to it for a period of seven days unless a longer or shorter period is deemed to be appropriate by order of the court: see section 27(3).

Thus, section 27(1), (2) and (3) provide as follows:

"(1) A constable or, in Scotland, the procurator fiscal may, for the purpose of an investigation into drug-trafficking, apply to a Circuit Judge or, in Scotland, to the sheriff for an order under subsection (2) below in relation to particular material or material of a particular description.

(2) If on such an application the judge or, as the case may be, the sheriff is satisfied that the conditions in subsection (4) below are fulfilled, he may make an order that the person who appears to him to be in possession of the material to which the application relates shall:

(*a*) produce it to a constable for him to take away, or
(*b*) give a constable access to it,

within such period as the order may specify.

This subsection is subject to section 30(11) of this Act.

(3) The period to be specified in an order under subsection (2) above shall be seven days unless it appears to the judge or, as the case may be, the sheriff that a longer or shorter period would be appropriate in the particular circumstances of the application."

Section 30(11) of the Act is concerned with the disclosure of information held by government departments. Accordingly, by section 30(11) an order granted under section 27(2) may require an officer of the department (whether named in the order or not) to comply with the order, and "such an order shall be served as if the proceedings were civil proceedings against the defendant."

No order may be made under section 27(1) unless the conditions in subsection (4) are fulfilled. These are:

"(a) that there are reasonable grounds for suspecting that a specified person has carried on or has benefited from drug-trafficking,

(b) that there are reasonable grounds for suspecting that the material to which the application relates:
  (i) is likely to be of substantial value (whether by itself or together with other material) to the investigation for the purpose of which the application is made, and
  (ii) does not consist of or include items subject to legal privilege or excluded material, and

(c) that there are reasonable grounds for believing that it is in the public interest, having regard:
  (i) to the benefit likely to accrue to the investigation if the material is obtained, and
  (ii) to the circumstances under which the person in possession of the material holds its,

that the material should be produced or that access to it should be given."

It will be noted that the order may be made against any individual (named in the order) who appears to be in possession of the material to which the application relates: see section 27(2). It is not necessary to show that he is suspected of having benefited from drug-trafficking or that he is suspected of having committed any offence. An order of a Circuit Judge under section 27 will have effect as if it were an order of the Crown Court (section 27(7)).

By section 27(9)(a) an order under subsection (2) shall " . . . not confer any right to production of, or access to, items subject to legal privilege or excluded material." "Items subject to legal privilege" and "excluded material" have the same meanings as in the Police and Criminal Evidence Act 1984: see section 29(2).

Thus, by section 10 of P.A.C.E. 1984:

"(1) Subject to subsection (2) below, in this Act "items subject to legal privilege" means:
  (a) communications between a professional legal adviser and his client or any person representing his client made in connection with the giving of legal advice to the client;

   (*b*) communications between a professional legal adviser and his client or any person representing his client or between such an adviser or his client or any such representative and any other person made in connection with or in contemplation of legal proceedings and for the purposes of such proceedings; and

   (*c*) items enclosed with or referred to in such communications and made:

      (i) in connection with the giving of legal advise; or

      (ii) in connection with or in contemplation of legal proceedings and for the purposes of such proceedings,

when they are in the possession of a person who is entitled to possession of them.

(2) Items held with the intention of furthering a criminal purpose are not items subject to legal privilege."

So far as "excluded material" is concerned, section 11 of P.A.C.E. 1984 reads:

"(1) Subject to the following provisions of this section, in this Act 'excluded material' means:

   (*a*) personal records which a person has acquired or created in the court of any trade, business, profession or other occupation or for the purposes of any paid or unpaid office and which he holds in confidence;

   (*b*) human tissue or tissue fluid which has been taken for the purposes of diagnosis or medical treatment and which a person holds in confidence;

   (*c*) journalistic material which a person holds in confidence and which consists:

      (i) of documents; or

      (ii) of records other than documents.

(2) A person holds material other than journalistic material in confidence for the purposes of this section if he holds it subject;

   (*a*) to an express or implied undertaking to hold it in confidence; or

   (*b*) to a restriction on disclosure or an obligation of secrecy contained in any enactment, including an enactment contained in an Act passed after this Act.

(3) A person holds journalistic material in confidence for the purposes of this section if:

   (*a*) he holds it subject to such an undertaking, restriction or obligation; and

   (*b*) it has been continuously held (by one or more persons) subject to such an undertaking, restriction or obligation since it was first acquired or created for the purposes of journalism."

"Journalistic material" as it appears in P.A.C.E. means, by section 13 of that Act:

"(1) Subject to subsection (2) below, in this Act "journalistic material" means material acquired or created for the purposes of journalism.
(2) Material is only journalistic material for the purposes of this Act if it is in the possession of a person who acquired or created it for the purposes of journalism.
(3) A person who receives material from someone who intends that the recipient shall use it for the purposes of journalism is to be taken to have acquired it for those purposes."

An important decision of the Divisional Court (but unfortunately only briefly reported as a "news item" in *The Times* on December 22, 1987) resulted in a ruling that solicitors, holding clients' documents which may be of evidential value in a criminal investigation, could not lawfully withhold that information from police on the basis of a solicitor-client relationship. Accordingly, Lord Justice Lloyd sitting with Mr Justice Macpherson ruled that a firm of Solicitors were compelled to comply with an order to produce files in connection with the sale of a house which the police suspected was purchased from the proceeds of drug-trafficking.

An order under section 27(2) will override any obligation as to secrecy or other restriction upon the disclosure of information imposed by statute or otherwise (section 27(9)(*b*)) and may be made in relation to material in the possession of an authorised government department (section 27(9)(*c*)).

Where the material to which an application under section 27(2) relates, consists of information contained in a computer then, the data must be produced in a form in which it can be taken away and which it is both visible and legible: section 27(8).

Where an order is made under section 27(2)(*b*) then the constable (or Procurator Fiscal) may order any person who appears to the court to be entitled to grant entry to the premises to allow a constable to enter the premises to obtain access to the material.

Authority for search

By section 28(1) a constable (or, in Scotland, the Procurator Fiscal) may apply to a Circuit Judge (or Sheriff) for a warrant in relation to specified premises authorising (by virtue of subsection (2)) a constable to enter and search premises if the court is satisfied that:

"(*a*) an order made under section 27 has not been complied with; *or*

(*b*) the conditions in subsection (3) are fulfilled; *or*

(*c*) the conditions in subsection (4) are fulfilled."

By section 28(3) the conditions referred to in subsection (2)*b* are:

"(*a*) that there are reasonable grounds for suspecting that a specified person has carried on or has benefited from drug-trafficking, and

(*b*) that the conditions in section 27(4)(*b*) and (*c*) of this Act are fulfilled in relation to any material on the premises, and

(*c*) that it would not be appropriate to make an order under that section in relation to the material because;

   (i) it is not practicable to communicate with any person entitled to produce the material, or

  (ii) it is not practicable to communicate with any person entitled to grant access to the material or entitled to grant entry to the premises on which the material is situated, or

 (iii) the investigation for the purposes of which the application is made might be seriously prejudiced unless a constable could secure immediate access to the material."

Again, by section 28(4) the conditions referred to in subsection (2)(*c*) are:

"(*a*) that there are reasonable grounds for suspecting that a specified person has carried on or has benefited from drug-trafficking, and

(*b*) that there are reasonable grounds for suspecting that there is on the premises material relating to the specified person or to drug-trafficking which is likely to be of substantial value (whether by itself or together with other material) to the investigation for the purpose of which the application is made, but that the material cannot at the time of the application be particularised, and

(*c*) that:

   (i) it is not practicable to communicate with any person entitled to grant entry to the premises, or

  (ii) entry to the premises will not be granted unless a warrant is produced, or

 (iii) the investigation for the purpose of which the

> application is made might be seriously prejudiced
> unless a constable arriving at the premises could
> secure immediate entry to them."

A constable who enters premises in the execution of a warrant issued under section 28 may seize and retain any material other than items subject to "legal privilege" and "excluded material" (see section 29(2) of the Act and sections 10, 11 and 13 of P.A.C.E. 1984) which is likely to be of "substantial value"—whatever that may mean—to the investigation for the purposes of which the warrant was issued: see section 28(5).

Disclosure of information held by Government departments

By section 30(1) the High Court may, on the application of the Prosecutor, order material in the possession of an authorised government department to be produced to the court within a period specified by the court. The material must first have been submitted to an officer of the relevant department either by the defendant or by a person who has at any time held realisable property[81]; secondly, the material must have been made by an officer of that department in relation to the defendant or such a person,[82] or thirdly, the material is correspondence which passed between an officer of the relevant department and the defendant or such a person.[83]

No order may be made under section 30(1) unless the conditions specified in section 7(1) or section 7(2) are satisfied[84] and no material may be produced under section 30(1) unless it appears to the High Court that the material is likely to contain information that would facilitate the exercise of the powers conferred on the court by virtue of sections 8 to 11 of the Act or, alternatively, on a receiver appointed under section 8 or 11 of the Act, or in pursuance of a Charging Order: see section 30(4).

The court may order the disclosure of the material produced by the relevant government department to any member of the police force[85]; the Crown Prosecution Service,[86] or an officer within the meaning of the Customs and Excise Management Act 1979.[87-99]

However, the court must not disclose any part of the material

---

[81] Section 30(1)(*a*).
[82] Section 30(1)(*b*).
[83] Section 30(1)(*c*).
[84] Section 30(2).
[85] Section 30(8)(*a*).
[86] Section 30(8)(*b*).
[87-99] Section 30(8)(*c*); and see also s.30(7).

unless a reasonable opportunity has been given for an officer of the department to make representations to the court *and* it appears to the court that the material is likely to be of substantial value in exercising "functions" relating to drug-trafficking: see section 30(7).

The expression "authorised government department," as it appears in section 30, means a government department which is an authorised department for the purposes of the Crown Proceedings Act 1947: see section 38(1).

POWERS OF FORFEITURE
(Other Than Orders Under the D.T.O.A.)

FORFEITURE UNDER THE C.E.M.A. 1979

Reference has already been made to the fact that under the Customs & Excise Management Act 1979, the Commissioners have broad powers of forfeiture in relation to many activities embraced by the customs and excise Acts (see Chapter 2). Anything liable to forfeiture under those Acts may be seized or detained by any officer, constable, member of Her Majesty's armed forces, or a coastguard (section 139(1) of the C.E.M.A.) and dealt with in accordance with section 139 and schedule 3 to the 1979 Act.

Thus, goods improperly imported may be forfeited under section 49(1). Ships, aircraft and vehicles which are constructed, altered or fitted in any manner for the purpose of concealing "goods" (including stores and baggage; see section 1(1)) may be forfeited (section 88) as indeed may any ship be forfeited if any part of the cargo is thrown overboard, or is staved, or destroyed to prevent seizure (section 89) unless the ship is over 250 tons (section 142) in which case other penalties are imposed by section 143.[1]

Forfeiture proceedings under the customs and excise Acts are *in rem*.[2-10]

FORFEITURE UNDER THE M.D.A. 1971

Section 27 of the Misuse of Drugs Act 1971 provides:

"(1) Subject to subsection (2) below, the court by or before which a person is convicted of an offence under this Act may order anything shown to the satisfaction of the court to relate to

---

[1] See *A-G* v. *Hunter* [1949] 2 K.B. 111.
[2-10] See *Denton* v. *John Lister Ltd.* [1971] 3 All E.R. 669.

the offence, to be forfeited and either destroyed or dealt with in such other manner as the court may order.

(2) The court shall not order anything to be forfeited under this section, where a person claiming to be the owner of or otherwise interested in it applies to be heard by the court, unless an opportunity has been given to him to show cause why the order should not be made."

An order, under section 27, must be made within 28 days after passing sentence and cannot be varied, or rescinded, or made after that period.[11]

Section 27 will only apply to things shown " . . . to relate to the offence . . . " being an offence created under the M.D.A., whether substantive or inchoate.[12] Accordingly, a conspiracy to commit an offence under the Act is not an offence created by the Act itself and therefore section 27 can have no application to such an offence.[13]

Furthermore, only tangible things—capable of being destroyed—can be forfeited under the M.D.A., and not choses in action.[14] So where, in *Cuthbertson*, the appellants supplied illegal drugs on a massive scale and transferred a share of their profits into bank accounts in Switzerland and France, the court could not forfeit assets which had been traced as representing the proceeds of drug-trafficking. As Lord Diplock observed,[14a] orders of forfeiture under section 27 were not intended by Parliament to serve " . . . as a means of stripping the drug trafficker of the total profits of their unlawful enterprises."

However, where money is seized by police in specie, for example in the form of bank notes, and then put into a bank account by police for safe keeping, the money so seized is sufficiently tangible for the purposes of section 27. The relevant moment is the moment of seizure.[15]

The tangible item must relate to the offence

In *Cuthbertson*, the House of Lords emphasised the importance of ensuring that the tangible items relate to the offence. In *Hagard* v. *Mason*[16] the Court of Appeal quashed an order under section 27

[11] See *Menocal* (1978) 69 Cr. App. R. 147.
[12] *Cuthbertson* [1980] 2 All E.R. 401.
[13] *Ibid.*
[14] *Cuthbertson, ibid.* and *Beard* [1974] 1 W.L.R. 1549.
[14a] *Ibid.* at p. 406 f/g.
[15] *Marland and Jones* (1986) 82 Cr. App. R. 134.
[16] (1976) 1 All E.R. 337.

which related to the sum of £146 found in the defendant's possession. He had been convicted of offering to supply another with L.S.D. The £146 represented the remaining proceeds of M's illegal dealings which were not the subject of a separate charge. Accordingly, the money did not "relate" to the offences. Similar considerations resulted in a forfeiture order being quashed in the case of *Ribeyre*,[17] where R admitted that £700 was the proceeds of drug sales but the receipt of the money was not reflected by a suitable count on the indictment—R having pleaded guilty to possessing cocaine with intent to supply it—and the £700 did not relate to that purpose. Judges in other cases have fallen into the same trap: see *Morgan*[18]; *Cox*[19]; *Llewellyn*[20]; and more recently *Booth*.[21]

In *R. v. Maidstone Crown Court, ex parte Gill*[22] forfeiture order under section 27 had to be quashed in respect of a motor car which related to a charge to which the accused had pleaded not guilty and the matter was "left on the file."

Orders made against non-defendants

Section 27(2) gives the owner of goods, or an interested party in it, the right to have the opportunity of being heard before an order is made.

Where the evidence is that such parties were put on notice, or should have been, that the item in question was going to be used for some illegal purpose, then it might be proper for a judge to make a forfeiture order: *R. v. Maidstone Crown Court ex parte Gill*.[23]

FORFEITURE UNDER THE P.C.C.A. 1973

Section 43(1) of the Powers of Criminal Courts Act 1973 provides:

"Where a person is convicted of an offence punishable on indictment with imprisonment for a term of two years or more and the court by or before which he is convicted is satisfied that any property which was in his possession or under his control at the time of his apprehension—
(a) has been used for the purpose of committing, or facilitating the commission or any offence, or

---

[17] (1982) 4 Cr. App. R. (S) 165.
[18] [1977] Crim. L.R. 488; and see *Askew* [1987] Crim. L.R. 584 C.A.
[19] [1987] Crim. L.R. 143.
[20] [1985] Crim. L.R. 750.
[21] [1987] Crim. L.R. 349.
[22] (1987) 84 Cr. App. R. 96.
[23] *Ibid.*

(b) was intended by him to be used for that purpose;
the court may make an order under this section in respect of
that property."

In *Boothe*,[24] B was convicted of possessing a drug intending to
supply it and unlawfully possessing a drug. Officers, by
chance, stopped B's motor car and found packages of cocaine.
£1,489 was found in his possession. B was not a regular full-
time dealer.

Held (1) the forfeiture of his motor car under section 43
P.C.C.A. 1973 was valid.

Held (2) the forfeiture of the money under section 27
M.D.A. must be quashed.

It was contended in *Boothe* that the motor car was not essential
for the commission of the offence (see section 43(1)(a), and *Lid-
ster*).[25] The Court had no difficulty in concluding that the use of
the car was an "integral part" of the offence as it was being used to
transport packages of cocaine.

It follows from the above that a tenuous connection between the
item, and the commission of the offence, is not enough.[26]

If as in *Boothe*,[27] money found in the possession of the accused
cannot be forfeited under section 27 of the M.D.A., the court may
be able to justify an order under section 43(1)(b) if it can be
shown, for example, that the money was intended to be used by
the defendant to increase his stock-in-trade (*i.e.* to buy additional
drugs in order to supply them) and provided that the defendant
either pleads guilty, or is convicted of an offence which reflects his
intention. However, the matter is not clear.[28]

It should be noted that section 43(1) of the P.C.C.A., is confined to property used or facilitating the commission of an offence
(or intended to be so used) by the person convicted. It does not
apply in cases where someone other than the defendant intended
(or did) use the property.[29]

If, during the course of the trial, or plea in mitigation, the
defence make it plain that the prosecution case on possession is
not accepted, it is essential that the trial judge holds an enquiry
and (if necessary) hears evidence.[30]

[24] 1987 Crim. L.R. 347.
[25] [1976] Crim. L.R. 80.
[26] *Jones* (27590B85; October 10, 1985).
[27] See *Supra* 17.24
[28] *Tarpy* (5639C84; February 2, 1985).
[29] *Slater* (561B86; June 16, 1986); [1986] C.L.Y. 603; and see *Neville*
[1987] Crim. L.R. 585, C.A.
[30] *Braker* (3893C84; March 19, 1985).

Forfeiture orders, under section 43, should not be used as a method of ordering that the proceeds of sale be used to meet a compensation order which is not otherwise enforceable.[31]

SENTENCING

Maximum sentences for offences under the M.D.A. 1971

By section 25 of the Misuse of Drugs Act 1971, the maximum sentences which may be imposed in respect of any of the offences under the Act are set out in Schedule 4, as amended by the following enactments:

(a) section 27, and section 28 and schedule 5 to the Criminal Law Act 1977,

(b) section 32(2), section 32(3) and schedule 7 to the Magistrates Court Act 1980,

(c) section 46 of the Criminal Justice Act 1982,

(d) the Controlled Drugs (Penalties) Act 1985.

For ease of reference, Schedule 4 to the M.D.A. is set out at the end of this chapter.

In the ordinary way, by section 32(2) of the Magistrates Courts Act 1980, offences triable either way and which are not specified in schedule 1 to that Act, carry a maximum fine on summary conviction in the "prescribed sum" *i.e.* £2000 (see S.I. 1984 No. 447).

For reasons which are not entirely easy to understand, section 32(5) of the 1980 Act provides that section 32(2) does not apply (on summary conviction) in respect of an offence under section 5(2) of the M.D.A. if that offence involves a Class B or Class C drug. Moreover, section 32(2) does not apply to an offence under sections 4(2), 4(3), 5(3), 8, 12(6), or section 13(3) if the controlled drug involved falls within Class C. Accordingly, the appropriate penalties are set out in Schedule 5 to the Criminal Law Act 1977 as amended by Schedule 7 to the 1980 Act.

The maximum penalty of £400, in respect of an offence contrary to section 17(3) of the M.D.A., is set at Level 3 of the "standard scale," see section 46(1) of the Criminal Justice Act 1982 and S.I. 1984 No. 447.

The Controlled Drugs (Penalties) Act 1980 increased, from 14 years imprisonment to life imprisonment, the maximum sentences in respect of offences under section 4(2), 4(3) or 5(3) which involve a Class A drug.

---

[31] *Jarvis* (5742C84; February 5, 1985).

Maximum sentences for offences under the C.E.M.A. 1979

By Schedule 1 to the Customs & Excise Management Act 1979, where a person is convicted of an offence contrary to section 50 (unlawful importation) or section 68 (unlawful exportation) or section 170 (fraudulent evasion) and where the offence involves a Class A or Class B drug, then he shall be liable, on *summary conviction* to a penalty of the "prescribed sum" (*i.e.* £2000) see S.I. 1984 No. 447) or of three times the value of the goods, whichever is the greater, or to imprisonment for a term not exceeding six months, or to both. On conviction *on indictment,* he shall be liable to a penalty "of any amount" or imprisonment for a term not exceeding 14 years in the case of Class B drugs, or life imprisonment where the goods are a Class A drug (see the Controlled Drugs (Penalties) Act 1985 or to both.

Cases involving a Class C drug attract lesser penalties, namely (*per* para. 2 of Sched. 1 to the C.E.M.A. 1979):

"(a) on summary conviction in Great Britain, to a penalty of three times the value of the goods or £500, whichever is the greater, or to imprisonment for a term not exceeding 3 months, or to both;

(b) on summary conviction in Northern Ireland, to a penalty of three times the value of the goods or £100, whichever is the greater, or to imprisonment for a term not exceeding 6 months, or to both;

(c) on conviction on indictment, to a penalty of any amount, or to imprisonment for a term not exceeding 5 years, or to both."

Persons convicted of an importation/exportation offence can no longer expect "early release" from their sentences under section 32 of the Criminal Justice Act 1982 since such an offence falls into the category of "excluded offences" as specified in Part III of Schedule 1 to that Act. Moreover, parole will no longer be available for prisoners sentenced to five years, or more, in respect of an offence of drug-trafficking. The decision of the Home Secretary in this respect has not been effectively challenged.[32]

Valuation

It may seem strange that under Schedule 1 to the C.E.M.A. 1979 the court can order three times the value of drugs in the context of an illicit trade. How is the value to be assessed? The answer, which is not entirely satisfactory, is that the court may

---

[32] *Re Findlay* [1985] A.C. 318.

look to the "black market" value of the drugs as well as the legitimate value. This answer is the combined product of section 171(3) of the C.E.M.A. 1979 and the decision of the Divisional Court in *Byrne* v. *Low*.[33]

Section 171(3) reads as follows:

> "Where a penalty for an offence under any enactment relating to an assigned matter is required to be fixed by reference to the value of any goods, that value shall be taken as the price which those goods might reasonably be expected to have fetched, after payment of any duty or tax chargeable thereon, if they had been sold in the open market at or about the date of the commission of the offence for which the penalty is imposed."

Accordingly, the value is the value of the drugs " . . . if they had been sold in the open market." If one construes the words "open market" literally then section 171(3) can have no application since drugs unlawfully imported can not "openly" be marketed. If sold, their price can only be at the black market value. This problem was considered in *Byrne* v. *Low*.[34]

> B unlawfully imported prohibited goods, namely indecent articles. The invoice price of the goods was approximately £2,235. The magistrates sentenced B to a fine of £3,000 which was varied, on appeal to Quarter Session, to £100 on the basis that since the importation was prohibited there was no "open market" for them.

The Divisional Court allowed the appeal. Lord Widgery C.J. held[34a] that a court is not " . . . restricted by the distinction between the so-called black market and white market."
He said[34b]:

> "What is being sought is the price which a willing seller would accept from a willing buyer for those goods as landed at the port or airport at which they were originally landed."

The Court thought that the invoice price could be a very good guide to the open market value " . . . and may well be the conclusive and only guide."

---

[33] [1972] 3 All E.R. 526.
[34] *Ibid.*
[34a] *Ibid.* at p. 529.
[34b] *Ibid.* at p. 529 a/b.

"Assessing the street-value"

Of course, drug transactions are rarely committed to paper in intelligible form. Accordingly, evidence of value of a given substance will normally be given to the court by an expert—normally a police officer who has had many years experience in dealing with drug offences. His information will be obtained from a variety of sources. Prisoners or suspects may speak of the value; the officer may have been personally engaged in undercover drug operations during the course of which he has negotiated a price, or he may refer to records kept by the National Drugs Intelligence Unit at New Scotland Yard, which collates information concerning drug activities nationwide. The tables produced by the Unit are elaborate and frequently updated. Values are expressed region by region and will reflect a variety of important factors including the purity of the drug.

Until 1984, the point had been taken at the trial (sometimes successfully) that evidence of value was inadmissible on the basis that it was hearsay and so could not be tested by cross-examination. However, in *Bryan*,[35] decided on November 8, 1984 the Court of Appeal held that the evidence of a Drug Squad officer with experience of street dealing is admissible as to the fact of what happens on the street. He was therefore entitled to give evidence of the street value of drugs. However, this was not a matter for a pharmacist who would probably have less information concerning black market prices than a Drug Squad officer. Wood J. said:

> "The view of this court is that police officers with their experience of dealing with these problems, being on the streets and with their knowledge and meeting those having a drug problem and those pushing drugs, have a very wide experience and can give evidence of fact of what takes place on many occasions on the streets."

Expert evidence concerning the value of goods, chattels and property is not new in English Law: see *English Exporters (London) Ltd.* v. *Eldonwall Ltd.*[36]

SENTENCING GUIDELINES

Sentencing attitudes quickly change and it would be idle to pretend that the authorities do not reflect attitude "swings" over the years. Thus, in *Pardit*[37] a 35 year old man, with no previous con-

[35] (unrep., 3923B84).
[36] [1973] 1 Ch. 415.
[37] (1974) Crim. L.R. 60.

victions, was sentenced to 18 months imprisonment after he pleaded guilty to the importation of 27·5 *grams* of cannabis for his own use. His sentence was upheld on appeal. Again, in *Daher*,[38] a sentence of three years imprisonment was upheld where D unlawfully imported approximately 5 kilograms of cannabis resin in the false bottom of a suitcase. The defendant was then aged 19, and of good character, who had been recruited in the Lebanon to act as a "drugs runner." Such cases are rightly to be regarded as being out of line with current sentencing policy over the last few years. In order to achieve a consistent approach to sentencing in drug cases, guidelines were given by the Court of Appeal in *Aramah*.[39]

The decision in R. v. Aramah (1983)

Class A Drugs. The Court of Appeal took as its example heroin but described all Class A drugs as the most dangerous of all the addictive drugs, being easy to handle; involving enormous profits; attracting the worst type of criminal and causing heroin addicts to obtain supplies of the drug (costing hundreds of pounds sterling a week) to satisfy "the terrible craving." Lord Lane C.J. remarked:

> "It is not difficult to understand why in some parts of the world, traffickers in heroin in any substantial quantity were sentenced to death and executed. Consequently, anything which the courts of this country can do by way of deterrent sentences on those found guilty of crimes involving Class A drugs should be done."

The guidelines, regarding Class A drugs, may be summarised as follows:

(1) Importation of heroin, etc.
    (a) Amounts Valued Over £1,000,000 .... 12–14 years
    (b) Amounts Valued Over £100,000 .... 7 years or more
    (c) An "Appreciable" Amount .... normally 4 years.

The starting figures in (*a*) and (*b*) above, were restated in *Bilinski*[40] and raised to 14 years and ten years respectively.

So far as mitigation is concerned it was said in *Aramah*, that a confession of guilt coupled with considerable assistance to the police could properly be marked by a substantial reduction in what would otherwise be the proper sentence.[40a]

---

[38] (1969) 53 Crim. App. R. 490.
[39] (1983) 76 Cr. App. R. 190.
[40] [1987] Crim. L.R. 782; (1988) 86 Cr. App. R. 146.
[40a] See *Sivan*, *The Times*, July 6, 1988; (521/A3/88).

(2) Supplying heroin

"The sentence will largely depend on the degree of involvement, the amount of trafficking and the value of drug being handled."

A sentence of less than 3 years would seldom be justified.

The nearer the source of supply the defendant was shown to be, the heavier would be the sentence.

(3) Simple possession of heroin, etc.

"It is at this level that the circumstances of the individual offender become of much greater importance. Indeed the possible variety of considerations is so wide, including often those of a medical nature, that it is impossible to lay down any practical guidelines . . . The maximum penalty for simple possession of Class A drugs is seven years' imprisonment and a fine, and there will be very many cases where deprivation of liberty is both appropriate and expedient."

Class B Drugs. Cannabis was singled out by the Court of Appeal as being the drug most likely to be exercising the minds of the courts.

(1) Importation

Massive Quantities	10 years[40b]
Over 20 kgs	3 to 6 years
Up to 20 kgs	18 months to 3 years

(2) Supply

Massive Quantities	10 years
Other cases	1 to 4 years

(3) Possession

Small Amounts/Personal Use	Fines
Persistent Flouting	Possible Custodial

Is Aramah Out of Date?

Judicial concern that the level of sentencing for serious drug offences may now be too low, has long been voiced. It has to be remembered that since *Aramah* was decided, Parliament passed the Controlled Drugs (Penalties) Act 1985, which increased from 14 years to life imprisonment, sentences in respect of the supply and importation/exportation of Class A drugs. In *Gilmore*[41] the Court of Appeal felt that "the time had come" when it was necess-

---

[40b] But see *Sivan & Others*, *The Times*, July 6, 1988; *Mitchell* (1986) 8 Cr. App. R. (S.) 472.

[41] *The Times*, May 21, 1986.

ary to move up the level of sentencing for such offences. May L.J. expressed the same view in *Ansari*[42] and again in *Obliyaei*[43] although, in both of these cases, the Court of Appeal felt constrained to apply the guidelines in *Aramah*.

> In *Ansari*, a sentence of seven years was reduced to five years in respect of heroin addict who was in possession of 1/4lb of heroin—worth £12,000—presumably intending to supply it.
> The appellant supplied in the vicinity of young people which was a proper matter for the courts to take into account.

> In *Oliyaei*, May L.J. said that the street price of heroin appears to be falling and substantially more of it may exist. Therefore, "*Aramah* sentences" may have to be increased. A sentence of seven years varied to five years, but a sentence of six years was affirmed.

Again, in *Gomez-Osorio*[44] the Court of Appeal upheld a sentence of seven years for the importation of 1·16 kilograms of cocaine on the basis that a deterrent sentence was called for and *Aramah* may no longer be appropriate.

Such expressions of judicial opinion have not gone unheeded for in *Bilinski*[45] Lord Lane C.J. looked again at *Aramah*, but only in so far as it applied to Class A drugs, and advised that, (*a*) where the street value of the consignment was in the order of £100,000 or more, the starting point should no longer be seven years *but ten years,* and (*b*) where the street value of the consignment was £1 million or more the starting point should be increased from 12 years imprisonment to *14 years*. Accordingly, Bilinski, having pleaded guilty to importing 3·035 kilograms of heroin of 90 per cent. purity, had his sentence of 12 years imprisonment reduced to eight years.

The court in *Bilinski* made no other changes to the guidelines in *Aramah*. It is to be regretted that the Court did not use the opportunity to restate current sentencing policy in respect of all drug-trafficking offences and the possession of Class A and Class B drugs. This is because confusion has arisen as to whether the sentences suggested in *Aramah*, in so far as they relate to drugs in Class B and Class C are also now said to be too low: see, for example, *Beaumont*[46] a case concerning the supply of cannabis.

There is some evidence that the Court of Appeal will depart

[42] (1986) 7 Cr. App. R. (S).
[43] unreported, 14.10.85, 2267C85.
[44] (unreported; 5787/F/86).
[45] [1987] Crim. L.R. 782.
[46] [1987] Crim. L.R. 786.

from the guidelines in *Aramah* if it is appropriate to do so. Thus, in *Brown*[47] a sentence of five years imprisonment was upheld where B possessed less than 1 kilogram of cannabis resin intending to supply it. B had previous convictions for drug possession and supplying. Rose J. remarked that *Aramah* laid down guidelines only and that a deterrent sentence was appropriate in the circumstances.

The value of citing sentencing decisions

Aramah[48] represents something of a landmark in our law because it marks the first of a line of cases which offers guidance to sentencers in respect of a number of different areas of the law. In one sense everything said in these cases should be treated as *obiter*, but the judgments expressed are, of course, very persuasive and should do much to produce consistent sentencing in this country. However, as the Court of Appeal has remarked on several occasions, decisions such as *Aramah* provide guidance only and must not be seen as laying down rigid rules to be applied strictly in every case: see *Nicholas*[49] and see *Brown*.[50]

For this reason, the extent to which "guideline" cases, and other sentencing authorities, may properly be cited has yet to be satisfactorily resolved. The author once heard Lord Widgery C.J. severely castigate counsel for citing sentencing authorities to the Court on the grounds that each case had to be decided on its own facts. In *R. v. De Havilland*[51] Dunn L.J. fired "a warning shot" regarding the increasing practice of citing sentencing decisions of the Court of Appeal when he said:

> " . . . the appropriate sentence is a matter for the discretion of the sentencing judge. It follows that decisions on sentencing are not binding authorities . . . Indeed they could not be, since the circumstances of the offence and of the offender present an almost infinite variety from case to case . . . Occasionally this Court suggests guidelines for sentences . . . But the sentencer retains his discretion within the guidelines, or even to depart from then if the particular circumstances of the case justify departure."

By contrast, in *R. v. McEvilly*,[52] Lord Lane C.J. observed that

---

[47] (unrep., 16.6.86, 769B86, Rose J.).
[48] (1983) 76 Cr. App. R. 190.
[49] (*The Times*, April 23, 1986, *per* Lord Lane C.J.).
[50] (1986) (unrep., 769B86).
[51] (1983) 5 Cr. App. R. (S) 109 (at p. 114, Dunn L.J.).
[52] *The Times*, November 4, 1986, C.A.

public money expended on unnecessary sentence appeals might have been avoided if the *Encyclopaedia of Current Sentencing Practice* had been drawn to the trial judge's attention.

It is submitted that there can be nothing improper in the citation of "guideline" cases but the value in citing other sentencing cases must be a matter of professional judgement.

SENTENCING EXAMPLES

Heroin importations

In *Tim-Loy*,[53] T, aged 37 years, imported heroin worth £150,000. No previous convictions. Sentenced to ten years imprisonment.

Held, Appeal dismissed.

In *Poh and To*,[54] two appellants aged 64 years and 58 years imported 32 kilograms of heroin in two cars. Total value of the heroin was about £5 million. The appellants contended that they were not the prime movers. They were sentenced to 14 years imprisonment—*i.e.* the maximum sentence at that time.

Held, Appeal dismissed. They had allowed themselves to become involved in the moving of drugs on an enormous scale and therefore they had forfeited any rights to humanitarian considerations.

Heroin supplying/possession with intent

In *Ashraf and Huq*,[55] H stopped in a car and found to be in possession of 52 grams of heroin, worth £5,200, which he had obtained from A. A was found in possession of 45 grams of heroin. H admitted being concerned with drug deals. H was sentenced to ten years; A was sentenced to seven years.

Held, Beginners or not, anyone who trades in dangerous drugs, particularly heroin, must expect very severe sentences when caught. The sentences could not be criticised.

The court will of course take into account the period of time the defendant has been engaged in supplying heroin, the purity of the drug involved and the volume of business.

In *France*,[56] F was a modest supplier of heroin over a few

53 [1974] Crim. L.R. 59.
54 [1982] Crim. L.R. 132.
55 [1982] Crim. L.R. 132.
56 [1984] 6 Cr. App. R. (S) 284.

weeks and sold drugs to finance his own habit. Sentenced to four years imprisonment.

Held, sentence upheld.

In *Gee.*[57] A sentence of six years was reduced to four years where G sold heroin to feed his own addiction and not for profit. He supplied on a small scale on a social basis.

Importation and supply of L.S.D.

In *Humphrey,*[58] the Court of Appeal held that a sentence of three years imprisonment, imposed on a man of good character who had unlawfully imported sufficient L.S.D. for 1999 doses, was neither manifestly excessive nor wrong in principle. This was so despite his good character, his determination to rehabilitate himself and his expression of remorse.

Again, in *McCullough,*[59] a sentence of six years imprisonment was upheld for conspiracy to supply L.S.D. He was found to be in possession of enough L.S.D. to make 8000 doses and planned to import and to sell L.S.D. on a substantial scale. Two thousand does had already been sold.

Importation of morphine

Cases involving the importation of morphine are relatively uncommon since it is not a substance popular with drug users.

However, in *Ahmad*[60] a sentence of seven years imprisonment was upheld for the importation of 991 grams of morphine even though the appellant was a man of previous good character who acted as a courier.

This case must now be viewed in the light of the guidelines in *Aramah and Bilinski.*[61]

Cocaine dealing

Although *Aramah* focussed its attention on heroin cases in fact no distinction is to be made between the types of Class A drugs: see *Martinez*[62] where the court drew attention to the dangers of cocaine.

---

[57] [1984] 6 Crim. L.R. (S) 86.
[58] (1981) 3 Cr. App. R. (S) 63.
[59] (1982) 4 Cr. App. R. (S) 302.
[60] January 22, 1980.
[61] [1987] Crim. L.R. 782.
[62] [1984] 6 Crim. App. R. (S) 364.

In *Martinez*,[63] a man of good character, sentenced to four years imprisonment for the importation of 23·7 grams of cocaine, worth £3,000.

Held, Appeal dismissed.

In *Parada & Others*,[64] six years imprisonment imposed on two couriers aged 25 and 26 years who imported cocaine worth £500,000.

Held, appeal dismissed.

In *Taan*,[65] a 12 year sentence of imprisonment was upheld for being concerned in the importation of £2·5 million worth of cocaine. T was involved in the organisation of the trade having booked and paid for the tickets of two co-defendants.
No assistance of any sort had been given to the customs and excise.

In *Suermondt*,[66] ten years imprisonment upheld for the unlawful importation of about ten kilograms of cocaine transported in three consignments. S bought the drug in Peru and intended to sell it in England. Value: £1,400,000. Aged 32; deep sea diver for six years; injured; fined £600 in Australia for the unlawful importation of heroin; visited Peru on business; pleaded guilty; gave information concerning a corrupt airline official.

The Court of Appeal in *Mariotti*[67] made it plain that severe punishment could only be expected if cocaine was imported for whatever reason. Accordingly, a mother who wished to bring her family to England and therefore imported £12,000 worth of cocaine, had her appeal against a 6 year sentence dismissed.

Supplying cocaine. In *Aramah* it was said that a sentence of less than three years is seldom justified in cases involving the supplying of Class A drugs.

In *Davies and Marshall-Price*,[68] D pleaded guilty to possessing 6·5 grams of cocaine with intent to supply and bought ten grams from M.
M was convicted of possessing 20 grams of cocaine with intent

---

[63] [1984] 6 Crim. App. R. (S) 364; and see *Ryan* 8 Crim. App. R. (S) 213, C.A.
[64] [1984] 6 Crim. App. R. (S) 219; and see *Van Hubbard* (1986) 8 Cr. App. R. (S) 228, C.A.
[65] (1982) 4 Crim. App. R. (S) 17.
[66] (1982) 4 Crim. App. R. (S).
[67] (unreported; December 14, 1984, 6203B83).
[68] (1982) 4 Crim. App. R. (S) 302.

to supply. D sentenced to 15 months imprisonment. M sentenced to four years imprisonment.
M had 14 previous convictions.
Appeals dismissed.

Marshall-Price was clearly more heavily implicated than Davies. Police raided Marshall-Price's flat which was plainly a safe house for drug-trafficking. The doors and windows were lined with steel. The court observed that "it is inevitable that people supplying hard drugs will be sent to prison and, as a general rule, the sentence of imprisonment is to be measured in terms of years and not months."[68a]

Importing or possessing cocaine for personal use. Clearly the fact that the drugs were intended for personal consumption is a mitigating factor but offenders, even if they are of previous good character, are in great danger of receiving an immediate custodial sentence. Where the amount involved is appreciable then such a result is almost inevitable. Thus, in *Keech (Walter)*,[69] K, a famous television personality, pleaded guilty to the unlawful importation of 36·7 grams of cocaine (worth £4,500) which was contained in a shaving cream can. K obviously knew the risks involved and took careful steps to evade the prohibition on importation. His appeal, against an immediate sentence of nine months imprisonment, was dismissed.

However, in *Diamond*,[70] a sentence of eight months imprisonment, of which six months were ordered to be suspended, plus the imposition of a £4,000 fine, was upheld where D, aged 34 years and of good character, was convicted of possessing cocaine.

Importation of cannabis

In *Price*,[71] a sentence of seven years imprisonment was reduced to five years in connection with the importation of 60·80 kilograms of cannabis. The quantity was substantial and clearly fell within the three to six year tariff suggested by the Court of Appeal in *Aramah*.

Again, in *Abdul*[72] a sentence of five years was reduced to three years imprisonment in respect of a man of good character, aged 43 years, who imported 43·65 kilograms of herbal cannabis. The

[68a] *per* Griffiths L.J. at p. 302.
[69] (1984) 6 Cr. App. R. (S) 402.
[70] (1985) 7 Cr. App. R. (S) 152.
[71] (1985) 7 Cr. App. R. (S) 190.
[72] (1981) 3 Cr. App. R. (S) 100.

court had regard to the fact what was being imported was not a Class A drug; that the appellant was a man of good character; a model prisoner who would be unable to have any visits from his family because they resided in Ghana as he normally did.

The court will obviously analyse the role played by the defendant in a smuggling venture. Thus, in *Chisti*,[73] the Court of Appeal reduced from nine years to six years a sentence of imprisonment imposed on the appellant for the importation of one-third of a ton of cannabis with a street value of over £600,000. The appellant was a Pakistani, of 47 years of age, of previous good character who was not the principal in the transaction.

> In *Forsythe*,[74] S aged 60 years, and of previous good character, suggested to his father a scheme for unlawfully importing into the United Kingdom cannabis packed into furniture. Some 152·7 kilograms had been imported in this way. The value to the importer (in 1980) was about £78,000 and some £200,000 at street level. He was sentenced to ten years imprisonment.
>
> *Held*, this sentence would be reduced to five years imprisonment.

The court accepted in *Forsythe* the appellant's contention that the original sentence was out of accord with sentences imposed in other cases which clearly it was.

A partly suspended sentence of imprisonment is not appropriate for either a courier or an organiser of a drug smuggling venture. The policy of the court is to deter other couriers and not simply to punish the individual.[75]

Importation of cannabis oil

Aramah[76] was applied in *Briggs & Malcomson*.[77] A sentence of five years imprisonment was held to be correct for the unlawful importation of 31/4 kilograms of cannabis oil. An estimate of its street value was given at £50,000. It was not possible to accurately equate the oil with an amount of cannabis resin of equivalent strength. The Court had to look at the case on broader lines.

[73] (1981) 3 Cr. App. R. (S) 99.
[74] (1980) 2 Cr. App. R. (S).
[75] *Dawson* [1983] Crim. L.R. 195.
[76] (1983) 76 Cr. App. R. 190.
[77] (392B84; June 12, 1984).

Importation and possession of cannabis for personal use

In *Atherton*[78] a sentence of nine months imprisonment was upheld on appeal, in respect of a consignment of 1·13 kilograms of cannabis which was sent to D in a parcel for D's own use.

Ordinarily, possession of a very small amount of cannabis for the defendant's personal use would not result in a custodial sentence but a continuous or persistent flouting of the law might justify a short custodial sentence: see *Aramah*; and see *Osbourne*[79]; *Jones*[80] and *Robertson-Coupar*.[81]

The court's attitude towards couriers

In *Aramah*,[82] the Court of Appeal remarked that the good character of a courier, as he usually was, is of less importance than the good character of a defendant in other cases. In the judgement of the court, the reason why this should be is that drug smuggling organisers deliberately recruit persons who will exercise the sympathy of the court. Thus, students and the sick and the elderly were (and are) often employed as couriers. They are vulnerable to suggestion and vulnerable to the offer of quick profit. The Court was concerned that such smugglers would also believe that the courts might be moved to misplaced sympathy in their cases. Similar considerations had been voiced a year earlier by Lawton L.J. in *Hamouda*[83] and see also *Anderson*.[84]

It is a fact that many couriers are extremely vulnerable. Many of them are foreigners; often astonishingly uneducated, poor, naive, and they frequently have never travelled beyond their own region let alone to another country. Obviously they are therefore easy targets for the smuggler. Furthermore, they are often expendable for three broad reasons. First, despite the best endeavours of the law enforcement agencies, only about one in six couriers are apprehended. Second, although the smuggled drug may have a high street-level value in this country, the same drug will often be readily available (at very low cost) in the producing/exporting country. This is particularly true of herbal cannabis which grows naturally, in abundance, in several regions of the world. Third, the courier is often not paid for his/her efforts until the drug is

---

[78] (1271C84; June 14, 1985).
[79] [1982] Crim. L.R. 834.
[80] (1981) 3 Cr. App. R. (S) 51.
[81] [1982] Crim. L.R. 536.
[82] (1983) 76 Cr. App. R. 190.
[83] (1982) 4 Cr. App. R. (S) 137.
[84] [1981] Crim. L.R. 270.

delivered to the consignee. Accordingly, the major financial loss to the organiser if the courier is arrested, is frequently no more than the price of the courier's air ticket. Such couriers are also easy targets for the officers of Customs and Excise who quickly spot a bewildered, nervous, and sometimes plainly inept visitor. By imposing deterrent sentences on couriers, the courts in this country (and elsewhere) hope that the "word will spread" and so deter others from acting as couriers. But achieving success in this way perhaps depends on the making of too many assumptions which, given the vulnerability of the type of person being considered, cannot realistically be made. However, that said, the courts are undoubtedly put in a very difficult position.

"Newton" hearings/factual basis for sentence

It has to be remembered that a courier may not always know precisely what he is carrying. He may be told that it is something prohibited from importation into England but he does not always appreciate that the substance is, a controlled drug, or a drug of a particular description. We have already noted that although narcotics are expensive to buy in the United Kingdom, drugs such as heroin and cannabis, are astonishingly cheap to buy in the producing country and it would be idle to suppose that some organisers do not think it tactically advantageous to keep the courier "in the dark" as to the precise substance he will be asked to carry. After all, how much does the organiser really stand to lose, compared to the vast profits which he may expect to make, sooner or later? For the purposes of a charge under the Customs & Excise Management Act 1979, it does not matter what the defendant believes the goods to be so long as he knew them to be prohibited from importation.[85] Again, for the purposes of a charge under the Misuse of Drugs Act 1971 an accused's ignorance (subject to section 28 of the M.D.A.) as to the quality of the thing, will afford him no defence. But, a mistaken belief, that the offending drug is of a different kind from that which he had been told it was, is a mitigating factor.[86] Similarly, a mistaken belief that the goods imported were of a totally different character, for example, pornographic videos, is also a mitigating factor.[87]

However, in *Bilinski*,[88] B pleaded guilty to importing 3·036 kilograms of heroin. He claimed that he believed the packages con-

---

[85] See *Hussain* [1969] 2 Q.B. 567; and *Hennessey* (1978) 68 Cr. App. R. 419.

[86] See *Ghandi* (1986) 8 Cr. App. R. (S) 391.

[87] See *Ellis, Street & Smith* (1987) 84 Cr. App. R. 235 at p. 248.

[88] [1987] Crim. L.R. 782.

tained cannabis although a book found in his possession seemed to relate to the topic of heroin. He was sentenced to 12 years imprisonment. The trial judge had taken the view that the appellant's view was irrelevant and therefore declined to hear evidence about it in accordance with the principles set out in *Newton*.[89] The Court of Appeal held that the appellant's belief was relevant to sentence and that the man who believed he was importing cannabis was less culpable than the man who knew it to be heroin. However, to what extent such a belief mitigated the sentence would depend on the facts in each case including the degree of care exercised by a defendant. In *Bilinski* the mitigating effect of B's belief (if held) was small and his appeal was therefore dismissed.

If a defendant's story is patently false then the judge is entitled to reject it without hearing evidence.[90] The decision of *Makenzie*,[91] which suggested a contrary proposition, may no longer be a good law.

Furthermore, the calling of evidence if disbelieved, or if it only repeated an absurd and spurious explanation given by a defendant, may considerably nullify any discount to be gained from a plea of guilty.[92]

If the trial judge does accept the defendant's explanation, the next question is to what extent is the sentencer bound to sentence the defendant on the basis of his explanation? This is particularly important on the question of the value of the goods involved—or believed to be involved—because the guidelines in *Aramah* are based substantially on the street value of drugs. Suppose a smuggler believed that he was importing 1 kilogram of cannabis worth, say £1,500 whereas he imported 2 kilograms of heroin worth, say, £200,000. If he were truly to be sentenced accordingly to his belief then, the sentence he might expect to receive, is a maximum of 18 months imprisonment and not (if his belief were otherwise) a sentence of ten years imprisonment or more.

The answer seems to be simply this: that a mistaken belief as to the type of goods imported or handled is only a mitigating *consideration*. It does not entitle the defendant to be sentenced on that basis at all. The relevant consideration is therefore the "street-price" of the drug involved. The defendant's error merely entitles him to a discount which, depending on the facts of the case

---

[89] (1982) 4 Cr. App. R. (S) 388.
[90] See *Hawkins* [1985] 7 Cr. App. R. (S) 351 and *Bilinski, ibid.*
[91] (1985) 7 Cr. App. R. (S) 441.
[92] See *Walton* [1987] Crim. L.R. 512; *Stevens* (1968) 8 Cr. App. R. (S) 297; *Jauncey* (1986) 8 Cr. App. R. (S) 401 and *MacKenzie, supra.*

(including the degree of care exercised by him), may be substantial or it may be negligible.[93]

Not every contentious issue raised during mitigation is a suitable matter for enquiry by the trial judge. So where a defendant with many previous convictions alleges that he has changed his lifestyle and reformed himself a "*Newton* hearing" is not appropriate.[94]

Burden and standard of proof. The defence version must be accepted unless the judge, or the jury, is sure that it is wrong and, the Court of Appeal will not interfere with the finding unless, for example, no reasonable tribunal could have reached that result.[95]

Curiously, in *Hall*,[96] Lincoln J. remarked that where the sentence is likely to be the same whichever version is accepted, it is undesirable that the trial judge should be seen to be adopting the prosecution version. If Lincoln J. meant no more than that the benefit of the doubt should be resolved in favour of the accused, then clearly there can be no complaint, but any tribunal, which is required to resolve conflicting versions, should not be slow to frankly express the version it accepts or rejects. This is so even where the judge considers that the sentence is likely to be the same; after all, the Court of Appeal may take a different view.

No challenge by prosecution. Where an explanation is put forward by the defendant, which the prosecution then choose not to challenge, the judge may consider it appropriate to sentence on that basis. Thus in *Lawless*,[97] L pleaded guilty to possessing 960 grams of cannabis resin with intent to supply. He claimed that he bought the drug on behalf of a syndicate of five or six persons, and not with a view to resale. The prosecution did not challenge this version. The Court of Appeal reduced his sentence of two years imprisonment, so as to allow his immediate release (after having served nearly 12 months), on the grounds that the case could not be safely treated as a commercial venture.

Of course, if the trial judge feels uneasy about the matter he may, of his own volition, assess the defendant's version in accordance with the principles set out in *Newton* above.

Acceptance of pleas. When a defendant pleads guilty to "lesser counts" he is entitled to be sentenced on that basis. So where, in

---

[93] See *Bilinski, supra.* n. 90.
[94] *Odey* (unreported; October 18, 1989; 697C84).
[95] See Ahmed (1984) 6 Cr. App. R. (S) 391; Parker L.J.
[96] (1984) 6 Cr. App. R. (S) 321.
[97] [1981] Crim. L.R. 845.

Lawrence,[98] the appellant pleaded guilty to one count of cultivating cannabis plants, and two counts of possessing cannabis resin, but pleaded not guilty to a further count of possessing a controlled drug with intent to supply (which pleas were accepted by the court) the judge was therefore bound to deal with the appellant purely on the basis that the drugs were for his own consumption.

Specimen counts, etc. Frequently the evidence in the case paints a picture of a defendant who is more heavily implicated in drug dealing than the specimen counts on the indictment actually demonstrate. In such cases there can be no objection if, having evaluated the evidence put before the jury, the judge comes to the view that the defendant should be sentenced in a way which marks that greater degree of involvement.[99]

However, the above is very different to cases where the prosecution either fail to include sufficient or appropriate counts on the indictment to reflect the extent of an accused's involvement, or where there are sufficient counts but the defendant either pleads guilty to, or is convicted of, only some of them. In these circumstances the courts are bound to sentence on the basis of the facts of the particular offence or offences.

> In *Ayensu and Ayensu*[1] the appellants pleaded guilty to one count of unlawfully importing 46·87 grams of cannabis. Their passports showed that they had made frequent trips between Ghana and the United Kingdom. They admitted to customs officers that they had smuggled cannabis into the United Kingdom on other occasions. A count alleging a conspiracy to import drugs was not proceeded with. Their counsel submitted that the plea represented the whole of their admissions.

The Court of Appeal held that it was the task of the Crown Court to sentence on the basis of the particular offence. The court could not take into account matters which were hotly contested and the court could not take into account the alleged admissions given to the customs officers.

Ayensu and Ayensu is in accord with the decision of *O'Conner*[2] but not, it would seem, with *Russen*[3] where the court remarked that:

---

[98] (1981) 3 Cr. App. R. (S) 49.
[99] See *Ghanderi* (unreported; October 16, 1984; 1291B83; Watkins L.J.).
[1] [1982] Crim. L.R. 764.
[2] (1981) 3 Cr. App. R. (S) 225.
[3] (1981) 3 Cr. App. R. (S) 134.

" . . . the court is perfectly entitled to look at a man's statement in order to discover if the incident in question is an isolated incident or not. When it appears perfectly clear from the statement that the event in question is not an isolated incident, the court is entitled to take that into account when sentencing."

It is submitted that *Ayensu and Ayensu* and *O'Conner* are to be preferred.

Social supplying

Many cases have considered the extent to which a supply of drugs to a small circle of friends of other drug users is a mitigating factor.

In *Bennett*,[4] the Court implicitly regarded such a feature as amounting to some mitigation: see also *Smith*[5] where a sentence of 12 months was upheld for an offence of possessing cannabis with intent to supply a small circle of friends for modest profit.

In *Spinks*,[6] A 23 year old male of previous good character, pleaded guilty to one offence of heroin. He and a friend agreed to buy £10 worth of heroin which they both duly consumed. Sentenced originally to 12 months imprisonment.

Held, too severe; sentence reduced to effect immediate release—*i.e.* equivalent to a sentence of about three months.

Although every case involving the supply of a controlled drug is a serious matter, nevertheless, the court will give credit for the absence of a commercial motive.

In *Daudi and Daniels*,[7] sentences of three months detention and six months imprisonment were upheld on two appellants who purchased £600 worth of cannabis on behalf of 50 members of the Rastafarian sect who had each contributed £12.

The court remarked that it would be "a denial of justice" for the Court to say "because you are a Rastafarian you are entitled to be treated entirely differently from other members of the community if you chose to break the law . . . "[7a]

In *French and West*[8] sentences of three and a half years imprisonment and two and a half years were said to have erred on

[4] (1981) 3 Cr. App. R. (S) 68.
[5] (1980) 2 Cr. App. R. (S) 18.
[6] [1987] Crim. L.R. 786.
[7] (1982) 4 Cr. App. R. (S) 306.
[7a] *Ibid. per* Griffiths L.J. at p. 307.
[8] (unreported; May 12, 1986; 7476C85).

the side of leniency in respect of two appellants who had supplied drugs to fellow students even though they had pleaded guilty and had been frank with police.

The presence of a commercial motive, even if the drugs were to be supplied to friends, is an aggravating feature. In *Bowman & Powell*,[9] a sentence of four years imprisonment was upheld in respect of the possession of 12 doses of L.S.D. which the appellant intended to supply to friends.

The fact that a person supplies other drug users or addicts is something of a "double-edged" sword. In *Guiney*[10] a sentence of six years imprisonment was reduced to four years where G had supplied other addicts with heroin. G was a "small-time supplier": and see *Hyams*[11] and *Gee*.[12]

Importing drugs intending to re-export them

There is in fact no mitigation at all in the argument that the drugs were merely in transit to another country, or were not intended for distribution in the United Kingdom.[13] See *Mbelu*; and *Winter*.

The drug trade is an international business carried on to the detriment of citizens of all civilised countries. Accordingly, this country owes a duty to other civilised countries to deter the trade; *per* Griffiths L.J. in *Otjen*[14] and see *Chukwu*.

Is police entrapment mitigation?

In *Sang*,[15] the House of Lords held that although a trial judge had no discretion, except in the case of confessions, to refuse to admit evidence merely because it had been improperly obtained, nevertheless, it could be a significant factor in mitigation. Lord Fraser of Tullybelton said[15a]:

> "The degree of guilt may be modified by the inducement and that can appropriately be reflected in the sentence: see *Birtles* [1969] 1 W.L.R. 1047 and *Browning* v. *J.W.H. Watson (Rochester) Ltd.* where Lord Goddard C.J. pointed out that

[9] (1985) 7 Cr. App. R. (S) 85.
[10] (1985) 7 Cr. App. R. (S) 200.
[11] (1983) 5 Cr. App. R. (S) 312.
[12] (1984) 6 Cr. App. R. (S) 86.
[13] See *Mbelu* (1981) 3 Cr. App. R. (S); *Winter* [1973] Crim. L.R. 63, C.A.
[14] 1981 3 Cr. App. R. (S) 186 and see *Chukwu* (May 10, 1984 Lawton L.J.).
[15] [1979] 2 All E.R. 1222.
[15a] *Ibid.* at p. 1238 b/c.

the court could even grant an absolute discharge in such circumstances."

So where, in *Petfield and Carresi*[16] Kennedy J., accepted that there had been police entrapment which led to P and C possessing 1·78 kilograms of cannabis and 27·62 grams of amphetamine, with intent to supply it. The judge took account of it and sentenced P and C to 21 months imprisonment and 12 months imprisonment respectively.

Each case will of course depend on its own facts. It is well known that many drug operations, particularly elaborately planned ventures, come to light and are successfully prosecuted as a result of police or customs and excise "under cover" work. This may include an officer posing as an interested purchaser of narcotics in order to ascertain who the suppliers (or importers) are in a distribution network. Such work is sometimes dangerous and without it many serious cases would go undetected. Is it therefore to be said, that in every case, entrapment is a significant mitigating factor?

In *Underhill*,[17] it is submitted that the Court of Appeal took a realistic view. The appellant was encouraged to sell a quantity of drug to a police officer who, on one view of the facts, instigated the offence. But the Court declined to treat this feature as mitigation on the grounds that the appellant was in any event ready to sell the drugs to anybody who was willing to pay the price. The court suggested that one would have to enquire whether the offence, or one like it, would have been committed notwithstanding the involvement of police and, secondly, whether investigating officers "crossed the line" between legitimate infiltration of criminal activities and conduct which could " . . . fairly be condemned as illegitimate instigation."

In *Beaumont*,[18] B pleaded guilty to being concerned in the supply of cannabis. Undercover agents asked B if she knew anyone who would supply them with cannabis. B suggested her father and took the agents to meet him whereupon he produced a quantity of cannabis and was arrested along with B. B was sentenced to two years imprisonment. The judge ignored the entrapment aspect. B was also pregnant.

Held, The trial judge was wrong to ignore entrapment and the sentence would be reduced to 12 months of which six months would be suspended.

[16] (unreported; 407E86).
[17] (1979) 1 Cr. App. R. (S) 270.
[18] [1987] Crim. L.R. 786.

It is not clear from the report whether B was a person of previous good character or not, or whether the prosecution alleged that she had been concerned in the supply of cannabis on other occasions. Clearly, where a person of good character is entrapped, and there is no reason to believe that the offence would have been committed but for the conduct of the officers (or agents), then the fact of entrapment must be quite substantial mitigation. However, on the facts of *Beaumont*, it is obvious that the appellant's father was ready and willing to sell cannabis and B undoubtedly acted in concert with him. Unfortunately, it is not apparent from the report whether the Court applied the principles expressed in *Underhill*[19] and therefore, *Beaumont* as reported, should be treated with caution.

SCHEDULE 4 TO THE MISUSE OF DRUGS ACT 1971

(as amended by the *Criminal Law Act* 1977, the *Magistrates Courts Act* 1980, the *Criminal Justice Act* 1982, and the *Controlled Drugs (Penalties) Act* 1985

Section	Offence	Mode	Class A	Class B	Class C	General
s.4(2)	Production	S	6 mths or [£2000] or both,	6 mths or [£2000] or both	3 mths or [£500] or both	
		I	Life or a fine or both	14 years or a fine or both	5 years or a fine or both	
s.4(3)	Supplying	S	6 mths or [£2000] or both	6 mths or [£2000] or both	3 mths or [£500] or both	
		I	Life or a fine or both	14 years or a fine or both	5 years or a fine or both	
s.5(2)	Possession	S	6 mths or [£2000] or both,	3 mths or £500 or both	3 mths or £200 or both	
		I	7 years or a fine or both	5 years or a fine or both	2 years or a fine or both	
s.5(3)	Possession with intent to supply	S	6 mths or [£2000] or both	6 mths or [£2000] or both,	3 mths or £500 or both	
		I	Life or a fine or both	14 years or a fine or both	5 years or a fine or both	
s.6(2)	Cultivation	S				6 mths or [£2000] or both
		I				14 years or a fine or both
s.8	Occupier	S	6 mths or [£2000] or both,	6 mths or [£2000] or both	3 mths or £500 or both	
		I	14 years, a fine or both	14 years or a fine or both	5 years or a fine or both	
s.9	Opium	S				12 mths or [£2000] or both
		I				14 years or a fine or both
s.11(2)	Safe Custody	S				6 mths or [£2000] or both
		I				2 years or a fine or both
s.12(6)	Practitioner Prescribing	S	6 mths or [£2000] or both,	6 mths or [£2000] or both	3 mths or £500 or both	

[19] (1979) 1 Cr. App. R. (S) 270.

Section	Offence	Mode	Class A	Class B	Class C	General
		I	14 years, a fine or both	14 years or a fine or both	5 years or a fine or both	
s.13(3)	Practitioner Prescribing	S	6 mths or [£2000] or both,	6 mths or [£2000] or both	3 mths or £500 or both	
		I	14 years, a fine or both	14 years or a fine or both	5 years or a fine or both	
s.17(3)	Information Relating to Supplying	S				£400
s.17(4)	Giving False information	S				6 mths, or [£2000] or both
		I				2 years or a fine or both
s.18(1)	Regulation Contravention	S				6 mths, or [£2000] or both
		I				2 years or a fine or both
s.18(2)	Licence Contravention	S				6 mths, or [£2000] or both
		I				2 years or a fine or both
s.18(3)	False Information	S				6 mths, or [£2000] or both
		I				2 years or a fine or both
s.18(4)	Obtaining Licence Falsely	S				6 mths, or [£2000] or both
		I				2 years or a fine or both
s.20	Assisting an offence under Corresponding Law	S				6 mths, or [£2000] or both
		I				2 years or a fine or both
s.23(4)	Obstruction	S				6 mths, or [£2000] or both
		I				2 years or a fine or both

S = Summary Trial
I = Trial on Indictment
[,] = Fine being the "prescribed sum",

PART VI

A PRACTICAL GUIDE TO
DRUG MISUSE

A PRACTICAL GUIDE TO DRUG MISUSE

Frequently the courts are asked to draw inferences of fact from "the surrounding circumstances" of the case. Yet, in a high proportion of "drug-cases," the relevant circumstances will display a way of life that is often totally alien to the majority of the population. Without some knowledge of drug misuse it is therefore no easy matter to find, let along accurately interpret, the necessary hallmarks that point the way to the truth. It is important to remember that many of the reasons for drug-taking, coupled with the methods of drug use and abuse, are as various, as they are personal, and liable to change as quickly as fashion and personal techniques bend with current market forces, medical and public influences, or other social or delinquent trends.

Accordingly, this section is included to provide a few basis facts and principles applicable to the types of drugs under consideration; the methods of their misuse and their consequential effects. The information is provided for *guidance* only and is therefore necessarily descriptive. Astonishingly, courts often find themselves trying drug-cases with little or no scientific help. The importance of adducing sound expert evidence (except in obviously straightforward cases) cannot be too strongly emphasised.

Having regard to the above, little is to be gained by describing every controlled drug. Instead, the main categories have been defined by their "type," for example, opiates, hallucinogenics and so on. Within each category, or "type," only the most popularly abused drugs are described. Nevertheless they serve as useful examples of other drugs of the same class.

I. TYPES OF DRUGS

(a) The opiates

These are some of the most dangerous drugs abused. They include heroin, opium, morphine, DF 118, methadone (physeptone), dipipanone (diconal), and pethidine. All were developed as pain relievers of varying degrees of strength. All share the fact that they are physically and psychologically addictive. Tolerance can develop alarmingly, and it is not uncommon to find heroin addicts who consume up to half a gram. of heroin *per* day in order to fight off the effects of withdrawal.

Heroin

Towards the end of the nineteenth century diamorphine hydro-chloride, a derivative of morphine, was synthetically produced to serve as a powerful pain reliever. Termed "heroin" in 1899 (from the Greek, "hero") the drug was recognised as having the ability to inflate the personality. Today, heroin is widely abused for that very reason.

All heroin must be imported, the majority of which now comes from Pakistan. In its purified form the drug will be a white powder; otherwise it will assume a brown or beige appearance. When put into soluble form it is then capable of being injected (*i.e.* "main-lined"), but this practice has several very dangerous aspects. First, a host of diseases including hepatitis and Aids may be transmitted by the use of unclean needles. Secondly, heroin is often "cut" with an inert substance in order to reduce the level of purity. Depend-ing on the integrity of the dealer, many substances are used to dilute the drug, for example, lactose or paracetamol. There have been rare instances of despicable dealers adulterating the drug with patently harmful materials such as Vim, Plaster of Paris, and talcum powder, which devastate the arteries and damage various organs. The reasons for "cutting" the drug are dealt with else-where.[1] Thirdly, the rate of absorption is instantaneous but toler-ance may develop more quickly.

The perils of injecting the substance have caused other methods of consumption to increase in popularity—particularly smoking the drug, colloquially referred to as "chasing the dragon." This involves putting heroin onto a piece of silver foil which is held over a small flame. The vapour/smoke is inhaled through a tube, for example, a milk-shake straw or a roll of paper. Occasionally, heroin is inhaled, ("snorted"). The rate of absorption is slower by reason of the mucous membranes which restrict the penetration of the drug into the bloodstream.

Over the last ten years the price of heroin (in real terms) has fal-len while its purity has increased from between 25 per cent.–30 per cent. (typical in 1976) to 50 per cent.–60 per cent. (or better) in 1987. "Fixes" can be bought in "deals" costing as little as £5 or £10 representing approximately one-eighth of a gram. A "deal" or "fold" is often a strip of paper (perhaps cut out of a magazine) measuring approximately four by four inches, wrapped to form a sachet. Because heroin is being imported in ever greater quantities it is now easier for a user to acquire "bulk purchases" at a much

[1] It is worth noting as heroin has become more plentiful and a greater number of "suppliers" are competing on the black market, the practice of cutting the drug with bad substances seems to be declining.

reduced price—an important point to bear in mind when considering an allegation of possession with intent to supply the drug contrary to section 5(3) of the M.D.A. 1971.

According to a recent survey carried out for the British Broadcasting Corporation,[2] most users will receive their first supply from a friend and then resort to a known dealer for a constant supply.

Opium

The unripe seed capsules of the opium poppy (*Papaver Somniferum*) are cut to release a brown liquid. Once dried and removed from the capsules, the result is a narcotic used as a sedative and intoxicant. Opium may be raw; prepared or medicinal.[3]

Morphine

There are many alkaloids of the opium poppy of which morphine is the most valuable. Aptly named "morphine" after "Morpheus," the God of Dreams and the Son of Sleep. It is highly addictive both physically and psychologically. Tolerance also develops. It is not a popular drug with drug abusers since it produces very unpleasant side effects.

Methadone and DF 118

In the treatment of heroin addiction one technique, widely used, is the substitution of methadone (physeptone) or DF 118 (dihydrocodeine), for heroin. The advantages are that these drugs block the effects of withdrawal and cause less dependence than heroin. It follows that by adopting a course of substitution, using drugs that are progressively less addictive, the addict is hopefully "weaned" off his or her addiction. The technique is not without its critics because it could *not* be correct to describe either methadone or DF 118 as a "safe" drug. Both are synthetic pain relievers but are also addictive. The effects, and side effects, of DF 118 are less severe than methadone. For that reason DF 118 is a Class C controlled drug while methodone is Class B.

Dipipanone (Diconal)

This is another narcotic pain reliever capable of causing morphine type dependence. Diconals ("dikes"), contain dipipanone and cyclizine hydrochloride (an antihistamine). Only the former is controlled by the M.D.A. (Class A).

---

[2] The BBC Drugwatch Survey 1985.
[3] See: definitions in Pt. IV to Sched. 2.

(b) Psychotic/hallucinogenic drugs

All such drugs are very potent and include L.S.D., "angel dust"; D.M.T. (dimethyltryptamine) and psilocin (from the so-called magic mushroom). All produce mind-bending, psychedelic effects and loosely mimic psychosis. They are not thought to be addictive but, mentally disturbing experiences may be encountered causing, in extreme cases, actual mental breakdown.

Lysergic Acid Diethylamide (L.S.D.)
First synthesized in 1938 in the Sandoz Laboratories in Basle, L.S.D. is one of the most powerful hallucinogens known to man. It has been used, clinically, to treat acute alcoholics. Psychotherapists originally expressed considerable interest in the drug but tests produced few favourable results and interest in it fell away when it was realised that the artificial effect of L.S.D., on the mind, differed from schizophrenia and so could not be used by psychiatrists to effectively understand, let alone treat, that type of mental disorder. L.S.D. was extensively abused in the 1960s and in the 1970s. There are strong indications that the drug is again increasing in popularity. The drug is difficult to detect being colourless, tasteless and odourless; but a minute quantity produces a colossal effect. Tracing the "factories" has proved to be a monumental task involving a great deal of police time. Impregnated onto "dots" of paper, or small tablets, or onto lumps of sugar, L.S.D. is usually taken by mouth but can also be "snorted" or injected. Effects of the drug are unpredictable. Many cases have been reported of users engaging in bizarre conduct as they enacted their experiences—including attempts to "fly," with occasionally fatal results. Perhaps the most individual aspect of the drugs is its ability to cause "flash backs" or "ghosts," even months after the last dose, in which the user resumes his psychotic experiences.

Psilocin
The mushroom, *Psilocybe Mexicana*, had been used by the Aztecs in some of their religious ceremonies. Today, it is better known as the "magic mushroom." The active constituent is *psilocin* which was first synthesized by Hoffman in the 1950s. The mushroom itself is probably not controlled. When picked, and chewed, the effect is mildly hallucinogenic. If the drug is extracted then it is classified as a Class A substance.

(c) Amphetamines

These are stimulants used in medicinal preparations for a wide range of purposes including the alleviation of depression, treating

alcoholism, slimming aids, or simply to maintain a state of alert-
ness. Their effects are not dissimilar to adrenalin. Subsequently
the user will experience a mood "trough" and other possible
effects, for example nausea, dizziness and weakness.

Abusers may administer amphetamines by injection, but they
are mainly taken by mouth or sniffed. The effect of the drug is
enhanced by injection but tolerance will develop more quickly.
The M.D.A. has controlled many amphetamines including amphetamine sulphate, methyl phenidate (Ritalin), dexamphetamine
(Dexedrine), and chlorphentermine (used as a slimming drug).

Cocaine

In recent years cocaine has come to be labelled as the "rich
man's speed." This is not new. Cocaine has always been expensive
to abuse. What is new is the extent to which the drug has swollen
in popularity in the last few years.[4] *Cocaine* has been with us for
over 100 years being an alkaloid obtained from the leaves of the
coca plant. In South America, particularly Bolivia, the coca plant
grows in abundance. When the leaves are dried, and then chewed
with powdered lime, the substance stimulates the nervous system
and reduces the desire to eat. For centuries, the leaves have been
used in this way by the natives of the Andes.

Formerly used a a local anaesthetic (particularly by dentists)
cocaine had been used in many preparations including chewing
gum and, to many peoples surprise, "Coca-Cola"[5] hence the
name. Although the drug was abused by certain elements of the
Victorian middle classes it was last significantly abused in Britain
in the 1920s. Today, cocaine is used to a very limited extent in
practical medicine by reason of its dangers and addictive quality.
Both *coca* and *cocaine* are controlled by the M.D.A. as a Class A
drug.

All cocaine is imported, mainly from South America, and
usually takes the form of a white powder. The drug is administered
by running a "line" of the substance along a flat surface, for
example a sheet of glass/mirror and then sniffed through a tube of
rolled up paper. The once popular method of injecting cocaine
under the skin has fortunately declined.

(d) Mood enhancers/cannabis

All narcotics will have an effect on mood but cannabis is
renowned for creating effects of relaxation, timelessness, changes
of perspective and apparent "happiness" or "distress." There is

___

[4] See: *Martinez* (*The Times*, November 24, 1984).
[5] Cocaine has long since been removed from the product.

much evidence that cannabis will accentuate pre-existing moods of happiness or tension which may, in turn, be linked to the prevailing environment. It is probable that the drug is not addictive and the evidence of physical or mental harm resulting from it use is equivocal.

In certain African countries, and in the West Indies, cannabis is regularly used and may even form part of the sub-culture. Some people use it as a medicine (for example, for colds); some will fry their fish in the oil; others will smoke the herb; or make tea from it, or sprinkle the herb into soups. Others even bake with it. Its use in the United Kingdom is, on average, less exotic being principally smoked.

Cannabis is grown in many parts of the world, for example, Morocco, Thailand, and India. The active constituent of cannabis is T.H.C. (tetrahydracannabinol). Extracted in its purest form, *i.e.* pure T.H.C., the drug is controlled as a Class A drug. Not all of the plant contains T.H.C. and therefore not all of it will be controlled. Section 37(1) of the M.D.A. (as amended by section 52 of the Criminal Law Act 1977) defined *"cannabis" as meaning*:

> *"any plant of the genus, Cannabis* or any part of any such plant . . . except that it does not include cannabis resin or any of the following products after separation from the rest of the plant, namely
> (*a*) mature stalks of any such plant
> (*b*) fibre produced from mature stalk or any such plant
> (*c*) seed of any such plant. Although it is not
> illegal to possess the seeds, it is an offence to sow them in order to cultivate the plant: see section 6 M.D.A.

The most popular forms of cannabis are:
    (i) cannabis oil—very potent.
    (ii) cannabis resin—less concentrated than oil and extracted from the leaves.
    (iii) herbal cannabis—weaker than resin; produced from the dried leaves, flowering and fruiting tops of the plant."

When smoked, cannabis produces a sweet, distinctive smell.

(e) Sedatives (Hypnosedatives)/Barbiturates

These drugs are the opposite of amphetamines. They all depress the operation of the brain. In large doses they will act as sleeping drugs (hypnotics); in small doses they will tranquillise. The drugs may be a *barbiturate* (for example, barbitone or phenobarbitone) or *non-barbiturate* for example, chloral hydrate (known as a "Mickey Finn" when combined with alcohol), chlormethiazole (Heminevrin), or methaqualone. In 1971 methaqualone (a sedative) was classified as a Class C drug but all barbiturates escaped control notwithstanding abundant evidence of widespread abuse and psychological dependence. However, the real peril of methaqualone was not in its use as a sedative, but as a powerful hypnotic when combined with diphenhydramine (an antihistamine). If taken with alcohol the effects are pronounced. "Mandrax" was the trade name of a substance that contained both these drugs. It has now been withdrawn in the light of widespread abuse as an hypnotic.

Barbituric Acid

On St. Barbara's Day in 1869, barbituric acid was discovered. Since then the acid has been combined to form several salts and esters (*i.e.* the barbiturates). Barbitone, barbitone sodium, phenobarbitone are long term sedatives. All substances containing 5,5 disubstituted barbituric acid are now controlled (Class B). As from April 1, 1986 other sedatives are controlled including:
   (a) Glutethimide (Doriden)—Class B
   (b) Ethchlorvynol—Class C
   (c) Nitrazepam (Mogadon)—Class C
   (d) Methyprylone (Noludar)—Class C

(f) Tranquillisers

Some of these drugs are also subject to control including (as from April 1, 1986):
   (a) Chlordiazepoxide (Librium)—Class C
   (b) Clobazam (Frisium)—Class C
   (c) Clonazepam (Rivotril)—Class C
   (d) Diazepam (Valium)—Class C
   (e) Flurazepam (Dalmane)—Class C
   (f) Meprobamate (Equanil)—Class C
   (g) Oxazepam (Serenid-D)—Class C
   (h) Temazepam (Normison)—Class C
   (i) Triazolam (Halcion)—Class C
All sedatives are highly addictive, particularly psychologically, and tolerance is liable to develop. When combined regularly with alcohol there is a marked increase in the risk of overdosing since alcohol is also a depressant. To a person *physically* dependant on a sedative, the symptoms of the sudden withdrawal can be most unpleasant including fear, sickness and delirium.

(g) Slimming drugs

Certain drugs are designed to encourage the loss of appetite or to "burn up energy." They may ostensibly accentuate the level of one's "awareness." The effects are therefore similar to amphetamine and indeed many slimming drugs contain amphetamine as an active ingredient. We have seen that amphetamine is controlled (Class A) and examples of other "slimmers" are:

(a) Phenmetrazine—Class B
(b) Dexamphetamine—Class B[6]
(c) Benzphetamine—Class C
(d) Chlorphentermine—Class C

(h) Solvents

In the last few years an alarming number of individuals, predominantly teenagers, have indulged in the highly dangerous practice of "sniffing" solvents, for example, glues. The glue is often put into a bag, the top of which is shaped to cover the nose and mouth. The vapours released are then inhaled. Many other toxic substances are abused ranging from typewriter correction fluid to nail-varnish remover. It is the relative ease and inexpense involved in obtaining these substances, which find favour with the teenage abuser, rather than the "satisfaction" derived from the abuse.

In attempting to control the abuse of solvents Parliament has been faced with a major practical problem. One option would be to control the chemical ingredient concerned under the Misuse of Drugs Act 1971 but this would adversely affect commerce and the everyday lives of millions of non-abusers. The alternative was to restrict the supply of certain solvents to persons likely to be affected. Parliament opted for the latter course which led to the passing of the Intoxicating Substances (Supply) Act 1985.

II. THE CONSUMPTION FACTORS

Administration

Section 37(2) M.D.A. 1971 the misuse of a drug involves:

" . . . misusing it by taking it; and the reference . . . to the taking of a drug is a reference to the taking of it by a human being by way of any form of self-administration, whether or not involving assistance by another."

---

[6] Dexamphetamine is omitted from Para. 1(*a*) of Pt. II of Sched. 2 but, it is still included in Pt. II by virtue of Para. 2 being a stereoisomeric form of Amphetamine: see S.I. 1985 No. 1995.

Drugs are principally taken by injection, by mouth and by inhalation into the lungs or the nostrils.

Injections may be *intravenous* (for example, heroin), *intramuscular* (for example heroin, if slow absorption is intended: rarely done and dangerous); or *subcutaneous* under the skin, for example, cocaine.

Different methods of administration determine different rates of absorption of the drug into the bloodstream. Intravenous injection produces a near-instant effect. Other methods are much slower.

Dosage

Assessing the amount of the drug to administer involves a very complex interaction between first, the rate of absorption; secondly, the rate at which the drug is destroyed/eliminated by the body; and thirdly, the desired effect. Dosage will also depend on many personal factors including the level of personal *tolerance* to the drug. An addict may consume heroin at a rate which might well kill a normal individual.

Drug metabolism

The body keeps certain drugs inactive until a chemical conversion has taken place or until it can be excreted. In this way the body keeps certain substances "in storage" until needed or eliminated from the body altogether.

Destruction/disposal

If the level of absorption exceeds the rate at which the body gets rid of the drug then there will be a build up of that drug in the body. Depending on the drug, and the amount consumed, it may be a matter of hours, or months, before the drug is totally removed or destroyed by the body.

Addiction

"Dependence" may be *physical* in which event tolerance develops. The body therefore needs the drug in order to prevent the effects of withdrawal if the regular administration of the substance is suddenly halted or interrupted. Alternatively, dependence may be *psychological*—resulting in a "craving" for the drug. Curing both forms of addiction is very difficult. Indeed treatment can only be successful if the addict displays a determined resolve to rid himself of the habit.

Synergistics—the drug cocktail

A combination of several drugs may have no more effect than if only one drug had been taken. Where the effect of any combination is greater than if only one drug had been taken, the drugs are said to act *"synergistically"*; if the effect produced is less, than they are said to act *"antagonistically."* Sometimes addicts will mix a "cocktail" in order to mimic the effects of a substance that they would prefer to use, for example, heroin, but which may be in short supply. Alternatively, the cocktail is intended to produce a totally different experience, or may be the product of an "experiment," or is intended to defeat certain side effects, for example, depression, sickness or trembling.

Perhaps it should come as no surprise to find that drug dealers have got on the bandwagon and now retail ready-made cocktails. Nevertheless this is a fairly recent development but a most disturbing one. Heroin, imported from Pakistan for example, has occasionally been found to contain phenobarbitone and methaqualone. The amount of heroin in the product may be no higher than 30 to 35 per cent. but, given the presence of the other drugs, the effect is largely similar to heroin of greater purity. The user may be totally unaware of the additives. If tolerance develops the user will therefore be unwittingly addicted to the additive(s) as well as to the heroin. He will be deterred from buying elsewhere since other supplies may not contain, for example, phenobarbitone (to which he is now addicted) and will experience withdrawal symptoms in consequence. Furthermore, the user wishing to cure his addiction will find the task far more difficult, since treatment must now attack addiction to more than one substance.

It follows that dealers peddling this type of concoction can only expect the courts to administer harsh penalties.

Other "drug" terms

It will be seen from the various Schedules to the M.D.A. and the current Regulations, that drugs are specified as "controlled" in Paragraph 1 of Part I, II or III of Schedule 2 to the M.D.A. However, the Schedules also refer to the "stereoisomeric forms," "esters," the "ethers," and the "salts" of various controlled drugs. These terms are not defined by the M.D.A. being terms of science. Without a reasonable knowledge of chemistry merely defining these terms is not very helpful. Nevertheless, if only to serve as an indication, here they are. *Isomers* consist of at least two compounds which are structurally different but molecularly identical. Because they differ structurally the compounds will have different chemical and physical properties. However, where the structure of the compounds are asymmetrically similar then they may be optically *stereoisomeric*; their chemical and physical properties are the same.

Esters are combinations of alcohol and acid to form organic chemicals. They often produce an appealing fragrance.

Common Ether is made up of carbon, hydrogen and oxygen. But *Ethers* is a generic term embracing compounds made by the interaction of alcohols and acids.

Expressed very loosely a *"salt"* is the resultant combination of a metal atom with other non-metal atoms, for example, chloride and sulphate.

III. THE TOOLS OF "THE TRADE" AND OTHER HALLMARKS

Proving possession of a drug is relatively easy. Proving allegations of supplying; possession with intent to supply; permitting premises to be used for smoking cannabis, and so on, frequently involves asking the courts to draw safe inferences from the surrounding circumstances. When assessing the relevance and the significance of certain facts the following points should be borne in mind.

(i) Users will often buy small quantities, but they may also buy in bulk, depending on their means and the state of the black market. Buying in "bulk" may result in a considerable financial saving for the drug user.

(ii) A large quantity of drug divided up into several small "lots," "doses," "deals" or "folds," *may* indicate an intention to supply the drug but it may either have been acquired in that form or may have been divided up by the user in order to regulate his intake.

(iii) The *place* where the drug was found is clearly relevant and may be highly significant. Thus, the finding of a large quantity of drug which, in certain circumstances, may be consistent with personal use might well be inconsistent with that purpose if the drug had been found in the suspect's pocket at a public house, place of work, or at school.

(iv) Unexplained "profits," in the hands of a suspect, is frequently a powerful weapon which often clinches allegations of supplying. "Following the money" is therefore an invaluable line of enquiry which is frequently neglected. However, it is an aspect that must be examined with care, for it is only too easy to make false assumptions. Where large "profits" received by the defendant are totally unaccounted for, being inconsistent with the known legitimate activities of the individual concerned, then such profits will clearly be relevant to charges of supplying or trafficking in controlled drugs. Again, where the cost of buying the drug (said to be for personal use) exceeds the users income then that fact will also be relevant to an allegation of supply or possession with intent to supply, because it may indicate that small quantities were sold by the user in order to feed his addiction.

Of course, monies may have been acquired by the accused as a result of other illegal activities (for example, theft, prostitution) in which case the suspect will be most reluctant to admit those offences. An accused's proceeds of crime may of course explain the existence of large sums of money in the possession of the accused which have not been invested with a financial institution. Secondly, there is always the possibility of the "hidden income" *i.e. credit.* Many drug-suppliers sell drugs on credit. It is sometimes their way of ensuring a continuity of trade with the recipient of the drug. Again, arrears of rent and other debts must be put into the calculation since one might discover that had it not been for the drug-habit the bills would otherwise have been paid.

(v) *Scales* used for measuring minute quantities, for example milligrammes and grams, may be of equivocal value if the suspect is a user of drugs who, typically, must measure his own supply in such small amounts or who wishes to check that he has purchased the correct amount.

(vi) Razor blades, panes of glass or mirrors bearing traces of drug, straws, tubes or rolls of paper, squares of silver foil, hubble-bubble pipes, may all be consistent with personal use but may also be consistent with supplying (save for the "pipe").

(vii) *Cutting Agents.* These are used to reduce the purity of certain drugs—notably heroin and cocaine. Thus glucose may be added to cocaine. The existence of a large quantity of drug coupled with a separate finding of a familiar cutting agent may be indicative of supply. Such a view may be reinforced if the drug is also found to be mixed with that agent. There are several reasons why the drug may be cut. First, to maximise profits. Secondly, to reduce the purity, from the addicts point of view, if a weaker dose is required, or in order to enforce an "economy," by padding out the quantity. And thirdly, with a view to adding another active substance to achieve a desired effect. In recent years the practice of cutting the drug with "rubbish,"*i.e.* a harmful additive such as cleaning powder seems to be on the decline. This is probably not because suppliers have become more scrupulous but simply because it makes good commercial sense given, that there is now much more heroin on the black market, sold by many more dealers. Since competition is tougher there is a disincentive to supply "bad" heroin.

(viii) The existence of a large number of strips of paper (perhaps torn from a magazine) or a number of small plastic "bank bags," may also suggest supplying.

(ix) An exceptionally large number of casual acquaintances visiting the suspects home, for seemingly unsociably short periods of time, may indicate supplying if other tools of the trade are found at the address, etc.

(x) Abbreviated records or calculations, for which no reasonable explanation is given, may suggest supply but may also be a record of sums owed to various drug creditors. This is another feature which must be examined with particular care.

(xi) A suspect, found in possession of a drug, who is not himself a user of that drug is a finding of fact totally inconsistent with personal use and therefore the suspect is either holding the drug on behalf of another (for example, for safe–keeping) or he is an outright supplier.

Articles and documents found by officers during the course of an investigation will be admissible if they are probative of any fact in issue in the case and subject, of course, to the discretion of the trial judge to exclude evidence that is more prejudicial than probative. Each case must be decided on its own facts. Thus, drug paraphernalia used by a heroin addict, and which was found at his home address may destroy his defence that he did not know that the substance he imported was heroin: see *Willis*.[7]

---

[7] C.A., January 29, 1979, unrep.; and see *Thrussell* (C.A. November 30, 1981, unrep.) and see *Madden* (C.A. July 25, 1986, unrep.).

PART VII

THE STATUTORY BODIES

STATUTORY BODIES

I. THE ADVISORY COUNCIL

The Advisory Council, created by *section 1* of the Misuse of Drugs Act 1971, is entrusted with the responsibility of keeping under review the situation in the United Kingdom with respect to drugs which are being abused or are likely to be abused or may have harmful effects sufficient to constitute "a social problem." It must therefore monitor the current situation; promote research (section 1(2)(e)) and, above all, advise the government on measures:
  (i)   which ought to be taken to prevent drug misuse.
 (ii)   to deal with resultant social problems.
(iii)   to restrict/supervise the supply of dangerous drugs.
 (iv)   to facilitate treatment.
  (v)   to promote co-operation between the community and the professions.
 (vi)   to educate the public.
It is apparent that the Advisory Council needs to pool the knowledge of many different disciplines. Accordingly, the Council consists of at least 20 members including practitioners from the field of medicine, dentistry, veterinary medicine and pharmacy. Other members must have wide and recent experience of social problems connected with drug misuse.

We have already noted how important it is that the law should be as certain as possible while being flexible enough to adjust to social and medical opinion. With every change of Government there may also be a change of policy or direction. Nevertheless, continuity is substantially maintained through the Advisory Council by virtue of section 31(3) which provides:

> "The Secretary of State shall not make any regulations under this Act except after consultation with the Advisory Council."

Again, the Advisory Council must be consulted before draft Orders in Council, intended to amend the classes of controlled drugs in Schedule 2, are laid before Parliament; see section 2(5); or before an Order is made under section 7(4) (restricting the use of certain drugs to research purposes only; or prohibiting a practitioner, pharmacist, etc from manufacturing, supplying or administering certain drugs other than by licence): see section 7(5).

283

II. TRIBUNALS

Where a practitioner is suspected of being in breach of certain provisions of the Misuse of Drugs Act 1971 (or is, in fact, in breach of any of them) the Secretary of State may contemplate issuing a *direction* to that practitioner not to prescribe, administer or supply drugs specified in the direction. In order to investigate the matter the Secretary of State should refer the case to a Tribunal who shall report on it to the Secretary of State: section 14(1). If the Tribunal finds the case "proved" it may indicate, in its report, the controlled drugs which it considers should be specified in the direction: section 14(4).

The Tribunal consists of five persons. The Chairman, who is a Barrister or Solicitor of at least seven years standing, is appointed by the Lord Chancellor. The remaining members are all drawn from the practitioners profession. Proceedings are normally heard in private unless the Respondent (*i.e.* the Practitioner) successfully applies to the Tribunal for a public hearing: see Schedule 3.

The Lord Chancellor may regulate the rules of procedure to be followed and the rules of evidence to be observed. All parties may be legally represented.

III. ADVISORY BODIES

If the Tribunal finds the case proved and the Secretary of State notifies the Respondent of his intention to give a direction prohibiting the Respondent prescribing, administering or supplying certain drugs, then the Respondent may within 28 days make representations in reply. If representations are made the case is then referred by the Secretary of State to an Advisory Body consisting of three persons chaired by a Queen's Counsel appointed by the Lord Chancellor. The Respondent may be legally represented. The task of the Advisory Body is, as the name implies, to advise the Secretary of State: see section 14(6) and section 14(7). Their findings are not binding on the Secretary of State.

IV. PROFESSIONAL PANEL

The above procedure can be protracted. The Secretary of State may consider that prompt and decisive measures are required. Accordingly, by section 15(1) where the Secretary of State considers that a practitioner has been prescribing irresponsibly (hence the need for rapid action) he may give temporary directions to the practitioner. In order to protect the interests and rights of the Respondent, the Secretary of State *must* first refer the case to a

Professional Panel which in turn, must afford the Respondent the right to be heard. The Secretary of State may not give temporary directions unless the panel confirms that the information available "affords reasonable grounds" for thinking that the Respondent has been prescribing controlled drugs irresponsibly: see section 15(2)(*a*) and section 15(2)(*b*).

The Panel consists of a Chairman and two members all of whom are drawn from the ranks of the Respondent's profession. The Respondent is entitled to be legally represented.

APPENDIX

SCHEDULE 2 to the MISUSE OF DRUGS ACT 1971
(*as amended*)

CONTROLLED DRUGS
PART I

CLASS A DRUGS

1. The following substances and products, namely:

(*a*)[3]
Acetorphine
Alfentanil[6]
Allylprodine
Alphacetylmethadol
Alphamethadol
Alphaprodine
Anileridine
Benzethidine
Benzylmorphine (3-benzylmorphine)
Betacetylmethadol
Betameprodine
Bezitramide
Bufotenine
Cannabinol, except where contained in cannabis or cannabis resin
Cannabinol derivatives
Carfentanil[8]
Clonitazene
Coco leaf
Cocaine
Desomorphine
Dextromoramide
Diamorphine
Diampromide
Diethylthiambutene
Difenoxin (1-(3-cyano-3,3-diphenylpropyl)-4-phenylpiperidine-4-
   carboxylic acid)[2]
Dihydrocodeinone O-carboxymethyloxime
Dihydromorphine
Dimenoxadole
Dimepheptanol

287

Dimethylthiambutene
Dioxaphetyl butyrate
Diphenoxylate
Dipipanone
Drotebanol (3,4-dimethoxy-17-methylmorphinan-6β, 14-diol)[1]
Ecgonine, and any derivative of ecgonine which is convertible to
    ecgonine or to cocaine
Ethylmethylthiambutene
Eticyclidine[6]
Etonitazene
Etorphine
Etoxeridine
Fentanyl
Furethidine
Hydrocodone
Hydromorphinol
Hydromorphone
Hydroxypethidine
Isomethadone
Ketobemidone
Levomethorphan
Levomoramide
Levophenacylmorphan
Levomoramide
Levophenacylmorphan
Levorphanol
Lofentanil[8]
Lysergamide
Lysergide and other N-alkyl derivatives of lysergamide
Mescaline
Metazocine
Methadone
Methadyl acetate
Methyldesorphine
Methyldihydromorphine (6-methyldihydromorphine)
Metopon
Morpheridine
Morphine
Morphine methobromide, morphine N-oxide and other
    pentavalent nitrogen morphine derivatives
Myrophine
[Nicodicodine (6-nicotinoyldihydrocodeine)][1]
Nicomorphine (3,6-dinicotinoylmorphine)
Noracymethadol
Norlevorphanol

Normethadone
Normorphine
Norpipanone
Opium, whether raw, prepared or medicinal
Oxycodone
Oxymorphone
Pethidine
Phenadoxone
Phenampromide
Phenazocine
Phencyclidine[4]
Phenomorphan
Phenoperidine
Piminodine
Piritramide
Poppy-straw and concentrate of poppy-straw
Proheptazine
Properidine (1-methyl-4-phenyl-piperidine-4-carboxylic acid
    isopropyl ester)
Psilocin
Racemethorphan
Racemoramide
Racemorphan
Rolicyclidine[6]
Sufentanil[5]
Tenocylidine[6]
Thebacon
Thebaine
Tilidate[5]
Trimeperidine
4-Bromo-2,5-dimethoxy-α-methylphenethylamine[2]
4-Cyano-2-dimethylamino-4,4-diphenylbutane
4-Cyano-1-methyl-4-phenylpiperidine
N,N-Diethyltryptamine
N,N-Dimethyltryptamine
2,5-Dimethoxy-α,4-dimethylphenethylamine
1-Methyl-4-phenylpiperidine-4-carboxylic acid
2-Methyl-3-morpholino-1,1-diphenylpropanecarboxylic acid
4-Phenylpiperidine-4-carboxylic acid ether ester
(b)[3] any compound (not being a compound for the time being
specified in sub-paragraph (a) above) structurally derived from
tryptamine or from a ring-hydroxy tryptamine by substitution at
the nitrogen atom of the sidechain with one or more alkyl substituents but no other subsituent;
(c)[3] any compound (not being methoxyphenamine or a compound

for the time being specified in sub-paragraph (*a*) above) structurally derived from phenethylamine, an N-alkylphenethylamine, α-methylphenethylamine, an N-alkyl-α-methylphenethylamine, α-ethylphenethylamine, or an N-alkyl-α-ethylphenethylamine by substitution in the ring to any extent with alkyl, alkoxy, alkylenedioxy or halide substituents, whether or not further substituted in the ring by one or more other univalent substitutents.

(*d*)[8] any compound (not being a compound for the time being specified in sub-paragraph (*a*) above) structurally derived from fentanyl by modification in any of the following ways, that is to say,

   (i) by replacement of the phenyl portion of the phenethyl group by any heteromonocycle whether or not further substituted in the heterocycle;

  (ii) by substitution in the phenethyl group with alkyl, alkenyl, alkoxy, hydroxy, halogeno, haloalkyl, amino or nitro groups;

 (iii) by substitution in the piperidine ring with alkyl or alkenyl groups;

 (iv) by substitution in the aniline ring with alkyl, alkoxy, alkylenedioxy, halogeno or haloalkyl groups;

  (v) by substitution at the 4-position of the piperidine ring with any alkoxycarbonyl or acyloxy group;

 (vi) by replacement of the N-propionyl group by another acyl group;

(*e*)[8] any compound (not being a compound for the time being specified in sub-paragraph (*a*) above) structurally derived from pethidine by modification in any of the following ways, that is to say,

   (i) by replacement of the 1-methyl group by an acyl, alkyl whether or not unsaturated, benzyl or phenethyl group, whether or not further substituted;

  (ii) by substitution in the piperidine ring with alkyl or alkenyl groups or with a propano bridge, whether or not further substituted;

 (iii) by substitution in the 4-phenyl ring with alkyl, alkoxy, aryloxy, halogeno or haloalkyl groups;

 (iv) by replacement of the 4-ethoxycarbonyl or any other alkoxycarbonyl or any alkoxyalkyl or acyloxy group;

  (v) by formation of an N-oxide or of a quaternary base.

2. Any stereoisomeric form of a substance for the time being specified in paragraph 1 above not being dextromethorphan or dextrorphan.

3. Any ester or ether of a substance for the time being specified in paragraph 1 or 2 above *not being a substance for the time being specified in Part II of this Schedule.*[1]

4. Any salt of a substance for the time being specified in any of paragraphs 1 to 3 above.

5. Any preparation or other product containing a substance or product for the time being specified in any of paragraphs 1 to 4 above.

6. Any preparation designed for administration by injection which includes a substance or product for the time being specified in any of paragraphs 1 to 3 of Part II of this Schedule.

PART II

CLASS B DRUGS

1. The following substances and products, namely:
(a)[6]
Acetyldihydrocodeine
Amphetamine
Cannabis and cannabis resin
Codeine
[Dexamphetamine][7]
Dihydrocodeine
Ethylmorphine (3-ethylmorphine)
Glutethimide[7]
Lefetamine[7]
Mecloqualone[6]
Methaqualone[6]
Methylamphetamine
Methylphenidate
Methylphenobarbitone[6]
Nicocodine
Nicodicodine (6-nicotinoyldihydrocodeine)[1]
Norcodeine
Pentazocine[7]
Phenmetrazine
Pholcodine
Propiram[1]
(b) any 5,5 disubstituted barbituric acid.[6]

2. Any stereoisomeric form of a substance for the time being specified in paragraph 1 of this part of this Schedule.

3. Any salt of a substance for the time being specified in any of paragraphs 1 or 2 of this Part of this Schedule.

4. Any preparation or other product containing a substance or product for the time being specified in any of paragraphs 1 to 3 of this Part of this Schedule, not being a preparation falling within paragraph 6 of Part I of this Schedule.

Part III

CLASS C DRUGS

1. The following substances, namely:
Alprazolam[7]
Benzphetamine
Bromazepam[7]
Camazepam[7]
Cathine[8]
Cathinone[8]
Chlordiazepoxide[7]
Chlorphentermine
Clobazam[7]
Clonazepam[7]
Clorazepic acid[7]
Clotiazepam[7]
Cloxazolam[7]
Delorazepam[7]
Dextropropoxyphene[5]
Diazepam[7]
Diethylpropion[6]
Estazolam[7]
Ethchlorvynol[7]
Ethinamate[7]
Ethyl loflazepate[7]
[Fencamfamin][1, 8(a)]
Fenethylline[8]
Fenproporex[8]
Fludiazepam[7]
Flunitrazepam[7]
Flurazepam[7]
Halazepam[7]
Haloxazolam[7]
Ketazolam[7]
Loprazolam[7]
Lorazepam[7]
Lormetazepam[7]
Mazindol[7]
Medazepam[7]
Mefenorex[8]
Mephentermine
Meprobamate[7]
[Methaqualone][6]
Methyprylone[7]

Nimetazepam[7]
Nitrazepam[7]
Nordazepam[7]
Oxazepam[7]
Oxazolam[7]
[Pemoline][1]
Phendimetrazine
[Phentermine][1, 7(a)]
Pinazepam[7]
Pipradrol
Prazepam[7]
[Prolintane][1]
Propylhexedrine[8]
Pyrovalerone[8]
Temazepam[7]
Tetrazepam[7]
Triazolam[7]
N-Ethylamphetamine[8]

2. Any stereoisomeric form of a substance for the time being specified in paragraph 1 of this part of this Schedule *not being phenylpropanolamine*.[8]

3. Any salt of a substance for the time being specified in any of paragraphs 1 or 2 of this Part of this Schedule.

4. Any preparation or other product containing a substance for the time being specified in any of paragraphs 1 to 3 of this Part of this Schedule.

[1] Inserted by S.I. 1973 No. 771.
[. .][1] Omitted by S.I. 1973 No. 771.
[2] Inserted by S.I. 1975 No. 421.
[3] Inserted by S.I. 1977 No. 1243.
[4] Inserted by S.I. 1979 No. 299.
[5] Inserted by S.I. 1983 No. 765.
[6] Inserted by S.I. 1984 No. 859.
[. .][6] Omitted by S.I. 1984 No. 859.
[7] Inserted by S.I. 1985 No. 1995.
[. .][7] Omitted by S.I. 1985 No. 1995.
[7(a)] Re-inserted by S.I. 1985 No. 1955.
[8] Inserted by S.I. 1986 No. 2230.
[8(a)] Re-inserted by S.I. 1986 No. 2230.

INDEX